INTEGRATED RECOVERY PROGRAMMES MADE POSITIVE IMPACT IN THE LIVES OF THE PEOPLE

(Lessons Learned)

Overview of UNDP Recovery Programmes in Eritrea

Personal Perspectives

By

Techeste AHDEROM

(Prof/Eng Emeritus)

First Edition Published in New York, November 2020

"We must make greater efforts to listen to the people on the ground. We must be less eager to devise and promote United Nations initiatives, and more constructive in finding ways to support local, African initiatives"

Kofi Annan, UN Secretary General, Address to ECOSOC High Level Meeting,
Geneva, Switzerland, 25 July 2001

TABLE OF CONTENTS

Background/Context

i. PREFACE

I came to Asmara in 1991 immediately after independence, initially to participate in a Seminar on Higher Education in Eritrea, at the invitation of the then President of Asmara University, Mr. Andebrhan Woldegiorgis. I was later invited by the UNDP Eritrea to lead an external Evaluation of the Programme for Refugee Reintegration and Rehabilitation of Resettlement programme (PROFERI), together with Dr. Tesfai Haile, a national consultant, and Mr. Gebremichael Tesfaslassie, who was the UNDP staff member who spearheaded the opening of the UNDP Liaison office in Asmara (1992-1993). Upon successful completion of the evaluation, I was also invited to be part of a team to assess/evaluate the CCF of UNDP Eritrea together with Dr. Sadiki, an economist from Canada, in 1997.

Moreover, I came back to Eritrea on a longer assignment as United Nations Development Programme (UNDP) Senior Advisor on Recovery, soon after the Cessation of Hostilities Agreement between Eritrea and Ethiopia, which was signed on 18 June 2000. The Peace Agreement signed in December 2000 and the deployment of the United Nations Peacekeeping Mission in Ethiopia and Eritrea (UNMEE), and the subsequent establishment of the Temporary Security Zone (TSZ), ushered a period of relatively stable peace. Consequently an overwhelming majority of the estimated 1.1 million internally displaced persons (IDPs) began returning spontaneously to their places of origin which in most cases had been completely destroyed or in some cases partly ruined by the war. The need for rehabilitation, reconstruction and reintegration was then the most important agenda of the day. The UNDP and other development partners have undertaken a number of recovery programmes. The UNDP notable programmes after the cessation of hostilities include: Post-Liberation and Pre-Independence Project (PPP), Pre-Post War Emergency Recovery Programme (Pre-PoWER), PoWER I and II, Integrated Recovery Programme (IRP), Joint Programme on IDPs/Expellees return/ resettlement, and Transition and Early Recovery Programme (TER).

This publication is not a record of all the recovery activities undertaken in the country since independence, it is instead an attempt to present a comprehensive listing of all recovery programmes undertaken by the UNDP, in partnership with the Government of Eritrea, covering two decades (1992-2012).

This effort is an attempt, to partially capture from a personal perspective, many of the notable behind the scenes interactions with stakeholders, which are seldom reflected in official documents and reports. Moreover, it is also meant to point out some key achievements, highlight lessons learned and identify a few best practices. For more details, I will refer you to the tedious but commendable work undertaken by stakeholders and implementing partners, in collating numbers, outcomes, and outputs that are included in the official mandatory reports, which were issued by the UNDP Eritrea periodically. Furthermore, the annexes also capture the programmes and projects, with some level of detail, undertaken during the period under study.

It goes without saying that I have used extensively the reports of External Evaluations of the various recovery programmes undertaken and the mandatory financial and narrative reports of the projects/programmes as applicable. In 1996 there was an external Ex-post Evaluation of the PROFERI that I was the lead international consultant. There was also a review of the first CCF of the Country Office in 2001 that I participated as a team member. Moreover, in 2002, there was a mid-term external evaluation of the PoWER Programme that was undertaken by a team of experts led by Mr. Pardeshi. In regards to the UNDP led Social and Economic Reintegration of Demobilized Soldiers, I had access to the relevant portions of the World Bank interim-evaluation report on the National Demobilization and Reintegration Programme (NDRP). There was also an evaluation made on the Mine Action Capacity Building Programme (MACBP), in 2008 and an evaluation of the Joint Programme on IDPs/Expellees in 2010. The MTR of the UNDAF has also highlighted the achievements of the Transition and Early recovery Programme (TER). The CPAP 2007-2011 Evaluation has also extensive coverage of the recovery programme, since it was the flagship of the Country Office (CO) for two decades. In general the observations were extremely positive and highly encouraging. Of course, evaluations have their limitations since they try to undertake, in three to four weeks, the scope and depth of complex programmes. Yet they are important, even if they only tell part of the story. Moreover, there were also regularly issued Programme/Project Quarterly Reports. I also had access to reports that contained both narrative and financial statements which were supplemented by regularly issued Annual Consolidated Reports.

This attempt is a daunting task, since it was undertaken when the Author was still having a heavy load that included addressing high priority emerging issues in support of the UNDP CO. Nevertheless, the assignment was completed and hopefully will serve of informing the UNDP and stakeholders of what has transpired in the critical phase of the rapidly changing developments in Eritrea. It may be helpful to understand the perspective of evaluation teams of programmes, due to the brief time that they are expected to file their reports. For example, one of the PoWER Programme evaluation team members stated during the de-briefing session that when challenged about his comments on one of the components that was highly successful, that he and his colleagues had to write something negative at least in one area. Otherwise, he said, no one would be interested in reading the evaluation, if it was only full of praises. It would have been alright, if the evaluation team leader selected another activity which could have been more plausible. In another case and regarding the evaluation of the JP on IDPs/Expellees where one of the national counterparts insisted on inserting a paragraph describing how in one district seeds for farmers arrived late. He heard this from one of the farmers and had blown it out of proportion. In subsequent visits both the regional authorities and the affected communities reiterated that they have received the seeds on time, but in some places tractor services from the government did not arrive on time which were then substituted by oxen ploughing.

Finally, I have also included a brief narrative on the context giving a cursory look at the social, economic, political, and demographic situation in the country and the challenges and opportunities faced by the government and its people. It would have been remiss, if some reference was not made on this aspect of the presentation. On the other hand, one should not read too much into the brief remarks on a variety of issues, since the main purpose is to give a brief overview of the UNDP recovery programmes and their impact rather than on the situation in the country, which is adequately reported in other publications.

ii. List of tables

iii. List of figures

iv. List of boxes

v. ACKNOWLEDGMENT

The idea of writing a book on my personal experience on the formulation, design and implementation of Recovery Programmes in Eritrea, has crossed my mind a number of times. It was, however, Macleod Nyirongo, the former UNDP Resident Representative (2004-2008) and Tiblez Araia, DRR (O) who encouraged me to start thinking about putting in writing my unique experience in Eritrea, in the fast moving and complex area that has not been explored so far. The project, however, took shape when Dr. Mamadou P. Diallo took office as UNDP Resident Representative in Eritrea (2009-2012).

The concept was discussed at many of the regularly scheduled one hour briefing sessions (every Thursday of the week) that I had with Senior Management on the UNDP recovery programmes in Eritrea. Right from the beginning, I was empowered to write freely without any constraints and to prepare a manuscript that gives my own personal views and perspectives of the successes, constraints and lessons learned of the UNDP recovery programmes in Eritrea. I am thankful to the Senior Management for their encouragement, and this is the result of such cooperative efforts.

It would be difficult to list all the people that helped me in my research, but naming a few will suffice. Yodit Tesfagebriel who served as my research assistant for a few months compiled and updated a few of the materials at the recovery programme archives. She helped to compile archival materials on lessons learned excerpted from numerous project reports, updated an earlier drafts on the overall budget up to 2009. Yodit did a very good job and i am grateful for her assistance. I am also grateful to all who volunteered to edit the manuscript for consistency of language, coherence, and relevance of the various personal narratives and episodes to achieve the goals of the manuscript.

I am thankful to a number of other persons for many of their comments in discussing the relevant parts of the draft manuscript, in areas where each have comparative advantage of knowing more about a specific programme than others, at different stages in its preparation.

I have drawn generously from the myriad recovery unit's technical reports, external evaluation reports, annual consolidated reports, quarterly reports, terminal reports and from over one hundred project documents that were written during the course of the different phases of the Recovery Programmes. Acknowledgments have been made as footnotes, if I were not the primary author, where appropriate.

I am indebted to Teclemichael Woldegiorgis (ROSSO), Kidane Tsige, Gebremichael Mengistu, Mehreteab Fissehaye, Habtom Seghid, Dr. Tekeste Fekadu, Gebremichael Tesfasellassie (Padre), Gebremedhin Haile, Negheset Hagos, Ghirmai Woldemichael, Berthane G. Michael and Sergio Valdini, for their valuable insights and helpful comments during workshops organized on selected topics. I am deeply indebted to Dr. Tesfai Haile who participated in the design and evaluation of a number of recovery projects in Eritea for his advice and comments. I would also like to thank Dr. Tijan Jallow, an experienced international consultant, for his contribution in defining the initial components of the programme that dealt with the resettlement of Rural Expellees from Ethiopia, in Gerenfit, Gash Barka Moreover, I am also grateful for the comments of Beshir Mohammed, Tseggai Gebremichael, and Yonas Haile, UNDP project coordinators in Debub, Gash Barka and Southern Red Sea regions respectively, for their comments on the draft manuscript relating to certains aspects of the lessons learnt in their respective regions. Moreover, I would like to thank all of the Stand-alone project/programme consultants, including ROCCO for preparing Village Resettlement Site Plans; MY Consultant for modifying and improving the designs of the Technical Training Centers for use by IDPs/Expellees; Asmarom Legesse for his research on Honey Development in selected villages to be used primarily in the war affected Resettlement areas in Debub region; Woldu Tewoldebrhan for his professional and effective supervision of the construction of the Senafe Hospital; and Alem Tesfamariam for the well-executed design and supervision of all recovery water projects in Debub and Gash Barka regions; and finally the two national NGOs, HABEN and ESCA for efficiently and effectively executing the various projects they were entrusted with.

It goes without saying that I would like to thank my then colleagues in the Recovery Unit who were fully supportive of the project especially Eyob Ghezai whose advice on cash for work, sustainable livelihoods, especially in the agricultural components and Michael Tewoldemedhin on water, MDGs and the overall thrust of the manuscript were insightful, I am very thankful for the critical and vital role played by Rita Mazzochi in the planning, design, implementation, monitoring and reporting of the Mine Action Recovery programme, Shoa Gebreegziabher for her untiring help in typing the early drafts and especially those pertaining to budget aspects and annexes. I am also indebted to Tedros Abraha for his invaluable technical support to make the layout of the pages, pictures, tables and inserts more effective and attractive.

Finally, this project would not have been realized, without the full support and encouragement of the UNDP Senior Management, consisting of Ms. Verity Nyagah, whose interest in seeing this manuscript finished, if possible during her tenure as DRR (P) was invaluable and Ms. Tiblez Araia to whom I am deeply indebted.

Furthermore, Christine Umutoni, former UNDP Resident Representative in Eritrea, after reviewing the final edited manuscript in December 2013 stated that the book could be useful for other practitioners beyond the borders of Eritrea and may also be a tool for resource mobilization. It should be published soon, before it becomes an archival material, she added. Unfortunately, she left her post in Asmara without having the book published.

The ideas, views and contents of this manuscript are completely that of the author and do not necessarily reflect the views and policies of the UNDP and other development partners, unless specifically mentioned.

CHAPTER ONE

Background contents

1. BACKGROUND/CONTEXT

Historical and Political Context

Eritrea was a colony of Italy from 1890-1940 and was administered under the British as a UN Trustship from 1942-1952. It was federated with Ethiopia from 1952 until it was annexed forcefully by the then Ethiopian Government under Emperor Haile Selassie in 1960. It was in 1961 that a formal armed war of liberation was initiated.

Eritrea was liberated in May 1991 and gained its independence after an internationally monitored referendum in May 1993, inheriting a destroyed and neglected social and economic infrastructure as a result of 30 years of occupation.

Eritrea is a young nation-state, the second youngest after South Sudan in Africa.

After the 30-year war of liberation with Ethiopia, Eritrea attained de facto independence in May 1991 and de jure independence two years later. The initial years of independence were marked by impressive progress as evidenced by improved social indicators, macroeconomic stability and economic growth.

The development gains were interrupted when a border dispute with Ethiopia erupted into renewed conflict in May 1998. A temporary Security Zone (TSZ) monitored by a UN Peace Keeping force was established in accordance with the Peace Agreement on the border issue signed in 2000. The Ethiopia-Eritrea Boundary Commission (EEBC) made a final 'virtual'demarcation of the boundary at the end of 2007. This has been accepted by Eritrea though was initially rejected by Ethiopia but eventually accepted in principle. According to the UNMEE, tensions remained high and both countries had troops positioned alongside the border.

Self reliance was enshrined in the "National Charter for Eritrea"

which was drawn and approved by the Eritrean People's Libération Front (EPLF) in February 1994. The Charter describes self reliance as "another ***foundation for victory attained by our liberation struggle. If we had not relied on our own abilities, both developing in principles and in practice, we would certainly not have succeeded. Self Reliance in all fields – political, economic and cultural is a basic principle."***

The then Minister of Finance at the 2008 United Nations Development Assistance Framework (UNDAF) annual review meeting, emphatically made this point time and again. He declared that self reliance implies among others that donated grant contributions to national development should be marginal, minuscule, transitional and short-lived.

Trade and investment should be penultimate and perpetual sources of foreign capital inflows to Eritrea, he added.
The question of self reliance is an interesting topic and needs to be addressed extensively in another forum. But suffice to say, that in this twenty-first century, no country on planet earth, is an island. A good example is that of a recent case where a member of parliament (the Duma) in Japan raised the issue of aid given by Japan to China, which has now the second biggest economy in the world. For decades Japan was giving aid to China, a few hundred million dollars a year, on priority areas identified by the Chinese.

The member of parliament raised the issue by stating "how come this aid is continuing year after year without question, despite the economic rise of China". Before the Duma could take action to cut off the aid, the devastating earthquake followed by the destructive Tsunami happened, and the issue was dropped. Self-reliance while laudable should be carefully handled by countries with limited resources in the initial stage of their development.

Socio-Economic Characteristics

According to the latest EPHS 2010, Eritrea has an estimated population of about 3.2 million, out of which around 20% reside in urban/semi-urban areas. The annual growth rate of the population was estimated to be about 3 %, thus the current population is 3.4 million. The Eritrean population lives in an area of about 12.57 million hectares of land (93,680 Square Kms), of whom 80% live on crop production, livestock raising and fishing.

The Gross Domestic Product (GDP), had been registering an average annual growth rate of 11% between 1993-1997;

however, due to the border war with Ethiopia, that growth rate progressively declined to minus 8.3% in 2000.[1] During the period 2008-2011, Eritrea had mixed results. In 2008 the rate of real GDP was estimated to be, -9.8% for 2008, 3.6% for 2009, 1.8% for 2010 and it registered a growth of 2% for 2011.[2]

1 *Ministry of Finance Report*

2 *United Nations, World Economic Situation and Prospects 2008-2013. Regional averages are calculated as a weighted average of individual country growth rates of GDP, where weights were based in GDP in 2005 prices and exchanges) and back to 5.5% in 2012 (Partly estimated) and 5.2% in 2013 (Baseline scenario forecasts based in art in Project LINK and UN/DESA World Economic Forecasting Model)*

Increasing levels of poverty in the country remain a major concern, with more than two thirds of the population living below the poverty line[3]. Currently Eritrea is still facing a humanitarian crisis as a result of drought and the aftermath of the 1998-2000 war with Ethiopia that is yet to be resolved and continues to limit the government's ability to respond effectively. It is one of the poorest countries in the world. According to WFP, Eritrea produced 13-20% of the 628,000 MT annual food requirements during the period from 2000 to 2004.[4]

Moreover, approximately 80% of the Eritrean population lives in rural settings, and are predominantly subsistence farmers and agro-pastoralists. Hence, the large proportion of household production was destined for internal consumption. Of this, 60% were semi-nomadic, living in dispersed household (HHs) clusters. The arid areas of Eritrea have the highest incidence of poor and extreme poor population[5]. Agricultural products are normally stored for a limited duration and the local market was usually considered as a "place where goods are bought rather than stored." In exchange the interest remains a consumer interest, as their primary goal was to satisfy their immediate food needs.

3 *Interim Poverty Reduction Strategy (I-PRSP), GoSE, Asmara, April 2004*
4 *Food and Nutrition Situation in Eritrea- A brief Analysis – October 2005, OCHA*
5 *Dimensions of Poverty in Eritrea, Government of the State of Eritrea, May 2003*

Although GoSE had developed a number of policy frameworks (e.g. Macro Policy, Interim Poverty Reduction Strategy Paper, Food Security Strategy, etc),
adhoc assessments showed that human and institutional capacity gaps posed delays and difficulties in terms of the implementation of these key GoSE policy initiatives. National capacity issues and constraints were identified as key concerns underpinning most development challenges across all sectors. The issues were equally serious at the regional and local levels. Accordingly, a long-term effort was required to build capacity at the central, regional and local levels, as well as at a sector level. This was one of the main focus areas in the current UN/GoSE Strategic Cooperation Framework - 2013-2016.

As mentioned earlier, economic performance in the early years of independence (1993-1997) was impressive with an average GDP growth of 7.4 %, increases in per capita income and other marked improvements. Significant progress was made in rehabilitating and reconstruction of infrastructure (roads, seaports, schools, health facilities, etc.). However, the period after 1998 was adversely affected by the sudden eruption of the border war (1998-2000) with Ethiopia. Consequently the economy did not perform as well due to the border war and the lingering demarcation stalemate compounded by recurrent droughts, severe resource constraints, and human capacity gaps.

As a consequence of both the long war of liberation and the brief border war
with Ethiopia, there were still significant numbers of Internally Displaced People (IDPs) and expellees, who together with the urban poor, the disabled, pastoralists, female-headed households, orphans, and high-risk HIV/AIDS groups were particularly hard hit.

Within these groups, women and children were the most disadvantaged, both socially and economically. Estimates indicated that there were about 71,000 IDPs sheltered in camps and being assisted with emergency aid. The resettlement and reintegration process of this population which was underway had significant implications for extra resource mobilisation. At that stage, most of the IDPs were back to their original villages or other settlement areas; however, much remained to be done if they were to lead normal, productive lives.

Eritrea faces acute food security challenges.
While the contribution of agriculture to GDP was low (15-20%), about two thirds of the Eritrean population depends on subsistence agriculture for its livelihood. The sector was highly exposed to the vagaries of nature and its production levels were low that it hardly coverd subsistence consumption even in good harvests; the country faced continued chronic food deficits.

Even at times of good harvest, for instance in the crop year of 1998/99, Eritrea produced only 60-70 % of its domestic food requirements. In 2002, agricultural production was equivalent to 30% of the country's domestic food requirements and the quest for food security remains one of the key challenges facing the Country.

4 Monitoring Agricultural Resources Bulletin, Vol. 4 June 2009, JRC EC
5 Monitoring Agricultural Resources Bulletin, Vol. 1 March 2009, JRC EC
6 Baseline Survey Project: "Emergency Response Addressing Livelihood (Food) Security of Former IDPs/Expellees, Host Communities and Drought Affected Rural Populations in Eritrea". October 2010, EC, UNDP & GSE

National Grain Demand Vs Grain Production

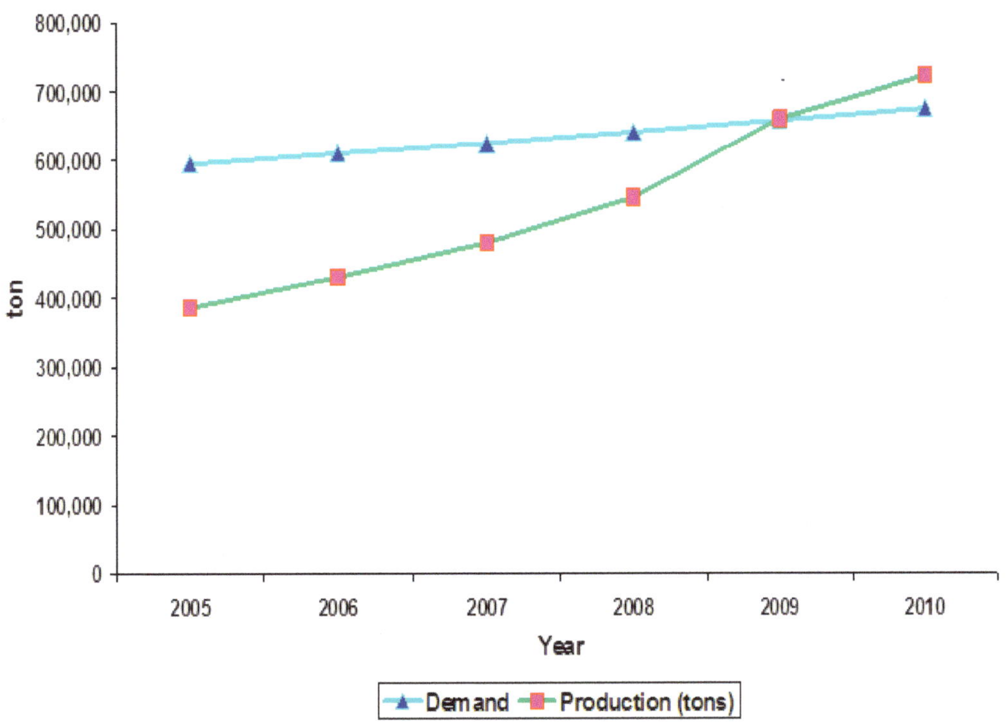

The agricultural sector registered an annual growth rate of 5.9 % of GDP between 1992 and 1999.
Its average share in the economy's GDP, at Constant Factor Cost, during those years, was 2.4 %.[6] Eritrea has always been a net food grain importer and was expected to continue to be so for some time to come. The share of imports in the total food grain consumption averaged 57% per annum during the period 1993–1999 (Ministry of Agriculture).[7] Even in the best years, Eritrea has to import about 40% of its total food needs, through commercial channels and via food assistance. In the worst drought years, that share rises to as much as 75 percent. During the years 2009 and 2010 Eritrea received favourable rainfall that resulted in relatively better harvests and thereby presumed to have enabled the country to meet at least 50% of its domestic food requirements.

Furthermore, there appears to be good economic prospects for the Country with the establishment of a joint mining venture at Bisha for gold, copper and zinc. A significant number of other mining companies are also licensed and/or are under licensing for mineral exploration.

Eritrea's arid and semi-arid climatic condition means a fragile environment and both natural and human forces have contributed to the relatively fast environmental degradation in the Country. Population pressure with its adverse impacts on the environment was intense, especially in the highlands. About 96% of energy consumption in the rural areas is biomass, thereby damaging further the disappearing forest stock of the country. Although, the demand for energy far outweighs the supply, the government was trying to address rural electrification by at least erecting the poles in selected rural communities for eventual connection to the national grid. Soil erosion was a serious problem and persistent droughts have caused soil to lose its vegetation cover and agricultural productivity has been adversely affected. Eritrea's accession to global environment and energy conventions, are among the country's attempts to reverse the worsening trends, which include: integrated land reclamation activities, a rural electrification fund, pilot wind power projects, preliminary geothermal studies, among others. However, extra efforts need to be embarked upon if these initial schemes are to be furthered and bear meaningful results.

The continuing humanitarian crisis Eritrea faces,
is a result of drought and the aftermath of the 1998-2000 war with Ethiopia that is yet to be resolved and continues to limit the government's ability to respond to the challenges effectively. Eritrea is one of the poorest countries in the world. The UNDP 2013 Human Development Index (HDI) ranked Eritrea at 181 out of 187 countries[8]. According to the National Water and Sanitation Action Plan (herewith 'Action Plan') of the Ministry of Land Water and Environment (MoLWE)[9] approximately 80% of the Eritrean population lives in rural settings. Of this, 60% were semi-nomadic, living in dispersed household (HHs) clusters.

6 *Government of Eritrea, Interim Poverty Reduction Strategy (I-PRSP), Asmara, April 2004*

7 *Government of the State of Eritrea, Draft Food Security Strategy, Asmara April 2004*

8 *Human Development Report, 2013, UNDP*

9 *National Water and Sanitation Action Plan, 2012-2017, Ministry of Land Water and Environment – 21 February 2012*

The arid areas of Eritrea have the highest incidence of poor and extreme poor population[10].

The Water, Sanitation and Hygiene (WASH) Sector Programme of Eritrea is designed to contribute to achieving National and Millennium Development Goals (MDGs). This programme was largely geared towards maintaining the gains made so far in capacity building and increasing access to improved drinking water supply, especially in the rural areas. It focuses on reaching the most vulnerable children and women, and aims at reducing the incidence of water borne diseases, in particular diarrhea among children under five.

Prior to the liberation of Eritrea in 1991, approximately 7% of the rural population (101,500 people) had access to safe water.
During the first seven years after liberation, significant progress has been made whereby, on average, an additional 35,000 rural people have received safe water services each year. Moreover, in the past 15 years, this yearly average has increased to almost 72,000. Today, it was estimated that slightly above 70% of the rural population (approximately 1,757,263 people according to the recently conducted survey) have access to safe water. However, the Southern Red Sea region has not fully benefited from this success, because of the harsh physical conditions and their remoteness from the main land.

Furthermore, social studies (KAP studies in 1998 and 2002) and a rapid assessment made in 2006 show that despite the provision of safe water services, most of the rural population have poor hygiene practices in water collection, storage and drinking. This calls for a concerted effort to raise awareness about the links between unhygienic practices and poor sanitation and that of disease transmission, including the need for skills development to identify and prevent such problems. Therefore, planning of future water development programmes must be integrated with those for sanitation and hygiene promotion including the carefully coordinated implementation of these activities to bring about synergy.

To address these challenges the 'National Water and Sanitation Action Plan' of the Government was intended to guide those working, to have a better plan, implement, manage and coordinate water and sanitation response interventions. Further guidance was also provided on technology choice, community participation, operations and maintenance, water conservation, recharge, maintaining of water quality, and for sanitation and hygiene promotion.

Moreover, the 'Action Plan' was considered an interim tool to meet the pressing water and sanitation needs over the next 5 years.
As noted earlier, this 'Action Plan' will also be guided by other key documents for Eritrea pertaining to sector planning and management and sector policies and legislative guidelines. Technical guidance for implementing the 'Action Plan' was also anticipated to be supplemented by pertinent and well tested, field manuals and tools already available to Eritrea through the Water Resources Department (WRD) of the Ministry of Land, Water and Environment.

10 *Dimensions of Poverty in Eritrea, Government of the State of Eritrea, May 2003*

The goal of this 'Action Plan' was, therefore, to ensure that all people in the Southern Red Sea are provided with at least a minimum supply of 20 litres of safe potable water/day, and that their basic sanitation needs are met over the next 5 years.

Despite the commendable progress since Independence, a lot remains to be done nation wide, to reach the goal of over 90 percent safe rural water coverage by 2015. Progress to date was seriously threatened by prolonged spells of drought which, if not tackled with appropriate strategies, will undermine future efforts and may even reverse service coverage and sustainability of water resources. Recognizing that almost 30 percent of the rural population does not have access to safe water, the task ahead was indeed a challenging one.

According to the 'Action Plan', a serious rethinking of overall water resources planning and management in the face of chronic drought, falling water tables and gaps in hydro geological data, is warranted. This necessitates an immediate sharing of all hydro geological, geophysical and hydrology studies and data to create a holistic understanding of the status of water resources in Eritrea and to identify critical gaps. A greater understanding of the hydro geological dynamics in various catchment basins and strategic aquifers was also needed to ensure that water extraction does not exceed that of water recharge. Furthermore, the rapidly falling water table in many agricultural areas where irrigation was practiced was a particularly worrying problem not only for agriculture, but also for human development needs.

Hence, this challenge forces policy decision makers to rethink how to utilize scarce resources better, work together effectively, better target setting and to make better use of proven and appropriate technologies and strategies, in order to reach the goals in an efficient, effective and sustainable manner.

Towards this end, in 2012 there was an effort, by the UNDP, to build capacity at the national level, so that the Water Resources Department would be capacitated to provide adequate technical leadership in setting of standards, formulating policies, strategy development, research and exploitation of water and the subsequent regulatory oversight. The necessary equipment has been secured in 2012, but more needs to be done in training of the professional staff in 2014 to complete the task.

Regarding the internationally committed development goals, Eritrea continues to make progress towards the MDGs.

As per the results of the First MDG Report (2006), the country was on track to achieve the MDGs relating to gender equality in primary education, child health, HIV/AIDS, malaria, and other major diseases, and access to safe drinking water. This picture has been reinforced by the latest DHS survey, the results of which has been officially released in September 2013. However, in the two crucial areas, namely eradication of extreme poverty and hunger and achievement of universal primary education, the country was below target. Though data paucity was still a major constraint which does not allow for complete assessment, the country appeared to have also made good progress in the crucial area of environmental sustainability according to first and only MDGs ever produced in Eritrea in 2006.

Recent information shows that Eritrea is one of the few countries in Africa that is making commendable progress towards achieving the health related MDGs 4, 5 & 6 reduce child mortality, reduce maternal mortality and combating HIV and AIDS).

It is now quoted as among 20 out of 46 countries in Sub-Saharan Africa (alongside Cape Verde, Mauritius and Seychelles) and one of 16 countries in the developing world, on track to attain MDG 4 (Reduce Child Mortality) by 2015[11]. The priority areas identified and subsequent interventions will enable the nation to consolidate and sustain the gains made and achieve the global targets of the MDGs by 2015.

Some of the recent achievements as reflected in the 2009 Annual Review Report for Basic Social Services include the expanded community based integrated management of child and newborn illnesses (IMNCI) whose coverage has reached some of the most affected regions (zobas) of Debub, Anseba, Northern Red Sea accounting for 50% from a baseline of 3%. There has been an increase of 48.5% in the number of deliveries at health facilities in Northern and Southern Red Sea. (to be cheked again and a footnote to be inserted)

In addition, a roadmap for Maternal and Newborn Health was developed to guide action in improving maternal and child health. In September 2010, the country launched the Campaign on Accelerated Reduction of Maternal Mortality in Eritrea (CARMME), an AU initiative aimed at assisting African countries to accelerate the reduction of maternal mortality and neonatal mortality in Africa. Coverage of antenatal care (ANC) has increased from 49% to 80%, while the HIV prevalence rate has declined from 2.38% in 2005 to 1.33% in 2008 among the general population (based on ANC and VCT centre visits).

Eritrea has also made commendable efforts in controlling communicable diseases. For example, by December 2010, about 14%[12] of HIV positive pregnant women were receiving a complete course of antiretroviral prophylaxis to reduce the risk of mother-to-child transmission; and PMTCT centers have grown from 91 in 2009 to 131 in 2010 giving pregnant women better access to HIV testing. Currently, 50% of the health facilities have the capacity and conditions to provide basic HIV counselling and testing and 80% of hospitals have the capacity and conditions to manage HIV/AIDS clinical services[13]. Furthermore, there have been several interventions and support programmes including development of policies and strategies and training of various health personnel in skills and management to enhance the capacity and quality of the health delivery system.

However, in order for Eritrea to attain sustainable quality and affordable health for all, persistent health related challenges related to nutritional deficiencies, diarrheal diseases, acute respiratory infections, malaria, HIV/AIDS and tuberculosis, and related infectious diseases, including rapidly increasing prevalence of non-communicable diseases, harmful practices, need to be continuously addressed.

---

11 The State of Africa's Children 2008, UNICEF

12 National AIDS and Tuberculosis Control Division (NATCoD) End of Year Review Report, 2010

13 NATCoD End of Year Review Report, 2010

Eritrea initially preferred to attain the MDGs through country contextualized approaches that primarily advance overall economic growth and development whereby the MDGs are implicitly linked to the country's development priorities and strategies. As part of its commitment to meet the MDGs, at present, the government was heavily engaged in the construction of rural infrastructure primarily aimed at the reduction of rural poverty through increased agricultural production and food security. In this connection, the government has also paid special attention to the development of rural health, education, roads and water supply facilities.

The key challenges in the government's efforts to processes meaningful socio-economic development process and achieve the MDGs (especially poverty reduction), inter alia, include: restoring macroeconomic stability, attracting quality investment, ensuring food security, achieving sustained and rapid economic growth, and mobilizing the required resources. Under such circumstances, the government's economic strategy tends to manage the macroeconomic imbalances using price controls and regulations until the security situation on the ground in connection to the border issue improves and allows transition to a market-based economy

Despite efforts made during the last two decades, Eritrea is still food insecure and as a consequence has relatively high rates of malnutrition, especially among children and women. Many households in the war affected areas of the country have been in the position of reducing expenditure on non-food items and depleting their household assets in order to meet their food consumption needs. A good indicator was an estimation made in 2002/2003 that an average of 66% of household expenditure goes for food in urban areas and 71% in rural areas[14].

Overall, the border war with Ethiopia and its lingering economic effects, coupled with the recurrent droughts eroded the immediate independence gains alluded to earlier.
The key challenges in the Government's efforts to promote a sustainable socio economic development and to achieve the MDGs, inter alia, included: restoring macroeconomic stability and sustained economic growth; ensuring food security; addressing environmental degradation; enhancing capacities for competent public service delivery; and mobilising the required resources.

Eritrea is prone to a humanitarian crisis as a result of drought and the aftermath of the 1998 - 2000 border war with Ethiopia that is yet not resolved and continues to limit the Government's ability to respond to the humanitarian crisis effectively. Since the end of the Eritrean-Ethiopian border war (1998 – 2000), the average growth in Gross Domestic Production (GDP), a key factor of poverty reduction and food security, has been low. Increasing levels of poverty in the country remain a major concern, with more than two thirds of the population living below the poverty line[15]. The UNDP Human Development Report 2011 Index (HDI) ranked Eritrea at 177 out of 187 countries.

14 Government of the State of Eritrea, National Statistics and Evaluation office, Dimensions of poverty in Eritrea, May 2003

15 Living Standards Measurement Survey, 2003, National statistics evaluation office

In 2008-2009, the prevailing variable global food price trends impacted local markets and caused high rates of fluctuation in prices of most market commodities, including staple grains, pulses, and animal feeds have been fluctuating at three figure rates annually: this has been aggravated by diesel fuel shortages that affect all economic activities. Due to poor crop and livestock yields, which are mostly caused by recurrent drought, supplies of agricultural produce to the local markets have been very low compared with the prevailing high demand for food. The above-mentioned changes on the supply and demand side of the food equation in the country have led to imbalances and drastic price changes in the local markets in unprecedented levels (50% to 100% increase in price of the common grains in 2008 & 2009). These facts have been recorded in the weekly local market assessment records, which have been ascertained during regular field monitoring activities of the on-going Joint Programme on IDPs, Expellees return and resettlement. The rising food prices further undermined the food security and threatened the livelihoods of the most vulnerable war/drought affected populations by eroding their already limited purchasing power.

The country is highly dependent on seasonal rainfall.
In general, precipitation ranges from 200mm -700mm throughout the country ;– it is torrential and of a short duration, despite the relatively good rain recorded in only few areas prior to 2007. In 2008 and 2009 rainfall was below average in most parts of Eritrea and the country experienced different levels of drought conditions. In 2008, there was nearly total crop failure in many places (in Debub region) and many farmers failed to harvest anything from their fields. The annual crop assessment internal report of the Ministry of Agriculture for 2008 showed that the total crop production was 108,000 metric tons, which was by far lower than the annual record of 400,000 to 600,000 metric tons during normal years. In 2009, average rainfall was below normal[4] and there was nearly total crop failure in many places (in Gash Barka and Debub regions). This resulted in much lower-than-average planting in the long season and higher yielding crops (sorghum, maize, and finger millet) and natural pastures failed to regenerate. Many farmers instead planted short cycle crops such as barley, wheat and summer ***taff*** which yield less, and legumes such as horse beans.

In Gash Barka region, although the 2009 main rainy season started on time (i.e. at the beginning of July), it stopped around the end of August and beginning of September which was earlier than normal by about two to three weeks. Crops did not receive the necessary moisture to complete their growth cycle and to fill up their grains. The 2008 and 2009 Bahri rains were not adequate as they were below average, consequently, crop fields dried up and livestock were starved, and death of livestock was prevalent in many parts of the country including Debub and Gash Barka regions.

As a consequences of the poor agricultural production, combined with the food price fluctuation and lack of income generating opportunities, many rural households did not have access to enough food sources for significant parts of 2008 and 2009. In some of the affected households, in return and resettlemnt areas of internally displaced persons and expellees, were forced to limit their food consumption, shift to even less-balanced diets, and consume or sell their assets, such as seeds and livestock and spend less on other goods and services that are essential for their health and welfare, such as clean water, sanitation, education, and health care. This means the people liquidated their very productive assets such as their seed reserves and livestock in order to cope with the crisis, a mechanism that weakens or even depletes the people's productive capabilities. As mentioned above, resource poor and women headed households as well as former IDPs/expellees who have been returned or resettled in 2008 were the most severely affected portions of the population in the country.

In responding to the above mentioned problems and the dire need to support the drought and war affected populations in the war affected regions of the country; the EC has signed three contribution agreements with UNDP in April 2008, in April 2009 and the last in June 2010. The first contribution agreement envisaged a component that supports the smooth and successful reintegration of IDP/expellee households in 2008-2010 to their villages of origin and designated areas of settlement. The second contribution was aimed at complementing the previous contribution by contributing to the on-going efforts in response to recurring problems of food insufficiency and retaining factors of agricultural production and integrating some 25,000 households from the former IDPs/ expellees and hosting communities to the society's productive strata through targeted and timely provision of support by employing Cash for Work program under the umbrella of Social Safety-net in semi/peri-urban communities.

By the same token the Norwegian Government has also signed three agreements with the UNDP. The first was signed in 2004 in support of the JP on IDPs/Expelees return/resettlement programme. The second was signed to support the Expanded JP on 2006. Finally the Norwegian Government supported the Transition and Early Recovery Programme supporting the on-going projects of the UNDP by signing an agreement in 2007.

The last multi-donor contribution was aimed at strengthening the livelihoods/food security and ability of drought and war affected agro-pastoralists by enhancing their farming systems productivity and resilience. In particular, the EC/UNDP/Norway contributions addresses economic rehabilitation and natural resources conservation, and contributes to the on-going efforts to achieve food security at household level through improved access to productive agricultural inputs and facilities; decreasing acute and growing animal feed as well as drinking water deficits and halt deteriorating conditions, including death of livestock in targeted areas.

There has also been great hope in the mining sector.

In the case of Bisha, extraction and export of gold has already started and the prospects for other minerals like potash in other parts of the country are claimed to be high. With the start up of gold production at the country's largest mine, real GDP was forecast to rise to 5% in 2010 (from 2.5% in 2009) and 7% in 2011 (EIU, 2010). With the opening up of the mining sector, there are also high prospects for new employment opportunities for skilled and semi-skilled manpower. However, with state control of most resources and little private sector involvement in the economy, it would be interesting to see how this evolves over time.

According to information extracted from the first MDGR (2006), the proportion of the population below the national poverty line was 53% during 1993-95 and the comparable figure for 2001-03 was 66%, mainly due to the undesirable effects of the border war and subsequent droughts. The highest incidence of poverty was realized to be in small towns followed by rural areas. According to the 2009 Human Development Report, Eritrea stood at a rank of 165 out of 182 countries in the Human Development Index with an index of 0.472. At the moment, there is no publically available national data that shows the current state of poverty in the country, as no recent survey has been undertaken to provide any update on poverty indicators.

Massive population displacements were the tragic consequence of both the war of liberation and the border war with Ethiopia.

Some 500,000 people fled the country during the war of liberation. Most went to Sudan. At the height of the border war with Ethiopia (1998 – 2000), as many as 1.1 million people, or a third of the population, were driven from their homes into internal displacement. In addition, over 75,000 Eritreans and Ethiopians of Eritrean origin were dispossessed of all property and forcibly deported from Ethiopia.

Hence, the border conflict with Ethiopia aggravated the already extensive socio-economic infrastructure damage as a result of the 30 years of war of liberation. In addition the border conflict had a devastating humanitarian impact. Some of the most serious problems caused by the border war were severe macro-economic imbalances, physical damage to infrastructure, decline in private sector activities and loss of agricultural output. The internally displaced persons were mainly from the Debub, Gash Barka and Southern Red Sea regions all located along the border with Ethiopia.

Evolving UN – Government Relations during the last two decades.

Before concluding the contributions of the Recovery Programmes in Eritrea, it would be appropriate to give a brief account on the evolving UN – GoSE relations over time, in order to indicate what would be the next chapter in this regard.

Government's Perceptions of the UN

The attitude of the Government over the last two decades has evolved from embracing it with open arms to subtle reservation. The most critical factor in the national context has been the perception of GoSE that the UN Security Council and the international community have failed to "force" Ethiopia to comply with the recommendations of the Ethiopia-Eritrea Boundary Commission and accept the virtual demarcation of the boundary coordinates that the Commission had established.

This together with the 2009 sanctions has caused irritation verging on frustration which have spilled over to the rest of the UN system, the value of whose contributions to Eritrea's development, in the view of the Government, are seen as marginal and miniscule vis-à-vis the political developments. It seems this situation has clouded the view and judgment of the Government in its attitude towards the UN Agencies in Eritrea.

The initial UN-Government relationship was excellent right from the beginning, with some ups and downs. The turning point, however, came in 2011. Eritrea was one of the United Nations Development Assistance Framework (UNDAF) roll-out countries for 2011; however the roll out process could not move forward as planned due to delays initially from our implementing partners and eventually by the Government.

Following the Finance Minister's return to Asmara from extensive absence abroad, and resumption of duties, a Joint UNDAF Mid-Term Review (MTR) workshop was held in September 2010, more than a year after its original due date. The UNDAF/MTR meeting was chaired by the Minister himself and by all accounts took place in a positive spirit of cooperation. The review of UNDAF accomplishments and subsequent deliberations were conducted in an open, transparent and constructive manner. While acknowledging the catalytic role that the UN system in Eritrea had played over the years and the critical transformational results achieved by UNDAF resources in promoting sustainable development, the Minister reiterated Eritrea's principle of self reliance and its desire to reduce its dependence on external financial flows.

In his view, the current UNDAF was too broad with many stakeholders and areas of intervention. In his closing remarks, the Minister underscored the need to develop a more focused UNDAF with results-oriented programmes that can make real impact on the ground and in the lives of Eritreans. He informed the meeting that the Government would take time to fully reflect on the deliberations of the MTR and further consult among its various bodies on the issues raised in the meeting, including the extension of UNDAF for one year (2012) to pave the way for an orderly UNDAF development rollout.

Following the MTR meeting, a series of follow-up meetings were held between the UN-RC and the Minister of Finance on a number of issues including the need for UNDAF extension, given that the time period for preparation of the new UNDAF and the deadlines for the approval by Headquarters could not be met. During these meetings, the Minister indicated in principle that the extension would be granted but stressed that he first wanted an exhaustive compilation of information from all UN agencies on their on-going interventions under the current UNDAF. Of particular interest for the Minister was data on financial flows and funds disbursed to national implementing partners (IPs) from the inception of the current UNDAF (2007) up to November 2010. This information was compiled by RC's office and forwarded to the Minister of Finance in early November 2010.

Much to the surprise of the United Nations, the Minister of Finance communicated to the United Nations Resident Coordinator (UN-RC) on 26 January 2011 informing UNCT that the Government of the State of Eritrea (GoSE) after assessing its past cooperation agreement would not be granting an extension of the current UNDAF and did not wish to enter into any new UNDAF agreement with the United Nations at the end of June 2011.

The principal objective of this decision as stated in the letter was the Government's intention to curbing financial aid flows in Eritrea as these are assessed to be harmful to the self-reliance national efforts.

The letter further requested all UN Agencies to complete on-going UNDAF projects/programmes for the year 2011 by 30 June and shift all remaining activities and financial resources in three specific areas (health, safe water supply and sanitation without due consideration of the annual work plans and budgets approved at the beginning of the year), and terminating before the normal UNDAF cycle was scheduled to end in December 2011. The letter also outlined the government's decision to only deal with a few selected agencies on a bilateral basis, namely UNDP, UNICEF, UNFPA, and WHO.

The principal objective underlying this decision by the Government was its intention to phase-out grant/aid financing and put in place its long stated goal of a development blue print based on its self reliance principle by relying on self-mobilized resources (domestic and/or foreign resources).

Moreover, the Governemnt had also sent two additional letters, namely a letter on 3 May 2012 stating that it had not yet decided on the options it had on the future GoSE-UN cooperations and that "GoE wants to know what the possible financial allocation for Eritrea will be before it can reach into a decision" and "whether the money can be used for productive capital Investments that augument sustainable development in some sectors."

On the other hand, the letter of 14 May states categorically that the GoSE had decided for quite some time to get rid of "aid" dependence gradually over a period of three years spanning from 2010-2012. Moreover, the Government reiterated that it will not submit a request for grant financial "aid" from the UN system for 2013 and all UN-funded projects carried forward to 2012 in health, water and sanitation should be completed within the year. In regard to extension or broadening of the current Framework Cooperation Agreement for 2013 until the Government clearly articulates the envisaged programme for productive capital investments, it stressed that no indication will be given to the UN Agencies at this time, "even at the risk of not having any UN Country Programme or financial allocation for 2013". This implied that the UN Agencies could not request for programme extension and bridge funding for 2013. Instead the Government directed that the UN should make new arrangements "to the realization of the changed circumstances in 2013.

Furthermore, these new areas fall outside UNDP's core competencies and organizational mandate. The fact that the UNDP programme could be adjusted to fit within this new framework for the 18 month period was remarkable and it shows the flexibility shown by the UNDP. The Recovery Unit was at the end of a series of fruitful cooperation programmes since 1992 culminating with the Transition and Early Recovery Programme scheduled to be completed at the end of 2012. The UNDP Recovery programmes will align itself with the goals of the UNDP Strategic Plan 2014 – 2016 and continue to move towards supporting fully the Government with its development efforts, in accordance to its national priorities.

Steps taken by UN to response to Governments directives

In response to the new policy directive, the UNCT has developed as an interim measure a Strategic Concept Note that outlined the UN response to the new priority needs of the Government. It was an interim measure, because the UNCT reiterated that some of the UN Agencies mandates and programmes (such as education, environment and sustainable development, food security, poverty reduction, recovery and others) were excluded in the new narrowly defined priorities set by the Government. However, if the UN system in Eritrea was to close all projects that are outside the new priorities by 30 June 2011, the interim measure gives breathing space until a more comprehensive UN policy decision was in place.

Consequently, the initial Concept Note briefly described the three priority sectors identified by the Government, namely health, safe water supply and sanitation drawing on the comparative strengths and mandates of UN agencies. The Government had modified the Concept Note so that its content complied with existing policies. Based on the concept note a GoSE–UN Cooperation Programme had been developed and agreed upon by the Government and UN. The new framework lasted until December 2012.

The agreement committed the Government to notify the UN system in Eritrea by the end of April 2012 at the latest, whether the present framework will be extended, modified, expanded or ended. By the same token, the Government would also commit itself to facilitate joint monitoring field visits to project sites which was now very difficult because of cumbersome processes to secure permits, especially for UN international staff.

Government's Principle of Self reliance

In a letter from the Minister of Finance to UN-RC on Government-UN Eritrea Cooperation, he emphatically stated that,

"national development will never be materialized if it is done by depending on grant financing from UN agencies and other bilateral resources ....Therefore, the Government of Eritrea has decided to curb financial flows to Eritrea.... and because of this Eritrea will not subscribe to another UNDAF....."

The Minister had previously stated in 2008 during the UNDAF annual review that,

*"due to the tempo currently unfolding in Eritrea and due to its desire for self-reliance, the UNDAF arrangement was likely not to have a long life span in Eritrea. As such, the UN system should thus start initiating an **exit strategy** that will enable it to squarely phase out eventually."*

Therefore, the recent position of the Government is just in a fulfilment of the statement made by the Minister in 2008.

The Government's goal still remains attaining food security and achieving a decent standard of living through growth and human resource development. To achieve this goal, however, the Government has stated emphatically that,

"aid only postpones the basic solutions to crucial development problems by tentatively ameliorating their manifestation without tackling the root causes".

Consequently, it was the Government's desire not to have a programme framework supported by grants and/or aid over a long period of time.

Despite this policy on self-reliance, aid/grant to the country to date has been very high considering the ratio of aid to GDP.

The Recovery Programmes of the UNDP alone has disbursed nearly USD 120 Million addressing the needs of war affected populations by rehabilitating/constructing over 40,000 housing units, tens of schools and health facilities, provision of potable water for human consumption and water for their domestic animals, as well as programmes focusing on sustainable livelihoods. Moreover, since the inception of the UNDAF in 2007 to October 2010, the UN System in Eritrea has supported Government with financial and technical assistance to the tune of USD 169.6 million.

UN Operations in Eritrea

The UN continued to operate in a very challenging environment in Eritrea. The Government had imposed a number of restrictions on UN operations including an embargo without notice on the sale of diesel to UN agencies in 2008 and restricted access to the field especially for international staff, and UN vehicles to monitor field-based projects. Field trips outside Asmara have become few and often preceded sometimes by tedious arrangements. The UN has had to adopt coping measures such as stocking diesel in limited amounts for emergency purposes and hiring vehicles from the local market which have increased operational costs. These coping measures in some instances run the risk of the UN not being safety and security compliant. Moreover, the lack of national statistics in the public domain, absence of macro-economic parameters and the absence of National Development Plans have hampered the development of appropriate responses by the UN system to the challenges faced by the Government.

Emerging trends in Development Assistance in Eritrea

Over the past few years, we have witnessed a consistent trend in declining development assistance to Eritrea. Bilateral and multilateral donors (USAID, DANIDA, AfDB and ECHO) who were present in the country are now virtually absent from the country and with very limited operations as it was the case with the AfDB, the WB and IMF. All international NGOs have ceased their operations and were instructed by the Government to wind-up their activities by 31 December 2011. The World Bank has ceased its lending operations in Eritrea, closed its offices and was currently using a small office space at the UNDP CO to wind-up its house keeping business.

THE CONTEXT OF THE UNDP RECOVERY PROGRAMMES IN ERITREA

Rehabilitation, Reconstruction and Reintegration of Social and Economic Infrastructure after the Thirty Year war of liberation

Recovery Programmes geared at war damaged infrastructure and the re-integration of displaced target populations as a result of Ethio-Eritrea border war.

The strategy followed for these two distinct but historically interrelated recovery programmes were similar, the latter building on the experience of the former.

Moreover, during the border war the mobilization of most men between the ages of 18-50 into national service, has resulted in women headed (70%) households in emergency camps and in return/resettlement areas. This disruption of the gender-balance in households and in the distribution of work placed an enormous burden on women, the elderly and children posed a major challenge for promoting sustaining livelihoods.

The war-affected areas constituted some 70% of the country's agricultural production. Other extensive destruction of major economic and social infrastructure was also incurred. These factors combined to set back the country's development significantly. The periodic/cyclical drought conditions in many parts of the country aggravated the magnitude of the emergency situation.

In addition, with the assistance of UNHCR, the Government of Eritrea re-started the repatriation of Eritrean refugees from Sudan in late 2001 as part of the continuation of the PROFERI programme. Furthermore, the Government had also demobilized over 100,000 soldiers and at the time made preparations for the demobilization and re-integration of another 100,000 soldiers.

Moreover, the villages and towns to which the IDPs and refugees from the Sudan have been returning were, in most cases, devastated by the effects of the war. In some areas, whole villages and towns such as Tsorona, Om Hajer were completely destroyed and looted.

The results of the Joint Rapid Assessment, conducted at the end of July 2000 by UNDP/ERREC/Italian Cooperation, indicated that the IDPs were spontaneously returning to their homes where they encountered lack of basic shelter, household utensils and means of production. By the end of July 2000, it was estimated that 760,000-1,260,000 IDPs out of the total 1.6 million had already returned to their homes in Gash Barka and Debub. Some 25,000 Eritrean refugees from Sudan had also returned to their homes in Gash Barka. The rest of the IDPs remained in camps, with host communities in or outside of their zones, or even took refuge in the nearby mountains. The figures on returnees constantly increased with the intensifying trend to move out of the IDP camps. A limited number of "new" refugees returning from Sudan also added to the numbers.

The overwhelming majority of the IDPs originated from farming households in the two agriculturally rich regions, Debub and Gash Barka. They faced several constraints to land cultivation on their return: they arrived too late in the season; invading forces occupied parts of the inland; the fear of land mines reduced significantly the available cultivable land; and there was a lack of draught animals, farm implements and seeds. In the majority of the ethnic groups in the area, women traditionally do not perform such tasks as ploughing. As women head the bulk of the returning households and there was – and still is - a severe shortage of male and machine power, land preparation was and is severely inhibited. Furthermore, some of the women in the affected areas have traditionally played a marginal role in non-agricultural income-generating activities and found it difficult to engage themselves in any other productive activities.

That was the grim picture facing the country in the aftermath of the border war with Ethiopia.

Before concluding this section, a word about the fluctuating Nakfa against the dollar would be appropriate. The value of the Nakfa against the dollar has constantly eroded over a period of ten years. The price of commodities was constantly getting higher and higher; cost of fuel was skyrocheting; labour-cost was rising disproportionately; and inflation, although a time series data was missing, was at an all time high (EC Report estimates inflation at 30 % per annum).

Although at the beginning of the Reovery programmes the exchange rate of the US Dollar was stable, it started to deteriorate after the border war with Ethiopia and the change of currency from Birr to Nkfa had also its own share.

The parallel (black) market gradually grew from one dollar to seven Nakfa to 50 Nkfa at the time of this report. This has great impact on the living costs of the people, especially those affected by war and drought. This has also a negative impact on the programmable budget for all recovery projets. This was especially true for projects that were dependent on commodities, especially construction materials, in the local market. In simple language, one US dollar was exchanged at the official fixed rate of 15 Nakfa, while the parallel market offered up to 50 Nakfa, which is a little more than three times the official rate. Hence, 2/3 of the mobilized funds were going directly to the government coffer while only as little as 1/3 was expended on programmes. By this estimation the number of projects could easily have doubled if not trebled. In the most critical period of the border war the price of one corrugated iron sheet, gauge 28, for roofing was about 110 Nakfa. This cost has escalated over time to 800-900 Nakfa per piece, for inferior quality corrugated iron sheets, with thinner galvanization.

Another important handicap was the state of the construction industry where licence of contractors and consultants were cancelled without notice in 2005. UNDP programme managers were forced to use semi-government entities (parastatals) as contractors in the implementation of infrastructure projects. In the absence of genuine competition from the private sector, these parastatals could dictate the price regardless of the quality of work they could offer. In those rare instances where recovery projects were allowed to make competitive biddings in the regions, the private enterprises won by a wide margin at competitive prices. These were exceptions rather than the rule. Moreover, the parastatal construction companies hardly finish projects in time or without cost overruns.

The interventions were always divided into support given at the household level (packages) and support given to communities as a whole (such as water system, health and school facilities, etc.

2.1 WHAT IS RECOVERY?

"It (recovery) is not only about rebuilding what there was – but building back better, creating safer and better communities… And it is about shaping the future relationship between the State, local government and civil society. The "early recovery clusters" coordinated by UNDP have the objective of bringing together all parts of the UN system and relevant NGOs in support of a country's effort to move as rapidly as possible from the humanitarian relief phase to the long-term reconstruction and development phase."

Kemal Dervis, UNDP/UNFPA Executive Board, 2006

In order to understand better the scope and impact of the varied UNDP recovery programmes in Eritrea starting from the opening of the liason office in Asmsra in 1992 to the Transition and Early Recovery programme ending in 2012, it would be helpful to define what recovery is.

Early recovery programmes represent the application of development principles – national ownership, capacity utilization and support, peoples participation – in a humanitarian setting. It is the interface at which humanitarian and development partners co-exist and interact and allows for the early initiation of recovery planning and key programming, thereby minimizing the gap between the end of relief and the onset of longer-term recovery.

UNDP as a policy[16] views its involvement in early recovery as an integral part of its support for poverty reduction, sustainable human development and the achievement of the Millennium Development Goals in crisis affected countries.

Early Recovery

In the words of the Inter Agency Standing Committee (IASC) Cluster Working Group, early recovery, therefore, is the term used to describe the application of development principles to humanitarian situations. It is intended to stabilise local and national capacities from further deterioration so that they can provide the foundation for full recovery and stimulate spontaneous recovery activities within the affected population. If such national capacities are used and strengthened, they are likely to reduce the overall burden of humanitarian support more rapidly.

"Early recovery is a multi dimensional process of recovery that begins in a humanitarian setting. It is guided by development principles that seek to build on humanitarian programmes and to catalyse sustainable development opportunities. It aims to generate self-sustaining, nationally owned, resilient processes for post-crisis recovery".[17]

While in a crisis situation, life saving relief is undeniably the most important priority, affected populations simultaneously start looking for ways to rebuild their lives. Support to stabilise the situation can reduce further setbacks for the affected population and pave the way towards full recovery. The situation in the area, (especially in the aftermath of the border war with Ethiopia that saw massive displacement of people, about 1.1 million, in a relatively small nation) was full of challenges.

This required actors to focus not only on saving lives but also on stemming further loss of livelihoods and security that were fundamental to the survival of the affected population, even as the humanitarian operations were underway.

16 UNDP Policy on Early Recovery, Bureau for Crisis Prevention and Recovery UNDP, New York and Geneva, 7 February 2008

17 Guidance Note on Early Recovery, IASC Cluster Working Group, October 2007

As will be illustrated later when describing the various programmes, the strategy followed at the outset was to support, sustain, and begin to rebuild the essential national capacities that are necessary to manage the situation in the longer term. The PROFERI programme was the case in point where the focal government agency ERREC was the focus of intensive capacity building.

This was achieved through distinctive early recovery activities to stabilise the situation, while identifying opportunities for longer term recovery and eventually development. In this sense, early recovery in Eritrea started very early during the humanitarian operation phase. Such strategy brought development principles into relief activities and seized the opportunities to go beyond saving lives and contributing to the building of national capacity, livelihoods and human security.

The nine recovery programmes in Eritrea (listed in Annex 10) that were spread over two decades, had some common characteristics that focused on interventions at the household level and interventions that affect the whole community including host-communities where applicable.

Interventions at the household level included support to vulnerable households with agricultural inputs (provision of seeds, farm tools, oxen, donkeys, support to shelter construction etc.) while the interventions at the community level included the rehabilitation and construction of water systems for both human and animal consumption, school and health facilities, water and soil conservation, reforestration, etc). It was obvious that with the exception of the relief distribution of items to save lives, the others such as the construction of micro dams that will have a life span of at least 30 years, could assist the long term development goals of the country beyond the immediate supply of potable water for the displaced populations.

In this regard, significant achievements have been registered as observed by numerous independent external evaluators of the various recovery programmes. Not every template developed at the global level applies to every country in a crisis situation and Eritrea is not an exception. Yet every avenue was explored during implementation of the various programmes and the best practices adopted to suit to the requirements and needs of the people.

The application of the early recovery guidelines, developed by the IASC, paraphrased below, were implemented in the following manner:

a) **There is no identifiable stage in a sequential "continuum" between relief and recovery.** We have noted that in the three most war affected regions in the country different vulnerable groups recover at different speeds. The Recovery team has therefore designed programmes for relief and recovery that are appropriate for each region, sub region and local communities. In most cases relief and recovery were taking place side by side, and simultaneously.

a) **In a humanitarian setting, the needs and opportunities for early recovery evolve over time and sometimes change very rapidly.** Situations may progress, creating new opportunities, or they may regress, stifling existing activities. There is therefore a continuous need for sensitivity and flexibility in implementing early recovery activities.

a) As cited in the earlier paragraphs, while early recovery paved the way for future longer term activities, **there was a need at times, to distinguish between early recovery and recovery programmes.** Early recovery programmes are foundational in nature. They restore and strengthen the capacities of governments at all levels to manage and lead the recovery process. They simultaneously facilitate the resumption of key livelihood, service delivery and community security programmes.

b) Recovery programmes, however, build on these early foundations and restore the social, political and economic fabric of a society while addressing the root causes of the crisis. These programmes are longer term and are normally derived from a systematic Post Conflict Needs Assessment (PCNA).

2.2 Framework for UNDP's Support to the Recovery Programmes in Eritrea

The Recovery Programmes supported by the UNDP spanned over two decades (1992-2012). The nine major programmes include: Pre-referendum Recovery Project (PRP), Programme for Refugee Reintegration and Rehabilitation of Resettlement Areas in Eritrea (PROFERI), Pre-Post-War Emergency Programme (PRE-PoWER), Post War Emergency Programme (PoWER I and II), Integrated Recovery Programme (IRP), Joint Programme on IDPs/Expellees Return/Resettlement (JP on IDPs/EXPELLEES Phases One and Expanded) and finally the Transition and Early Recovery Programme (TER).

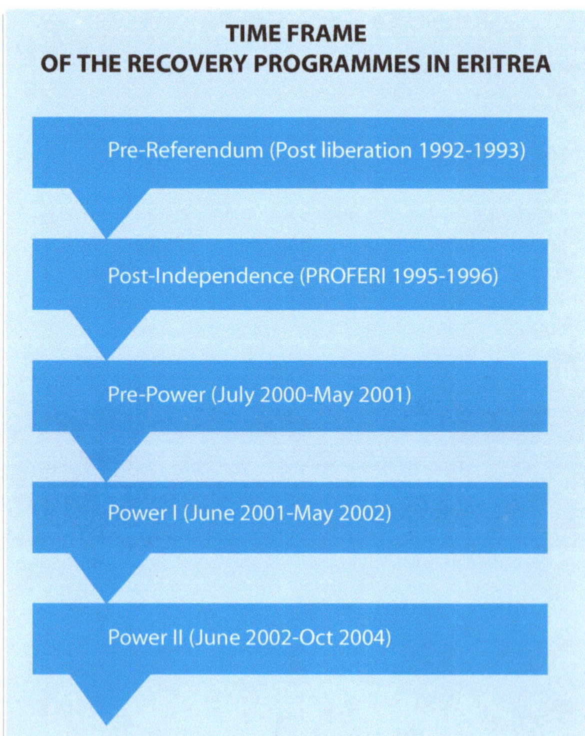

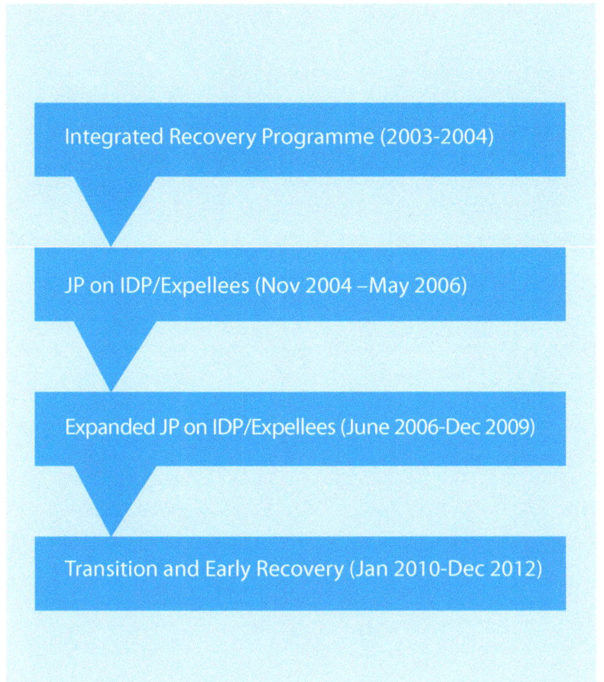

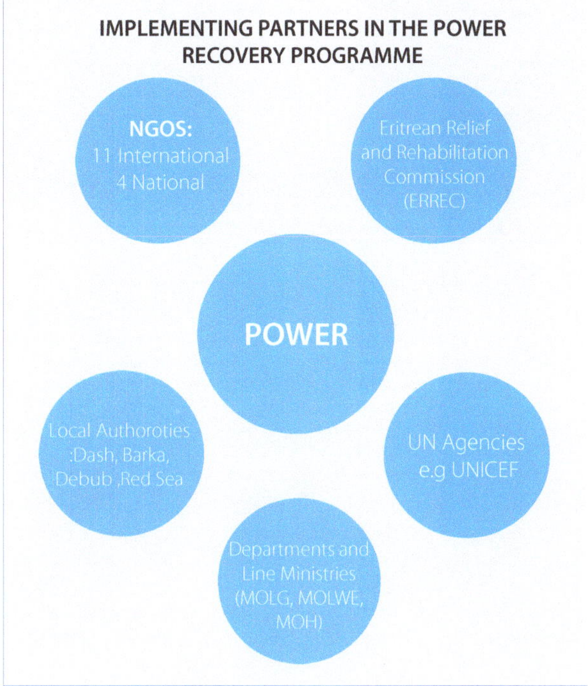

The United Nations Development Programme in Eritrea started supporting the Government of Eritrea almost immediately after liberation, in 1992 and before Independence in 1993. This was followed by PROFERI, the first major recovery programme in Eritrea 1995-1996. This was followed by a series of Recovery Programmes following the border war with Ethiopia.

The UNDP Recovery Programme in Eritrea was designed to help first with the emergency situation and then – more importantly – with the transition from relief to sustainable medium-term development. The beneficiaries of the Programme were to be the returning IDPs/Expellees, demobilized ex-combatants with a focus on female-headed households and host communities.

The Recovery Programmes covered the major sectors of an integrated recovery operation, namely shelter, non-food household items (NFIs), health, education, water and sanitation, sustainable livelihoods and capacity building. The shelter, sustainable livelihood and capacity building sectors were given particular attention and UNDP took a lead in those sectors together with the Eritrean Relief and Refugee Commission (ERREC) and the Regional Administrations of Debub, Gash Barka and Southern Red Sea.

The implementation of projects under the Recovery Programmes was undertaken by relevant Government agencies, regional administrations and national/international NGOs. The modality of using Non-Governmental Organizations (NGOs) has been carefully worked out by taking into consideration the on again and off again strained Government and NGO relations.

The decision making structure adopted allowed us to boldly introduce Government-endorsed NGO-implemented community interventions. In addition, the implementation of some projects through the structure of local administrations has greatly assisted in building the local authorities' capacities for efficient planning and implementation of recovery projects.

The Recovery Programmes have operated through a rapid, effective and flexible mechanism for approving and implementing recovery projects. Due to the then overstretched capacity of many of the Government departments, UNDP CO with the approval of the Government and UNDP HQs decided to assume responsibility for the direct execution of the early Programmes instead of the usual National Execution modality (NEX/NIM) in order to ensure expedient delivery of assistance through such a complex, multi-sectoral programme. UNDP, in consultation with the Government, was able to use different implementing agencies (the Government departments and/or NGOs) according to their comparative advantages and capacities. UNDP directly procured goods and equipment as necessary. This mechanism for approving and implementing recovery projects has allowed full ownership from the Government and flexibility in allocating resources according to emergency needs.

2.3 Resources Mobilized for the UNDP Recovery Programmes

Funding for the UNDP Recovery Programmes totalled USD 119,990,669.00 USD and it comprised of projects benefiting IDPs, host communities, returning refugees and expellees as well as targeting the economic and social re-integration of demobilized soldiers.

By and large, the resource mobilization strategy for Recovery Programmes has been highly succsseful except in one programme area, the Integrated Recovery Programme (IRP). Granted, resource mobilization at the CO level had its ups and downs, however, recovery fared better than the other CO programmes, because we tried our level best to divorce it from domestic political entanglements that the donors always raised.

There were drawbacks from time to time, because of the perception of donors and their tendency to attach it to the bilateral/multi-lateral problems they face with the government. Some donors have also used it as an excuse for not contributing, although they had no intention to be generous, whatever the circumstances.

There was one occasion when diplomats and donors from 16 countries (including 7 Ambassadors) were given a guided tour of recovery projects in Gash Barka. The area was flooded with cars of all brands (Land Cruisers, Land Rovers, Four Wheel Drive vehicles and others) and were marshalled to cruise noisily along quiet rural roads and settlements.

This was a big fiasco, since not a single cent was mobilized by this effort. On the contrary there was a negative reaction from the authorities.

It looked like the area was invaded by Donors ready for the ride, a term that we use to describe donors who join field trips to visit project sites but have no intention to seriously consider funding any. This term we coined after one of the village adminstrators complained that donors come and take photographs of our homes and our family members, but they do not even share a copy of the pictures with us, nor do we see concrete results from their visit.

There was one particular Embassy that made the UNDP Recovery Unit prepare five different project proposals in order to secure some emergency funds. In the period covering the years 2002–2009, not a dime was provided by the said Embassy. When there was a sixth attempt by the same Embassy to prepare yet another project proposal, the Ambassador was emphatically told not to waste our time and energy for promises of funds that were never kept.

The resource mobilization was successful when targeted to likely donors and countries. The tools used were multi faceted, including but not limited to field visits by selected donors to project sites, so that they can see first hand, the value of their money; 90-100% high delivery rate accompanied by annual consolidated reports, quarterly narrative and financial reports; visibility of the donor countries in UNDP publications and websites for the benefit of their constituents back home.

Resources Mobilized for Recovery Programmes in Eritrea: Both pooled by UNDP, and parallel by other partners (agencies)

Programme/Project		**Budget**	**Donor**
Post Liberation/Pre-Referendum Project - PRP (1992 1993)		6,000,000	UNDP
Sub Total		**6,000,000**	
PROFERI (1995-1997)		9,305,873	UNDP
		2,054,795	Swedish Trust Fund (managed by UNDP)
	Sub Total	**11,360,668**	
Pre-PoWER (July 2000-March 2002)	Emergency Assistance	1,334,661	Italy
	Emergency Assistance	314,150	USAID
	Sub Total	**1,648,811**	
PoWER (November 2000-October 2004)	PoWER I (Nov. 2000-Dec.2001)	14,934,882	Italy
	PoWER II	2,177,056	Italy
	Emergency shelter & HH Items	5,336,156	Netherlands
	Capacity Building and Mine Action	4,035,193	Norway, Holland, EU, UK, Canada
	Preparatory Assistance Demobilization	200,000	UNDP
	TA for Demobilization	580,000	USAID
	Sub Total	**27,263,287**	

IRP (*2003-2004*)	Jumpstart IRP	226,000	UNDP/BCPR
	Sub Total	**226,000**	
First Joint Programme (*November 2004-March 2006*)	Pooled Funding	1,000,000	UNDP
		2,061,088	Norway
		1,111,000	Netherlands
		1,000,000	USAID
		240,000	UNICEF
		829,384	Italy
	Parallel funding	3,030,000	WFP (In-knid)
		2,370,000	Norway (NGOs)
		1,300,000	Government (In-kind)
	Sub Total	**12,941,472**	
Expanded Joint Programme *(April 2006-December 2009)*	Pooled Funding	2,400,000	UNDP
		11,788,113	Norway
		904,000	Netherlands
		3,875,171	USAID
		1,600,000	Norway (transferred funds from Mine Action to IDPs)
		996,000	CERF
		240,000	CERF to IDPs
		240,000	CERF to Mine Action
		400,000	CERF to IDPs
		15,741,400	EC
	Parallel funding	300,000	UNICEF
		70,500	UNHCR
		In-kind	UNHCR
	Sub Total	**38,555,184**	
Transition and Early Recovery Programme - TER (January 2010-December 2012)		6,283,837 3,664,347 10,756,837 265,947 1,024,288	UNDP Norway EC UNOCHA GoSE (IFAD)
	Sub Total	**21,995,256**	
	Total	**119,990,669**	

It should be noted that there were extraordinary donors and diplomats that assisted the UNDP Recovery Unit achieve, time and again, its resource mobilization targets. They were not only supportive of the recovery programmes, they were people of compassion, committment and integrity who delivered what they promised. Prominent among these were: Sergio Palladini, Emma Gori (Italian Cooperation); Yoka Brandt, Annemarie van der Heijden, Marisa Pechaczek (The Netherlands); Paula Amadei, Jean-Paul Heerschap, Karin Jonsson, Tanith Bello, Stefanescu Bogda, Hilda Timmerman (EU/EC); Kari Bjrnsgrevink, Brita Naas, Rodney Lobo and Ellen Borchgrevink (Norway).

Donors visiting a project site in Endabastifanos, Debub region

Since 1994, the Recovery Programmes have rehabilitated schools, supplied school furniture and materials, refurbished health facilities (including hospitals) and purchased medical supplies, furniture and other equipment along with technical assistance in the health sector. It has also rehabilitated houses and market places/buildings, constructed new housing units, distributed semi-permanent shelters and upgraded permanent structures, supported projects for livelihoods of IDPs/Expellees and host communities.

Health Center including residence for staff rehabilitated in Omhajer

Middle School reconstructed in Omajer – Gash Barka

Furthermore, the programmes drilled boreholes, constructed hand-dug wells and built a variety of micro dams and water distribuition systems. The programmes have supported national safety net projects through cash-for-work programmes, provided assistance and NFI to several IDP camps, and implemented integrated community-based projects. The latter improved the living conditions in those communities, especially for women headed households, and successfully provided sustainable livelihoods through skills training and income-generating activities.

2.4 Implementation and Management Structures

The management structures varied from programme to programme. The latter programmes have gained from the experience of the earlier programmes. As a general rule, the ownership of the process was fully in the hands of the government right from the beginning. There was flexibility all along and the UNDP and other development partners were fully engaged in the planning and monitoring and evaluation of the various recovery programmes.

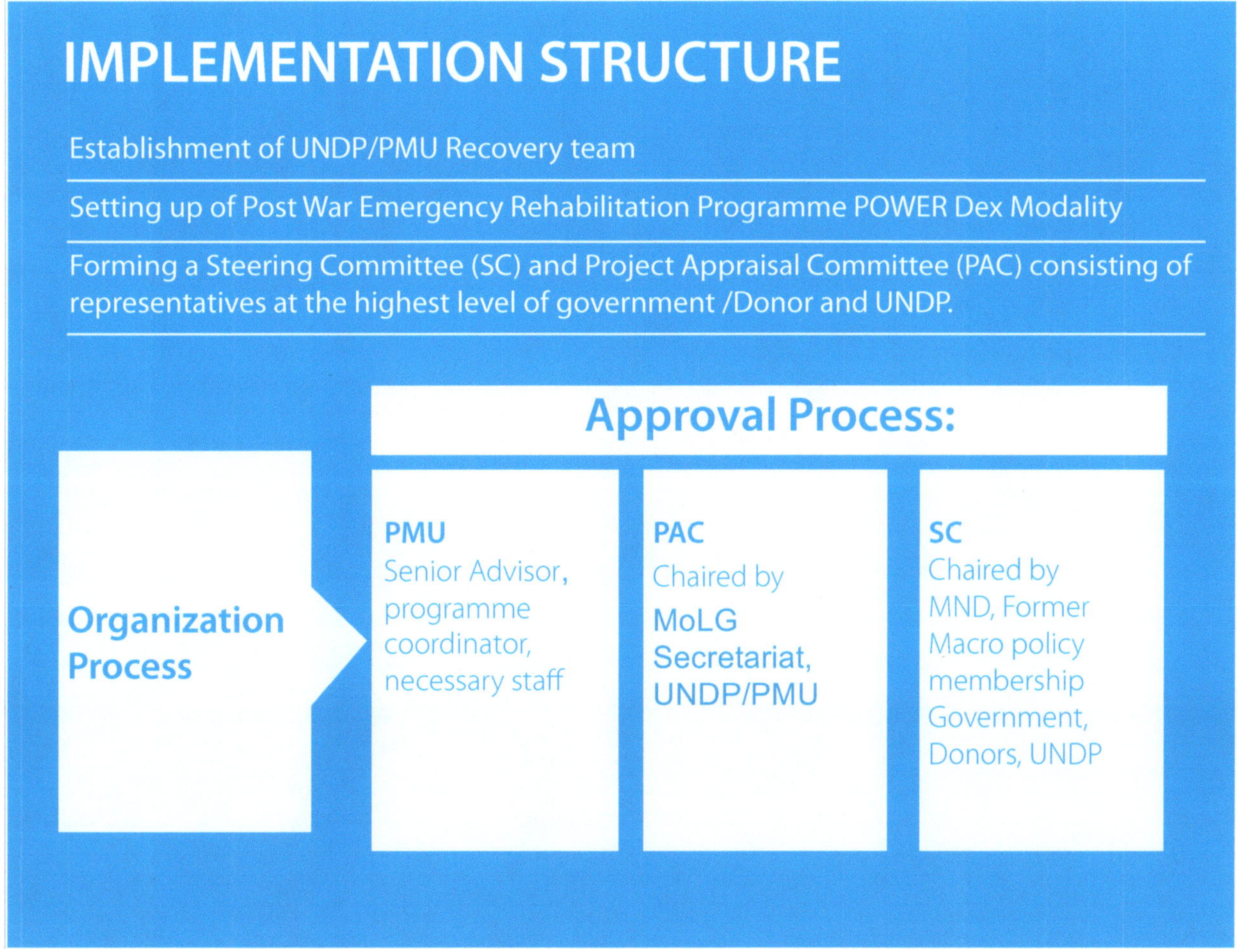

The management structures for making decisions consisted of the following main elements: Establishment of Programme Steering Committee (SC) comprising of representatives from the Department for International Cooperation, Macro Policy and Economic Coordination later replaced by the Ministry of National Development (MoND) (Chair), the Ministry of Local Government, Eritrean Refugees and Rehabilitation Commission (ERREC), United Nations Development Programme (UNDP) (Secretary), Italian Cooperation (as a major funder) and the Programme Management Unit of the Government run Emergency Recovery Programme (ERP). The SC met once a month to oversee the overall activities of the programme. Duties included: policy decisions, including resource allocations; approval of projects; review of periodic project progress and evaluation reports; and participation in the periodic reviews of the projects. The SC had the responsibility to review and respond to the evolving emergency situation, if warranted, through reallocation of funds based on identified priority needs.

The Project Appraisal Committee (PAC), was established for the appraisal of individual projects. The Committee consisted of representatives from the Ministry of Local Government (Chair), ERREC, UNDP and Italian Cooperation (by far the major contribution at the time). Other Donors were also allowed to attend, on a case by case basis, if they show in interest on a project(s) under consideration. The PAC submits its recommendations, before implementation, to the Steering Committee for final review and approval.

The Programme Management Unit (PMU), responsible for the day-to-day management of the programme included a senior advisor on recovery, programme coordinator, community development specialist, a technical specialist, a finance officer, a logistics/procurement officer and support staff.

During the early period of the implementation of this programme, other recovery activities, such as projects implemented with funding from the Netherlands and USAID, were processed through the standard UNDP procedures for review and approval of projects.

For projects to be considered by the SC, respective regional administrations and relevant line ministries must give their written endorsement for the proposed activity. Without this endorsement the SC cannot consider or approve any project. This process ensured that the Government has complete control of the programme and hence its support was unconditional.

Coordination in the Humanitarian Sector

Under the overall leadership of the Government, represented by ERREC, activities of the various humanitarian players in Eritrea were coordinated in the framework of a humanitarian coordination forum that held on the average monthly meetings. Under this forum, five sectoral working groups (SWG) monitored the humanitarian situation and harmonized activities in their respective sectors, namely: Shelter and Household Items, Water and Sanitation, Food Aid and Food Security, Education, and Health and Nutrition. In addition to meetings of the main sectoral working groups in Asmara, inter-agency coordination meetings were also held at the regional level in three of the affected regions, namely: Gash Barka, Debub and Southern Red Sea[18].

The UN system in Eritrea played a prominent role in the above-mentioned coordination forums. The UN Resident Coordinator, who also serves as the UN Humanitarian Coordinator, co-convenes the monthly forum with the Government. Similarly, each of the sectoral working groups was co-chaired by a representative of a UN agency most active in the particular sector. For example, UNDP facilitated and hosted the shelter SWG, while ERREC co-chaired it. The UNDP Recovery Programme participated regularly in working groups that are more relevant to its work, like Shelter and Water and Sanitation. In his humanitarian coordination functions, the Resident/ Humanitarian Coordinator (R/HC) was supported by the Office of the Coordination of Humanitarian Affairs (OCHA).[19]

At a later stage the UN Country Team also took the initiative of establishing an inter-agency working group on recovery. This group was expanded to include relevant Government representatives and other partners. This action was necessary for effective coordination in the area of recovery, which increasingly took precedence over the emergency phase.[20] The lead agency was the UNDP and the secretariat of the sector was the PMU.

18 United Nations Development Assistance Framework (2002-2006), Eritrea. May 2002

19 United Nations Development Assistance Framework (2002-2006), Eritrea. May 2002.

20 United Nations Development Assistance Framework (2002-2006). Eritrea. May 2002

During the implementation phase of the PROFERI programme, however, a National Project Coordinating Committee (NPCC) was set up and chaired by the Commissioner of the then Commission for Eritrean Refugee Affairs (CERA) and members were drawn from the Line Ministries and UNDP which met regularly to monitor and evaluate the programme and assess the progress of project implementation. Donor participation in the NPCC meetings was once every six months. A Project Management Unit (PMU) was also built within the CERA structure to coordinate and direct the overall implementation of the programme. The programme required that all the various institutions whose services are essential and critical to the well-being of the refugees, implement the aspects of the programme which fall within their mandate and domain. Hence, close coordination by CERA through NPCC and the PMU was vital to the success of the programme.

The CERA-PMU was mandated to implement the overall technical and financial responsibilities of the repatriation and reintegration programme. These responsibilities included the management of the transit and reception centres and transfer of returnees from these centres to the various resettlement sites. The CERA-PMU also acted as the operational instrument of the NPCC in as far as day-to-day programme management was concerned.

On the other hand, the implementation arrangements of the Pre-PoWER programme was the Direct Execution (DEX) modality of the UNDP, created with a trust fund contributed by the the Italian Government. The Trust Fund was managed by the UNDP and the implementers were mainly NGOs (CRIC, APS, CESVI, MANITESE and ESCA) and the Ministry of Health.

The PoWER programme began its operations immediately after the agreement to start the PoWER programme was signed on November 2000. UNDP established promptly the Programme Management Unit (UNDP-PMU) responsible for the programme. The first group of nine projects were reviewed by PAC on 7 December and approved by the Steering Committee on 8 December 2000. Most activities started in early January 2001.

The first projects approved were in the following sectors: five in the area of social infrastructure rehabilitation (schools and health facilities), two projects to improve water and sanitation services, and the remaining two were targeted at improving shelter, health and sanitation conditions in IDP camps as well as distributing non-food items. Most projects were intended to meet the most urgent needs created by the emergency, with respect to IDPs and the physical rehabilitation of social infrastructure. Focus on rehabilitating infrastructure and improving water services also laid the groundwork for more long-term development activities, such as the improvement of health and education services in general.

NGOs implemented all of the first set of projects mentioned above. In line with UNDP's policy, which prioritizes area-based development, some of these projects were interrelated and targeted the same areas in the country for maximum impact. For example, a project improving the health infrastructure in the Molki sub-region received funding to upgrade the education infrastructure in the same area as well. The endorsement by relevant line ministries and regional administrations of the projects was mandatory.

General Criteria for Selecting Projects

At the beginning, the criteria for selecting projects was laid down as follows:

At the outset it was agreed that recovery projects should:

- Use labour-intensive methods and benefit all the communities;

- Promote community participation in planning, monitoring and implementation, and ensure full transparency in the selection of workers;

- Give priority to vulnerable groups (female-headed households, orphans, the elderly and the disabled).

There were also additional criteria for appraisal and approval of projects:

- Activities should focus on war-affected populations, either displaced in camps or back in their communities of origin;
- Overhead cost of the activities should not exceed 15% of the total cost;
- At the explicit request of Government representatives, expatriate staff should be kept at a minimum, to reduce inflated salary payments, and that expertise found among different Government implementing partners should be seen as common assets;
- Implementing partners should focus on areas and/or sectors of intervention so as to reduce logistics costs and improve efficiency;
- Local authorities and counterparts as well as central authorities and line ministries should endorse projects.

As detailed in Annex 1 of this publication, the SC approved the second set of projects in January 2001 using the criteria shown above. These projects focused on two housing projects, two cash-for-work projects, one integrated recovery scheme and one project on children in IDP camps. The housing projects were implemented in the geographical areas where PoWER already supported activities through other projects, consistent with the UNDP policy in favour of area-based development and following the criteria for meeting urgent needs as well as addressing more long-term needs. This time, however, half of the projects were implemented directly by local government authorities, which also helped in building their capacities for recovery related activities.

Responsiveness to Community Needs

The Recovery Programme has responded to the needs of the emergency situation extremely well, as it has been very flexible in planning the activities and in rapid and timely disbursements. It has been able to redirect funds easily to legitimate areas not foreseen in the original project document but later discovered as newly identified communities deserving of and warranting assistance.

The management structure for appraisal and approval of the projects was put together within one month of the programme's approval, facilitating the early approval and implementation of the projects. In general the programme has been able to approve projects and release funds without delays. Many of the NGOs have also been very prompt in responding with new proposals and implementing the activities accordingly.

Involvement of the Beneficiaries in the Planning Process

The Recovery Programmes have deliberately fostered the involvement of beneficiaries and local administrations in the identification, formulation and implementation of the recovery projects. In nearly all cases, the local administrations have been actively involved in the planning of the projects that they implement. In fact, approval of the projects required evidence that the regional administration was involved and had endorsed the proposed project. In particular, during both the planning and implementation the integrated community development, projects involved their beneficiaries in a meaningful way.

Moreover, the PoWER programme operated right from the beginning with a rapid, effective and flexible disbursement mechanism, which proved to be ideal for emergency circumstances. This capacity has been well recognized and appreciated by the overwhelming majority of the partners in meetings and workshops organized to assess and review the annual programmes. Moreover, because of this very unique characteristic the PoWER programme had also followed initially an essentially reactive planning mode. PoWER-funded projects were usually presented directly by the implementing agencies themselves, mostly by regional/local authorities, UN Agencies, international/local NGOs, and appraised and approved on a project-by-project basis, without relying on a comprehensive, overall planning process, but within a common agreed framework with the Government.

However, the Recovery Programmes gradually moved to a more proactive planning approach as evidenced by the fact that the programmes were actively undertaking more field visits and discussions with local officials as well as conducting periodic rapid assessments of the areas of need. Thus, the programmes participated actively and even took the lead in the discussion of the needs assessments of the war-affected areas and populations.

An important characteristic for an emergency rehabilitation programme is its ability to efficiently approve projects and release the required funding in a timely manner. Given the need for speedy action, combined with the fact that some of the government structures of the war-affected countries are not necessarily in a position to execute the recovery projects themselves, UNDP Headquarters has granted its country office in Eritrea the authority to execute projects directly. Consquently, and at the the request of the Government of Eritrea, the UNDP country office used this authority to approve projects and release funds without any unnecessary delays. This modality has helped in responding to the most urgent needs very promptly.

Special Partnership with the Governments of Italy, the Netherlands, and Norway, the European Commission and UNOCHA

The Recovery Programmes had also forged a new kind of partnership with donors—especially the above four in which they actively kept abreast of the management and oversight of the programme. Italy has had a long presence in Eritrea and Norway's relationship dates back to the war of liberation days and both were sources of information to other donors, on the country in general. The Italian Cooperation was instrumental in helping to identify the first implementing international NGOs as well as in attracting some of them to the country.

CHAPTER THREE

3 LESSONS LEARNED – BEST PRACTICES

"We must make greater efforts to listen to the people on the ground. We must be less eager to devise and promote United Nations initiatives, and more constructive in finding ways to support local, African initiatives"

Kofi Annan, UN Secretary General, Address to ECOSOC High Level Meeting, Geneva, Switzerland, 25 July 2001

3.1 introduction

Lessons learned and best practices are experiences acquired in the execution of programmes and projects, which can provide value-added direction to the formulation, and execution of future development and unique operational initiatives. The purpose of documenting lessons learned is to share and use knowledge derived from experience to promote the recurrence of desirable outcomes and preclude the recurrence of undesirable results. Best practices are attributes demonstrated to be effective guidelines for the successful management of programmes and projects. The main purpose of identifying best practices is to share innovative and effective ways of developing and carrying out recovery programmes and projects, as well as encouraging continuous learning and improvement.

The lessons learnt from the Recovery Programmes in Eritrea over the last two decades were significant and each contributed to the refining in the design of subsequent programmes/projects. In total there were nine UNDP Recovery Programmes during the period 1992-2012. In most cases lessons learned from each programme were used to adjust the planning and design of subsequent programmes/projects, thus making the latest most effective, efficient and sustainable.

The first part will deal with selected issues that are common to all the UNDP recovery programmes implemented in the last two decades. If the lessons learned are only specific to one programme, it will be narrated later in subsequent chapters at the appropriate section for that specific programme(s).

3.2 Snapshot of Common Lessons Learned – across all recovery programmes: Selection of Beneficiaries

The criteria for selection of the beneficiaries cited above, especially in relation to cash for work programmes and others was elaborate, egalitarian and democratic. When the resource allocated to a particular village or cluster of villages is not enough to cover all the interested and needy residents, the sub-region administrator calls a general meeting of the villagers and in cooperation with the village administrator(s) announces the resources available for a particular project.

The administrator(s) set the initial criteria for selection of the beneficiaries that gives priority to the needs of women headed households, the elderly, the disabled and the absolute destitute. The general meeting was then asked to add, subtract or completely replace the initial criteria but all the time within the parameters mentioned earlier. One such addition put forward at one of the typical meetings in Tsorona sub-region was to take into consideration by excluding from the potential pool of beneficiaries, when the situation warrants, those households that have relatives abroad and who have been observed to receive remittances from them, from time to time. After the crucial consultations, the general meeting approves the names of the selected beneficiaries based on the criteria agreed.

What was remarkable however, was the openness and transparency of the whole process, which the United Nations can learn from. This procedure has given the vulnerable heads of households, extra cash in their pockets, to helped them cover costs for extra food, as well of non-food items, such as school materials for their children and sugar, coffee, salt and other similar items.

Women have been observed to be the best managers for handling the money, since most men tend to be inclined to drink part of the income by going to the market entertainment places.

Women in the planning, implementing and follow-up decision making processes

Another landmark achievement across many of the programmes was the active involvement of women in the decision making process beyond the rhetoric often voiced as "equal rights for women," by translating into practical application those often stated rights. A significant number of women were selected to be members of water management committees, in the beneficiary identification taskforces, soil and water conservation management committees etc. Granted these are limited inroads to the domain where men have the monopoly.

Such practices have also enabled women headed households to be the main beneficiaries in the variety of packages given in such areas as provision of shelter, re-stocking, tractor ploughing services, etc.

At the community level, where there are no visible privileges to be gained; election results are generally speaking a reflection of the wish of the villagers. In exceptional cases, there may be a few that may slip in and are motivated to be elected to the various committees mentioned earlier, not so much to serve but to be served. These tendencies are corrected almost immediately by the community, since traditionally, leaders at the community level are elected for their integrity, experience and wisdom and are universally recognized to serve the people well.

Tractor ploughing vs ploughing by oxen

Experience has shown in a number of the recovery programmes that tractor ploughing is preferred in flat farmlands like in Goluj and Om Hajer in Gash Barka region, if adequate diesel fuel could be secured on a timely basis. This was not always possible; due to the intermittent supply of diesel to far away communities where access to fuel is not always guaranteed.

Restocking (Oxen) in Ambeste Geleba

In mountainous communities like Kinito, Lahyo and Adi shihu, in the Southern region, oxen ploughing is the only and most desirable option. It also allows the farmer to plough his/her land at their convenience, without the fear of if the tractor will arrive on time or not. The drawback is once the two months ploughing season is over, the farmer has to feed and take care of the oxen until the next season. In drought prone areas, this was a challenge when they may not have adequate water supply to offer their livestock and adequate fodder to feed them.

The villager and town man – varying treatments at the hands of local authorities in recovery projects

During monitoring trips to project sites, we have observed one or two beneficiaries who feel they have suffered or been subjected to harsh and arbitrary treatments at the hands of some local authorities. They raised specific grievances and issues and requested that the wrong doings by the village/local authorities be corrected or re-addressed. Those who complain are not, in general, afraid to express their views and do so without the fear of retaliation after the monitoring team leave the village or Kebabi.

This observation was not unique to this specific place, similar things were happening in other local communities as well. We were curious to know what makes this practice work in villages but not in towns/cities. We asked an elderly man from this village for his insights on the situation. "As you know he said" in villages, everyone knows everybody else, hence, the people are treated with dignity; whilst in towns, authorities could be arrogant and fail to live up to the expectations of the society that put them there, and they treat those they administer with disdain and without accountability and with impunity".

The town was an assortment of people coming from many places, cultures and backgrounds. There are very few things that bind them together. Rule of law would have been the binding agent, but at this stage in their history, it does not exist. This lends us further food for thought and we also reflected on our own observation that the individual in the village was a person with a name, and distinct personality endowed with human identity, whilst in towns, the individual was just a number to be dealt with without recourse to fairness and protection which normally would have been given to him under the law.

CHAPTER FOUR

4.1 Unique Episodes that have added value
Monitoring trip to Gerenfit-Gash Barka – an encounter with a herd of elephants

4.1 Unique Episodes that have added value

Monitoring trip to Gerenfit-Gash Barka – an encounter with a herd of elephants

On one of our monitoring visits to Gerenfit in Gash Barka, a resettlement area for rural expellees from Ethiopia, we chanced to pass through the riverbed of the Gash River.

Gerenfit village after the Expellees move from Shelab cam

GERENFIT RESETTLEMENT VILLAGES FOR EXPELLEES

Gerenfit village Community Centre

A community centre built under the PoWER programme to serve as meeting place for the former expellees and a training centre for income generating activities. The structure was erected through a generous contribution from the Government of the Netherlands.

GERENFIT VILLAGE Community Centre – overlooking the resettled expellees' farmlands

As we were inspecting the newly dug borehole, we saw at a distance, about a hundred meters away, a herd of elephants about 23 of them drinking water from the river bed which was then at its lowest level. The elephants had their young ones all around them. Yoka Brand, the then Dutch Ambassador to Eritrea, was pleasantly surprised and slightly astonished to see the herd. Unfortunately, we did not have our cameras to record the historic moment except one of our party. He volunteered to go near the elephants and take a picture that he could then share with all of us. He braved the group and came much closer to take a close-up when the leader of the herd was moving around uncomfortably. The locals warned Hagos that the Leader might charge suddenly and crush him under his huge feet. He withdrew from the scene without noise and without any incident.

We were all surprised to see elephants in this part of the country. Nobody would have believed us, if we said we saw elephants on the riverbed of Gash. Several decades have passed, since they were last seen in the area. The war, the smell of gunpowder and the noise and rapid urbanization had driven them away to distant lands where they felt safe. We happened to read a few years earlier of an edict issued by the first Italian civil governor of Eritrea, Martini (1895-1921) stating that it was forbidden to kill elephants without a license. We then learned that there were indeed elephants in Eritrea over a century ago.

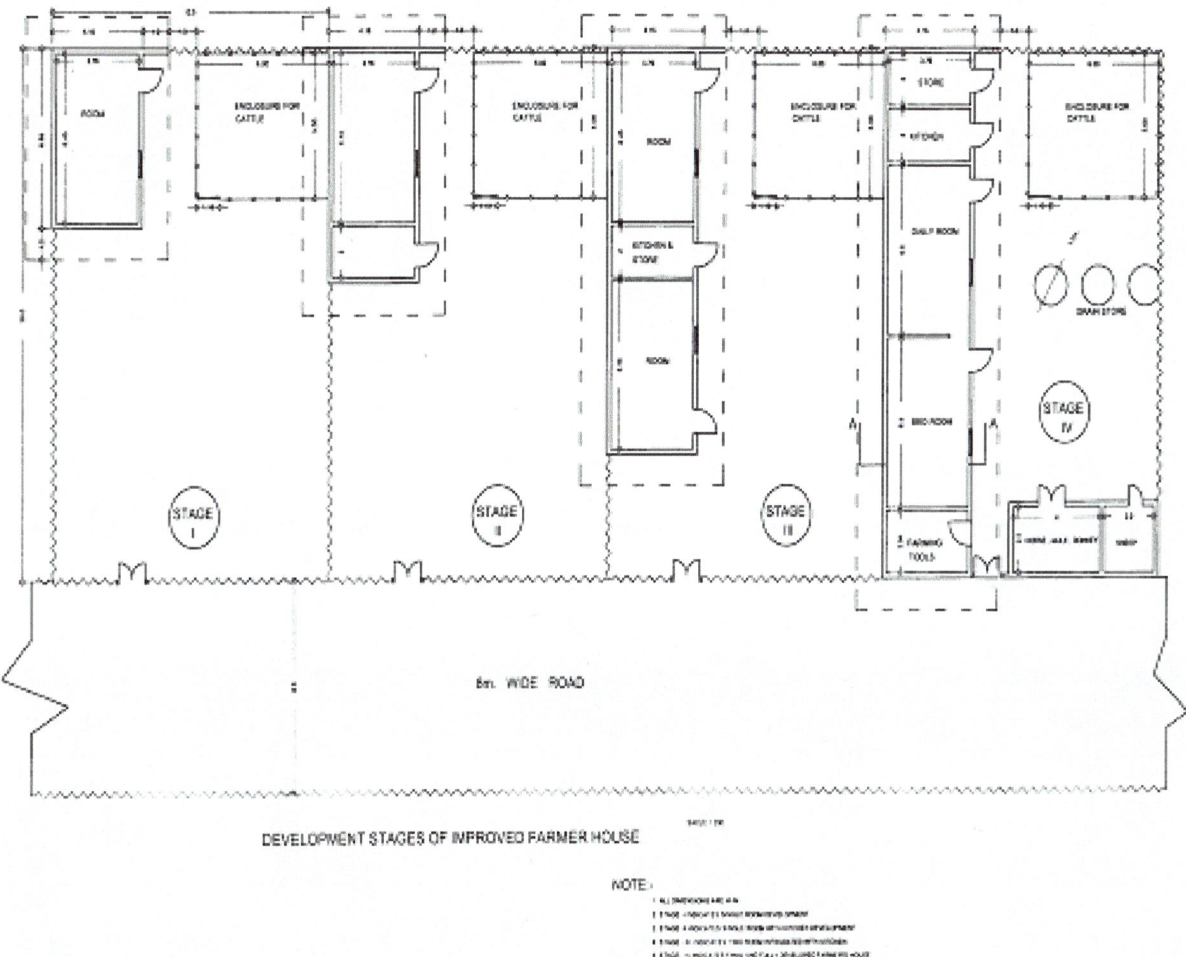

Prototype of Expandable Farmer's House built in Gerenfit

The then Governor of Gash Barka immediately sent a film crew to the site, after our return to Barentu the regional capital, and dispached a copy of the video to the Ambassador in recognition of her unstinting support to the resettlement of IDPs/Expellees all over the affected regions in the country. This incident was narrated, because we were informed a few weeks earlier that the farmers in the area were complaining that a herd of elephants were thrashing their farmland and their maize as they pass the riverbed to drink water. It was unbelievable at the time but we took note of it and consulted with experts who were mapping their path. We found out that the ancient trail of the elephants indeed passed through their land. It was then arranged to leave a wide elephant-pass to allow them to pass unhindered to the riverbed to quench their thirst. The elephants were not deliberately thrashing the farmland to consume their maize but it was an opportunity they could not pass.

Expandable Farmer's House under construction in Gerenfit village

Gerenfit Farmlands – Expellees first fruit of their resettlement

Solar Panels for pumping water from a bore hole for the benefit of IDP return villages in Gash Barka

Monitoring Trip to Shelab camp with a Donor

Based on our past experience with donors, we planned focused field trips for donors that were sympathetic and earnestly wanted to visit the IDP/expellees emergency camps.

This strategy was crowned with success and the results were overwhelming. One such visit was by an Ambassador who was taken to see the Shelab emergency camp that temporarily sheltered the rural expellees. The Ambassador was deeply saddened to see the expellees suffering from wind and dust blowing in their faces constantly. The tents were tattered and they did not have any personal belongings of substance.

The Ambassador from the Netherlands, Mrs. Yoka Brandt, expressed the desire to interview a person at random. An old woman who happened to be passing in front of the group was selected by the Ambassador, in the presence of the then Deputy Commissioner of ERREC Mr. Teklemichael and the UNDP Senior Advisor on Recovery, Prof. Techeste Ahderom. The old woman was accompanied by her 10 year old grandson. The Ambassador asked the old woman where she came from and what her living conditions were at the camp. She narrated a sad story. She and her family were rural expellees from Ethiopia.

Her son died in the border war and her daughter in law was sick on her trip from Ethiopia to Eritrea and died also, leaving her only son with his grandmother. They were then moved to the Shelab camp a God forsaken place, since they came from a relatively fertile and green-land that they and their ancestors lived on for centuries. She finally remarked that she was waiting for her turn to join her family in the next world.

The Ambassador was deeply moved by the story and shed a few tears in front of the group. This is a true story and unadulterated because the Author was the interpreter for the interview. It was rare to see a seasoned diplomat espress such deep emotion for the needy in a foreign setting. Misery was everywhere in the world. But it was a rare happening for people to have empathy and humanity in public.

The Ambassador then challenged the Deputy Commissioner and the Senior Technical Advisor to come up with a project soon and she would get the necessary funds from The Hague. Within a week a Project Document was developed and the finance was secured from the Netherlands for the first phase of the move from Shelab Camp to Gerenfit.

"If the UNDP would have given me the money in cash, most probably I would have spent it on coffee and sugar and it would have been spent by now with nothing to show today." Again the Author was the official interpreter for this dialogue and the event was covered by a number of international news agencies.

The lesson of the effectiveness of targeted resource mobilization strategy was noted. This bore fruits and the UNDP Recovery Programmes mobilized a cumulative of 119,990,669 USD for all the nine recovery programmes mentioned earlier.

Resource Mobilization for the Integrated Recovery Programme

Moreover, we have also a different experience relating to the mobilization of resources for the Integrated Recovery Programme (IRP). We have learned that meticulously prepared, appraised and beautifully bound documents, do not necessarily bear tangible results.

The road to successful resource mobilization is more complex than meets the eye. The Recovery programmes succeeded in raising 3 USD for every one dollar of UNDP core resources. We always made appropriate preparations to know exactly the priorities of the individual countries and their representatives in the country. Following this, we carefully nurtured the trust of key donors and countries and established excellent working relationships with the Ambassadors and their technical staff.

We have always been truthful in our approach and transparent in our presentations. We have told them truthfully what the opportunities are, as well as the constraints and challenges. We have also succeeded in taking the donors to all project sites that they helped co-finance for them to see the value for their money. The countries in this category included, Italy, Norway, the Netherlands and EC from the multi-lateral agencies. The countries that we could not persuade were the UK and the French representatives for reasons that have been spelled out in other sections of this narrative.

Food Insecurity

There have been ad hoc studies to assess the food security and nutrition situation in target communities. This helped us to target communities with the greatest needs.

We learned that the most appropriate response options to support livelihoods in IDP/Expellees return/resettlement areas was to identify food insecure households; the level of their food consumption, food access and coping (mechanisms) strategies they followed.

Food access and the household's ability to acquire adequate amounts of food through one or a combination of own home production and stocks, purchasing bartering, selling assets, eating seeds reserved for next farming season, gift borrowing and as a last resort food aid initially was then substituted by Cash for Work projects.

People were many a time reluctant for cultural reasons, to state clearly their assets. Hence, livestock ownership was very hard to measure, as people were reluctant to provide accurate information for traditional reasons.

It is clear and evident that household security plays an important role in child nutrition; the core concepts in household food security encompass availability, access and utilization. There was therefore a direct relationship between food insecurity and malnutrition.

Social safety net: Infrastructure development, social protection, has it worked or did it create dependencies? What are the lessons learned. The remarks of a farmer in one of the target communities for recovery interventions was noteworthy. "Is it raining in Canada" he is reported to have said. "God has always his ways to take care of us. It is good that we are not all affected by drought" he added.

The advantages of advance and adequate preparation vs Return/Resettlement of IDP/Expellees to villages of origin or new areas, before the infrastructure was ready for their use

Livelihoods: A livelihood comprises the capabilities, assets (material and social) and activities required for a means of living.

Sustainable Livelihoods: A livelihood is sustainable when it can cope with and recover from stresses and shocks, maintain or enhance its capabilities and assets, while not undermining the natural resource base

In the case of the return of IDP temporary sheltered in Adi Keshi emergency camps, in Gash Barka, advance preparations were made. There was adequate water and temporary schools in the resettlement sites, before they were moved. In other return to villages of origin cases like Tselim Kelai and Adi Maelel, the IDPs were moved without advance preparations, resulting initially in great dissatisfaction. After four months of their return to their original villages, there were no basic social services in place and their farmlands were surrounded by landmines and UXOs. Some of the resettled IDPs were heard to say that "they prefer to be in the emergency camps than in the return/resettlement areas that do not have any facilities including health and schools.

Tselim Kelayo Micro dam for livestock

Adi Maelel Microdam, Gash Barka

Provision of Shelter in Adi Maelel

Provision of Shelter in Elala

Kinito had a shortage of water and a no access road. They fetch water from Ruba (River) Belesa. The Ethiopian villages on the other side share the same river for their water needs as well. It takes an hour and half for women in Kinito village to haul water, about 20 liters on their back from the Belesa River. Occasionally there were conflicts and insults were exchanged across the river but no serious incidents followed. They did not have dependable roads for water tankers to be sent to alleviate their situation.

The only health station in Hadish Adi was destroyed during the border war and no access road was available as well to take critically ill patients to the nearest Health Center in Tsorona semi-urban center.

In Una Argena resettlement site, the IDPs from Kinin and other nearby villages, have been given one hectare of agricultural land each, but it was not enough to sustain their subsistence farming. Yet the UNDP supported them with all the packages given to other IDPs in the area.

Sorting out those who left their villages and those who stayed "Stayees"

The priority for the distribution of packages, such as tarpaulins. donkeys, Jerba (water bags made of hides) was given to those who were living in emergency camps. Those who did not abandon their homes, however, were initially not given the packages, on the assumption that they remained behind to protect their homes and property from the occupying forces. While those who were evacuated lost everything they had.

Cash for Work and Monetizing Food Aid

At one time, food aid had been turned into a political tug of war between the government and the donors. In the meantime the vulnerable people in the middle suffered.

Mr. Roger Moore, EC Director, East Africa/ Southern Africa region, had a working visit to Eritrea amidst a row between the Government and some key donors. He was clear in his messages and sided with the Government on its interpretation of the use of Cash for Work programmes. He had to pay a heavy price. He was chastised after his return to Brussels. There was a solidarity among key Donors stationed in Asmara not to buckle under Government pressure. But he stated that that there was no problem of using Cash for Work programmes. It was used in many African countries, he added.

This created an uproar in those Embassies and donors who were opposed to it. The Minister of National Development at the time said that the new interpretation was music to his ears. We can have an excellent cooperation, the Minister added. Unfortunately, EU- GoSE relations were characterized by mis-understandings and mis-apprehensions. According to the Donors, capacity to absorb massive infusion of resources was missing; the question of self-reliance, ownership and leadership had also a different meaning to both sides. Despite the above clarifications by Roger Moore, on the donor side there was no flexibility. In the meantime, to add fuel to fire, some 60,000 tons of food were impounded by the Government. WFP then temporarily suspended its activities in Eritrea. Despite some positive moves, the situation remained the same for some time. On monetizing food aid, no agreement was reached.

4.2 Synergy with other Major Initiatives in Recovery Programmes in Eritrea

The UNDP Recovery Programme was very prompt in initiating major recovery and rehabilitation activities in Eritrea. In fact, it was an active participant in helping to prepare the groundwork for other complementary recovery programmes, in particular the Emergency Recovery Programme (ERP) and the National Demobilization and Reintegration Programme (DRP), both partially funded and led by the World Bank.

Components of the ERP included balance of payments support, infrastructure rehabilitation (roads and energy sectors), private sector development and agriculture and social protection. The social protection component included a social safety desk within the Ministry of Local Government (MoLG), a housing unit and replenishment of the Eritrean Community Development Fund. Total financial requirements were USD 287 million. The funding for the ERP came from the International Development Agency (IDA) of the World Bank, Italy, European Union, African Development Bank, Denmark, France and the Government of Eritrea.

The World Bank and UNDP jointly supported the National Demobilization and Reintegration Programme (DRP) for the demobilization of up to 200,000 soldiers. The DRP targeted three components: demobilization, reinsertion and reintegration. The demobilization element was directed at defining a civilian identity for the ex-soldiers; the reinsertion component comprise cash or in-kind payments; and reintegration include both social and economic reintegration activities. Social reintegration activities include disseminating information to the community, as well as counseling and community activities for the demobilized soldiers. Economic reintegration activities cover skill development and training micro-enterprise development, rural development and employment promotion. The total cost of the programme was estimated at USD 196 million.

FOCUS OF THE INTERVIEW IS ON UNDP Recovery Programmes only

There were a number of other Parallel recovery programmes in Eritrea during the same period led by:

Multi-lateral Agencies (EU,WB,ADB)

Bi-Laterals (Italy,Dutch,Norway,etc)

Government (ERP,DRP,ECDF,SMCP)

Civil Society Organisations including national and International NGOs

UNDP had assisted the DRP Commission with conceptualizing the Social and Economic Reintegration component, including the formulation and elaboration of core documents addressing the issues related to, for example, training and small-scale enterprise development. UNDP also assisted in organizing and funding the first workshop on Social and Economic Reintegration and provided three international facilitators for this purpose.

The demobilization of 200,000 soldiers from the armed forces started in May 2002. A significant number of the soldiers are skilled and educated people—many of the others make up the agricultural work force. Their absence from the private and public sectors has had an adverse impact on the socio-economic situation in Eritrea. It was assumed that speedy demobilization will also facilitate the return to normalcy for families throughout the country.

Other Major Recovery Initiatives

The International Community have been generous in their response to the various appeals of the Government and the UN System.

The GoSE and its development partners have launched a range of recovery initiatives and programmes since the end of the 1998-2000 war. The leading initiative in terms of size and scope is the Emergency Reconstruction Programme (ERP), a government/multi donor multi-sectoral program with a budget of US$ 287.7 million. The ERP was approved in 2,000 and was initially scheduled to close at the end of December 2004. ERP Funding, however, has reached--at the time of the this writing--about 70% of the pledges. The main donors to the ERP include the Italians, ADB, and EU[21].

In the face of the urgent need to assist populations not covered by ERP and other recovery interventions, the Government and UNDP with the initial support from Italy formulated the Post-War Eritrean Recovery (PoWER) as a bridging programme of USD16.8 million to deliver the needed assistance expeditiously. Since November 2000, the PoWER program focused in the areas of rehabilitation of social services, the promotion of sustainable livelihoods, and national capacity building in mine action. Additional contributions also came from: Italy, Netherlands, the EU, Norway, Canada and the UK, which brought the total to USD 28 Million. PoWER was on schedule to be successfully completed at the end of 2004.

UNHCR has helped address the immediate needs of the returning refugees and their host communities. UNHCR has assisted, at the time, the repatriation and reintegration (through community based rehabilitation and reconstruction activities) of over 118,000 returnees from Sudan. Total UNHCR funding for reintegration of returnees was over USD 15 Million for 2001-2003. In regard to the Returnees, the IRP will build on UNHCR initial reintegration activities.

Other UN agencies (UNICEF, WFP and UNFPA) as well as several International NGOs (including Oxfam, CARE, Dutch Inter Church Aid, Africare, LWF, Movimondo, Manitesse, COSV, ISCOS, Conern and Refugee Trust) made important contributions to the recovery efforts in the country in general and in Gash Barka in particular.

The Government's other initiatives include the Transitional Economic Development Plan (2002-2005), the Interim Poverty Reduction Strategy Paper (I-PRSP 2004-2006) and the National Food Security Strategy (NFSS). The IRP together with the other initiatives mentioned above were being incorporated into the country's Medium Term Development Plan. Under the PRS, the GOE aims to pursue a strategy of rapid, sustainable, widely shared economic growth and poverty reduction. It aims to promote economic growth through the promotion of a dynamic private sector, attracting private sector investment; privatizing government-owned enterprises; and developing a sound financial system, increasing agricultural productivity and achieving macroeconomic stability.

21 ERP PMU, General Manager Report June 2004

4.3 Interview with Selected Beneficiaries

Keshi (Priest) Ghebrekidan

Keshi Ghebrekidan Berhe is 66 years old married with four children. Before the border war, he was among the relatively rich households of the village of Kinito on the border with Ethiopia which is 38 kilometers from Tsorona semi-urban center. Before the border war, he had 300 – 400 goats, 15 draught animals and 11 bee colonies. Like most of the villagers he lost all his property and stayed in the Metera emergency camp for eight years.

Agriculture and animal husbandry is the main livelihood in the area. Keshi Ghebrekidan states that "the survival of my household depends on the revival of agriculture. I am grateful for the agricultural support I received from the UNDP, such as the provision of oxen, seeds and farm tools" He said "Oxen are kept mainly as a source of draught power in agricultural production especially in the hilly parts of my village. That is, we use them for ploughing and threshing. They are a key input in the process of crop cultivation". Indeed, Keshi Ghebrekidan noted that "the oxen can plough our farm land - and thus they feed us. The oxen also produce" he added "valuable dung, which can be used as either fuel or manure or both".

Keshi Ghebrekidan is farming through a strategy called ***Lifinti*** (literally "working together"), a type of mutual assistance system, whereby two persons agree to assist each other in their respective fields in a sequential manner. This system is often used by male headed households, who only possess a single ox, and who therefore need to borrow a "partner ox" from somebody else to be able to plough their land. Each person will keep the produce from his field for himself.

"The farm tools are multi-purpose" he added. He further said "I use these tools for farming as well as during the Cash for Work activities". We have also noted that the tools were useful during the construction of shelter. Furthermore, he recalls the benefits he reaped from Cash for work. "Even though, I had so many needs to satisfy, I used the income for clothing for my children in order to motivate them to study in school" said Keshi Ghebrekidan.[1]

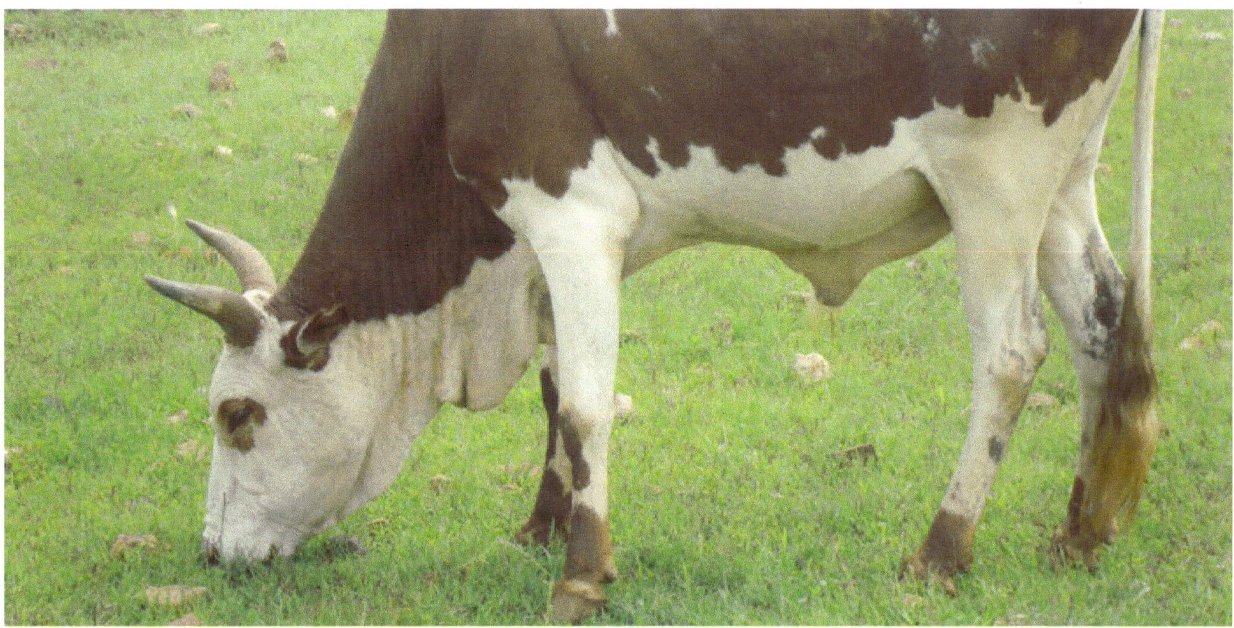

2. Qib'at Haile

Qib'at Haile is a young woman with a pleasant and smiling face. She is 27 and has two daughters aged 12 and 10. She is from the village of Lahiyo, 32 km from Senafe town. Qib'at and the residents of this village had stayed in three different emergency IDP camps from November 1999 up to May 2006. Qib'at was pregnant with her second child during the time of displacement. Being pregnant and holding her first born on her back, she could not manage to take any of her property, as she left her village in a hurry. She gave birth in the caves near the village of Rokhoito, Sub region Senafe. She lost all her properties during the border war. Moreover, and above everything else, she lost her husband who was killed during the second round of the border war with Ethiopia.

Earth micro dam - Rokhoito, Senafe Subregion, Debub

Stone masonry micro dam, Ham village-Senafe Sub region, Debub

Access to water is a national humanitarian and development priority. Programmes that lead to improved access to water are considered to contribute positively to the raising of living standards, reducing poverty level and enhancing social wellbeing of the target communities. In particular the reduction in time required to collect water and reduction in water borne diseases is expected to make available significant labour resources that can be utilized for other productive activities. Women of the Lahiyo village used to travel for about three hours to fetch water from the nearest river bed. Besides they had to spend one hour in the water source for the water source is very weak and had to wait in a long queue. "When I was busy with agricultural and domestic chores, my girls assume the task of fetching water" says Qib'at. There were so many instances that her children missed classes to collect water for the household. She states " now thanks to the Government and its partners (UNDP) we are getting tap water at the heart of our village. [2] Hence, my daughters are attending school on a more regular basis. My energy and time is saved and after the tiresome farming and domestic chores, I can now easily get water and prepare food for my family on time." Besides, access to safe water is secured, Qib'at noted that the improved water quality enables her village to reduce water borne diseases.

3. Solomon Meles

The livelihood of the sub-region entirely depends on crop and animal production. The core aim of the UNDP's sustainable livelihood component of the joint programme on IDPs/expellees is to assist the beneficiaries to stand with the sustainable way on their livelihood base. Based on this, according to the information given by the sub-region head of the Ministry of Agriculture (MoA), Mr. Solomon Meles, the support provided to IDPs in this sub-region among the others include the following:

1. Crop Production

Draught power: Most of the farm lands of the villages in the Southern region where IDPs have returned is not suitable for tractor use due to its topography. Hence, the provision of oxen was the only option available, and farmers able to purchase oxen through the cash amounted Nakfa 6,000 delivered to them. According to the information given by the sub-region head of MoA, Ato Solomon Melese, the farmers were able to plough their farm land on time by fixing their ox with the other ox of other farmer. The same will go for the other farmer too. Under these circumstances both framers benefited equally including female headed households.

Provision of seeds: The strategy taken in the provision of seeds was through delivering the required amount of funding to farmers to purchase seeds themselves from the market, taking into consideration the experiences and confidence of the farmers in identifying the suitable seeds for their respective farm lands.

In addition, the MoA was involved in securing the right types of seeds through physical observation only. Furthermore, he added that, it would have been preferable that the seed distribution was handled by the MoA, if equipped with some assisting apparatus like 'a'percentage seed fertility rate" identifier. The identifier apparatus assisted in identifying the fertility percentage of the seed, as it is very important to know the productivity of crop production before seeding. The final output of crop production is more determined by the percentage of seed fertility rate as compared to the other inputs.

Provision of Farm tools: The provision of farm tools was based on the pre-identified types of tools suitable to the farm areas. The types of farm tools distributed to the direct beneficiaries were Plough, Hoe, Sickle and Shovel. The farm tools distributed were correlated to the farm activates namely for ploughing (plough), weeding (hoeing), harvesting (sickle) and threshing (shovel). Moreover, the farm tools were utilized for cash for work program and house construction apart from their prime objectives.

2. Restocking – Building the Assets

Provision of goats: The provision of goats is inclusive to those who do not undertake crop production (provided with ox), if their localities are not favourable to crop farming. Based on this, the beneficiaries' choice were mainly in purchasing of goats. The preferences of goats were due to the nature of feeding of the goats on browsing rather than grazing, where the goats could browse the whole year round compared to grazing (sheep) which is limited to some months.[3]

4. Fathma Mohammed

Fathma is a mother of four and a good entrepreneur and articulate woman. She lives in Melhin Digo, Gollo Kebabai. She is one of the beneficiaries of the Honey Development scheme of the UNDP which was aimed at assisting the Saho community in the Soira mountain range whose livelihoods are based on rearing of goats and honey production. The border war has devastated their neighborhoods and their livelihoods. They were one of the groups that were displaced.

The project was meant to revive their honey production by giving them two modern Beehives and adequate training on their use. She was asked to speak frankly on the success or failure of the project and whether she and her family have benefited from this intervention. She and a group of five women were interviewed in November 2013 on the benefits they have gained, if any, in improving their livelihoods.

Fathma said emphatically that the UNDP project was "timely and has improved their lives, in a short period of time". This statement was echoed by Radia Omar who said from the proceeds of the honey she produced, "I bought solar equipment that gave my family and especially my children the chance to study in the evenings, and to recharge the battery of my mobile and listen to the radio, with a single socket installed in my home". She added that she was also able to cover the cost of education related expenses of her children, including school fees, books and supplies.

See'ida Mohammed added that she also paid with, the extra money in her pocket, the school expenses of her children and basic food supplies for her family. Moreover, See'lda Ali shared the information that in addition to covering her incidental expenses she was able to buy a sheep, who is expecting. She also bought clothes for her children and herself out of the sale of the honey she produced. Another beneficiary, Hawa Abdela, has also stated that she bought two sheep and could not have done it without the opportunities opened up by the project.

The men who were present also stated that they all benefited from the project and wished that the others who were not included in the first phase would also get a chance to benefit from this worthwhile project.

When asked what advice they would like to offer in light of their experience, they gave freely their opinion on improving the technical specification of the beehives by making the top sieve narrower in order to protect the Queen bee from insects; improving the mechanism for the release of smoke in the beehives when harvesting the honey to make it more efficient and effective. They all suggested that water and flowers are important for the bees to produce honey and that this could be done by SWC schemes (such as check dams) to preserve the moisture and plant new local flowers; as well as providing extra Extractors. These feedback has already been shared with the relevant departments of the MoA and the Regional Administration of the Southern region.

Honey Development in Gallo Kebabi – Senafe Sub-region

Local Beehive production

Beehive production and accessories

Livestock in the shade provided by trees, in the riverbed, before the Meghel Dam in Shilalo sub region was built

4.4 Sample Episodes / Noteworthy Encounters with Donors

Consultation on the Gash River bed near Gerenfit

Village administrators sometimes complained that few donors come and take photographs of our houses, and our families, but they do not even share a copy of the pictures with us nor do we see concrete results from their visits. There was one particular incident when one diplomat strayed from the guided tour and approached farmers on his own, with his driver as an interpreter. He came with a ridiculous story that the land that they have been re-settled on has been forcefully taken from other tribes and that the population to be resettled were not willing to move to it. He did not tell us about the encounter until he returned to Asmara.

Whenever misinformation circulates among the diplomatic community on our recovery programme, since it is harmful, we promptly respond to it by clarifying the situation. At the request of the UNDP Recovery Unit, the Regional Administrator of Gash Barka set up a committee of 7 individuals from the Shelab Camp that included three women and one priest to go to the proposed site in Gerenfit and come up with their findings. This task was done in an expeditious manner.

By the same token, a committee from the village of Ugumu (the nearest settlement) were also invited to come to meet the delegation from the Shelab camp. The meeting was held on the river bed of the Gash River about 20 kilometres from the village of Ugumu, and 10 Kilometres from the proposed sites at Gerenfit. The joint meeting was cordial and after a frank and extensive consultation an understanding was reached. Each reported their findings to their respective communities.

The UNDP was considered neutral; hence we chaired the meeting so that they could express their views without fear of repercussion.

The Shelab Camp delegation, through their spokesperson, said that they were happy with the selected area and especially about the fertility of the farming area. They had only one reservation of one of the four selected sites for resettlement. It was too close to the river, and they said that their children will be exposed to malaria and they may all die in 2-3 years time. The site they rejected was immediately cancelled and the population for that site were redistributed to the other three sites that they approved. We also made sure that each of the seven representatives were asked separately if they agreed with the proposal. They all confirmed one by one in the presence of everybody what their spokesperson said.

Moreover, the Ugumu delegation said that the land selected for the resettlement of the expellees is dominale (State owned) and that they have their own adequate land with the possibility for further expansion which they are not able to develop fully. They were delighted to have new neighbours and knowing that they are hardworking people they will all join hands to develop the land to the benefit of the two communities. They also remarked that their village of Ugumu which at the time had only 50 huts (about 50 Households) would also need help, as host community. Their request was duly noted and arrangements were made to have a water project that included the digging of a borehole, the installation of solar panels and a solar pump, the building of a water reservoir and the building of Public Water Distribution systems within the village. A make shift school was also built. Such a programme was under the auspices of the recovery designed to cater to the needs of host-communities. The population of the village grew by leaps and bounds and currently it stands at 500 HHs and is still growing.

Revolving Donkeys

In the Sosona and Koita project there was a UNDP component to assist selected beneficiaries to acquire a pack animal, in this case a donkey. The idea was to assist vulnerable women headed households to lessen their burden of fetching water and firewood if they acquire a donkey. Moreover, the donkey could also be hired to earn some money to bolster their meager income. In order to expedite the process the NGO in charge of the project (implementing partner) gave cash to the beneficiary family to purchase a donkey of their choice. In that way it was also felt that this may enable the project to acquire the said pack animals at a lower cost. It has, however, been observed that some of the beneficiaries who went to the market to buy donkeys used unorthodox ways to secure them.

Although the NGO in charge of the project did its best to monitor the process, it took some time to realize that some of the beneficiaries had better things to do with the money given to them than buy a donkey. Hence, there were people in the area who would take their donkey to the market and pretend to sell it to you so that you could take the donkey and the receipt to the NGO project manager as evidence that you have bought it. In reality it was a sale valid for a day or two for a nominal fee paid by the buyer (beneficiary) to the owner.

The root cause of this was sometimes the unavailability of enough donkeys for sale in the market or the price was too high to be covered by the money allocated for such a purpose or better things to do with the money. This was immediately remedied by resorting to other more transparent methods of providing the beneficiaries with pack animals. Similarly the price of oxen jumped from 6,000 to 8,000 Nakfa, when the sellers learned that the UNDP through the Ministry of Agriculture will buy a few thousand.

Backseat Drivers

In emergency situations you could not do what you have to do in the preparation of normal development plans/projects. There may be people who are dying of thirst due to the war displacement. You would be looking for water anywhere and everywhere. If there are already water systems in place, you may perhaps be expanding it only to relieve the additional pressure from more users. However, in areas where there was no trace of water, you may be forced to dig for water. It is obvious, you have to conduct a cursory survey and consult with local inhabitants to learn from their age-old wisdom. Obviously, if you succeed there was no complaint, however if you fail the back seat drivers will rush with their quick judgment and ask pointedly; did you have hydro geological studies, geophysical studies? Do you have surface water experts, etc.? The nature of the intervention was emergency relief to save lives to be followed by rehabilitation at a later date.

Leave alone in times of emergencies, even under normal conditions, there were still places in remote areas where there was hardly a useable road map leave alone hydro-geological maps. If there were water experts around you they generally could help you to making an educated guess based on their observations in similar situations elsewhere, which is better than leaping in darkness without any planning. Osman Mohammed showed us a carefully hidden abandoned well built during the Italian Colonial era.

This was done after they carefully examined our backgrounds and established beyond the slightest doubt that we were their friends and that they could trust us. We did not touch this site, and instead we advised the elders that they could keep it confidential for some time longer. Then they could decide what to do about it when the situation improves. In other cases the local authorities were forced to dig where they think water may be available by looking for traces of water, green vegetation and consulting with elders from the area. In Gash Barka for example, the local authorities out of desperation dug in one area around 47 wells without success. The objective was always to save lives.

Relations with some Experts from the Donor Community

In the early days of the recovery programmes, we encountered some challenges from the staff of donors. The staff did not have the requisite expertise, and yet they tried to speak with great authority. If you challenge them on their assumptions and facts they presented, it was likely that you would not get a penny from them. Some had experience in other crisis countries where they were treated as "lords" and what they say is considered sacred and final. They generally come with their proposals with a "take it or leave it proposition". They claim they are apolitical, but they were politicians from head to toe and there were many examples to cite to prove this point. Generally there was good will in their Capitals (Headquarters) and they were willing and eager to help but their young emissaries in the field were at times arrogant or merely incompetent.

We have also observed at times that some donors were more comfortable with their kind. Maybe the head of the implementing NGO or UN Agency is from their country or region. Personal likes and dislikes enter the decision making process. It was almost unbelievable to fathom the rationale for such a happening. They would like to give the impression that they have open minds when in reality they have made up their minds, and there is no way they will support the programme/project you may be proposing. Fortunately the overwhelming majority of donors were free from this particular behavior.

There were also those with political agendas of their own and in a subtle way they pursued them. Many a time they created stumbling blocks for the programmes rather than assisting in solving the problems of the war/conflict affected populations. We have discovered that one way of mobilizing resources for the recovery programmes was to invite potential donors to visit project sites in remote areas, so that they would be able to see for themselves what is being done and what the gaps are.

The case of one Ambassador accredited to Eritrea, but not resident in Asmara was a good example to illustrate our point. The said Ambassador was most of the time operating out of his Capital, but would visit Eritrea every three months. The first encounter was a meeting with the Ambassador at the UNDP premises, where he requested to be provided with a project within the scope of the Gerenfit resettlement project, a project that has resettled about 12 thousand rural expellees from Ethiopia. This request for a project out of the multi-faceted undertaking came after a field visit to the site together with other donors. A project document was prepared and submitted for his review and comments. A few months passed by without any response.

We have then learned that a similar request has been forwarded to the Eritrean Demining Authority on the same subject. Obviously since we were working together on Mine Action they requested us to help them prepare a Project Document for the an Ambassador. We complied with their request and the Embassy was provided with the required project document ready for signing. Again the EDA was informed that the documents were sent to his capital city for review and approval. Almost a year passed and again no subsequent response was received.

The last episode in this story is when accidentally we learned that the same Ambassador had promised resources to the late Minister of Health, if he could submit a project that could be approved on a fast track basis in the area of recovery in the health sector, in the Gerenfit area. Again and again, after a lot of hard work spent in designing projects that would fit their priorities, no luck this time as well.

One of the junior staff of the Embassy came once to our office for information on some other recovery programmes and said that he was a little bit embarrassed about the continuous requests that their Embassy makes for proposals without securing funding for any of them.

During the same period an overseas development minister from that country was visiting Eritrea, apparently to sort out certain regional issues that we were not privy to. On the occasion of this visit the Ambassador once again suggested that the UNDP Eritrea sign an agreement with the visiting Minister, so that the national/international press could cover it and give an added value to the visit. When asked where the money is, they said that some four years ago they had contributed to a Global Trust Fund to UNDP HQs in New York. We were then advised to apply for it. In order not to offend the Ambassador, we complied with his suggestion and soon discovered that the said Trust Fund was completely exhausted. Hence, we were advised by HQs in New York that there was no need to apply for an allocation.

We knew that Global Trust Funds are administered by Headquarters and sometimes they also have conditions attached to it. The donor may have indicated specific regions to benefit from their contributions, and sometimes even specific countries. The Ambassador was then informed emphatically that we could not sign for non existing funds with the visiting State Minister just for the sake of getting publicity. If the Ambassador was serious, he was told, he should help to secure financing for one of the many projects that upon his request were prepared but so far without any response. We would then be happy to sign such agreements within the guidelines set by the UNDP, at any time and at any place. This was the last straw that broke the camel's back.

At the end of our meeting with the Ambassador the then Resident Representative of the UNDP, concluded in unmistakable language, "Please do not give us more home work that don't result in any funding from your Embassy. We have enough real work of our own that we need to attend to, without any additional phantom projects to deal with".

That was the end of the story, the Ambassador never returned and he was shortly replaced by another Ambassador who resides in Asmara.

Lesson Learned: Eritrea is a special country with unique characteristics and needs and should be treated accordingly. Generally speaking, most UN agencies, bilateral and multi-lateral organizations do not send top of the line representatives to Eritrea. In fact, with few exceptions, we rarely observed diplomats or representatives who have the competence and relative experience to exert policy influence in the country. On the contrary, many of the assignees consisted of first time ambassadors or heads of UN agencies. They were ill equipped to confront and forge partnerships with their Government counterparts. In fact a few seem to have been assigned to the post as non-important or as a way to be promoted with higher salaries before they are retired. They were at times also given hardship allowances as incentives to come to Eritrea. This has to be corrected since Eritrea finds itself in a highly sensitive geographical situation. If you have a difficult adversary you send competent representatives and not trainees.

Needs Assessment Exercise – Seeking the Perspectives of Beneficiaries?

One of the 150 Projects that were under implementation in the Recovery Programme of the UNDP in Eritrea was the construction of a foot pass in the Southern region. The project cost was a little more than 250,000 US Dollars. When we saw the proposal we were a little concerned that we will be a laughing stock if this turns up to be a Mouse Elephant Project (as opposed to a White Elephant Project).

We visited the site and enquired why the inhabitants of this remote sub-region in Qohaito Kebabi selected the project. We were briefly informed that the people who lived in the escarpment below were cut off from the social and economic services that are provided a few Kilometers away in the adjoining plateau. They explained that there was an ancient pass from Qohaito to the low lands linking with the ancient Adulis Port over 2000 years ago. Over the centuries the path deteriorated and was not impassable and out of use. It was blocked by new boulders, the soil around most of the area was washed away and what remained was a steep cliff that could not even be climbed by skilled mountaineers with axes and robes to help them.

Over the last century they said, if one of their women has complications with her pregnancy, she was taken to the lowland area first and then through a rough detour sometimes lasting a day or two to reach the Health Facility on the Plateau. Most don't make it; they die en route. Moreover, their children could not have access to the educational facilities and they did not have resources to have them in boarding schools in the highlands or to provide them with enough resources to rent a house and cook for themselves.

The village leadership then unanimously decided that they prefer the footpath over many other priorities that were equally urgent. We then recalled the story of one of the Bretton Woods Institution Assessment Missions to a remote area of Mexico where most of the native Indians live. It was reported that when the mission reached its destination they rested in a small semi-urban area which was the trading centre for the surrounding population. It was the fad for development practitioners at the time to routenly ask what the beneficiaries want. The village elders in unison said a Dancing Hall. The Assessment Mission members were flabbergasted with the request.

Ancient Foot Path Sefira- Port of Adulis

They were also condescending in their attitude. We know the Mission leader said that the natives like dancing. They could even dance for days, if the occasion warrants it, he added. But they could not swallow the gist of their request, since they observed all around them poverty and lack of school and health facilities. The Mission left without identifying a viable project.

In a year's time they came back with another mission. They asked again what their priorities were. The elders restated the same request – a Dancing Hall. One of the team members wanted to know why. This time the elders explained that the trading centre is the nearest place for all the villagers around to come and sell their produce and buy some industrial goods to take home. There was no entertainment or recreational facilities that the farmers could part of their income to spend on, within 100 Kilometers from the Trading Centre. The villagers would welcome such a facility and spend a little of their extra income. The trading centre will then get considerable income from the weekly market. The elders then said with such income it would be possible to build whatever they want, such as schools, water and health facilities etc.

If we ask you to build us now a school or health station, we do not have the resources to maintain it, they said. If one of the windows gets broken it remains broken almost forever. You can see all around you the dilapidated facilities which are never maintained. Hence, the new Dancing Hall will provide the Trading Centre with sustainable income to do all the work the communities identify as priorities.

We then, without hesitation, bought the idea and recommended it to the Steering Committee for approval. The contract was signed with an Irish NGO "Project Concern" and work progressed rapidly. Initially the project envisaged to build about 42 Kilometers of footpath. Eventually they were able to construct over 62 Kilometers of footpath connecting all the villages in the surrounding areas. The immediate highland area social and economic facilities were accessible and all took advantage of the new situation. It was a sharp escarpment. The project also provided Saho women work on the foot path to earn income. Traditionally they would hardly leave their homes, let alone go to work. It reminds us of the award winning Film "The Guns of Navaron", where the cliff could only be climbed by expert mountaineers.

On the day of the opening, traders were seen with their camels and donkeys going to the market with their produce and others coming back to their villages. Moslems predominantly inhabited the sub region. As mentioned earlier, the traditional Moslem women were engaged in the construction of the footpath. Some taking the traditional role of providing food and drinks such as water and tea, while other were engaged in non traditional activities, while others were participating in the actual construction activities, such as breaking of stones, laying down the dressed slates on the footpath etc.

On one of my monitoring trips to the region, the Minister of National Development and his staff came to view the project. Among the field visitors was Gebre Michael Tesfaselassie (Padre), the Eritrean-American who facilitated the opening of the UNDP Liasson Office in Asmsra, who remarked before we arrived at the scene. "Wei good" what are you going to show us,"a Foot Path for a village at a cost of a quarter Million US Dollars?". At the end of the trip everyone was impressed at the objectives of the project and the way it was implemented. The story of this project was picked up in the UN CHRONICLE JOURNAL in 2004.

An Episode during the visit of the UN Security Council to Ethiopia and Eritrea

In order to encourage Ethiopia and Eritrea to speedily demarcate their common border as per the decision of April 2002 by the Border Commission, the Security Council decided to have a meeting outside its normal venue. There was a brief Border crossing ceremony at Mereb Bridge. They then proceeded to visit one of the camps in the Senafe area. The members and their entourage wanted to interview some of the IDPs in Metera camp. The United Nations officer who organized the visit requested the Author if he could be the official interpreter for the Security Council vistors when they talk with the IDPs in camps, since the Author had the advantage of knowing Tigrinya, one of the local languages.

Poultry Development project in Senafe for IDPs

Donors also accompanied the Security Council members to this field trip. In the course of the visit, they singled out a woman who was standing in line and asked her how she has benefited from being in the camps. She told them that she has been assisted by the UNDP in developing a sustainable livelihood project. It was how to raise poultry she said. She informed the group that she was given training on how to keep chicks and how to build them cages as well. She was also provided with an initial supply of 25 Chicks and the building materials necessary (corrugated sheets, wood and nails) to build them a shelter.

A Nairobi-Kenya based donor asked her, "Wouldn't it have been better if the UNDP gave you the money in cash so that you could spend it in whatever manner you please". The peasant woman replied unhesitantly that she has lost all her property and her personal jewels when she left her village in a hurry, as a result of the relentless shelling caused by the border war. "I have been mentally affected by this sudden happening in a village I lived all my life" she said". I was first trained on how to take care of the one month old chicks and construct a shelter for them. I was provided with the building materials necessary to build the structure with my own hands. When I was doing this it gave me a break from constantly thinking about my unfortunate fate and the things I lost. It gave me a temporary relief to think clearly. The chicken will provide me with more resources to feed my children with milk. It is my hope that with God's will, I will be self supporting eventually."

As for your specific question, had the UNDP given me the money in Cash, I would have already spent it on consumable items such as sugar and coffee. Instead since I have been given training and some one month old chicks as you can see they are growing and I have already started selling eggs. Eventually, I will buy with the proceeds some goats and increase my assets which I lost during the border war. She added that during the Invasion of her village she lost everything. There is still some scar in my heart for the harsh treatment I received at the hands of the invading troops. This Socio-economic project has now given me an opportunity to be busy with the chicken and that has some therapeutic effects on me, she added. It is healing my wounds. I like the kind of assistance I received she concluded. The only request I have is that the project has only reached 700 women headed households in my area and many are waiting to get their turn.

We were all stunned by her answer. She was not prepared for this interview, as is customary in such situations. She was selected at random and yet she knew what she wants.

Distribution of materials to IDPs to build Chicken Boxes

Metera Emergency camp - Senafe

4.5 Media, Government and Donors

The Media and the attitude of the Government towards donors who try to get credit for their contributions for consumption of their constituents in their home countries needs to be mentioned.

The media could be an important asset if wisely used. In some instances it could also be an impediment to what you would like to achieve. We have real-life examples to illustrate our point. The Recovery Programme in Eritrea had over 150 projects spread over two decades. One such project was in Tsorona semi-urban centre. The urban centre was devastated by the border war with Ethiopia. It used to be a thriving regional trading centre covering a market with a radius of 25 Kilometers in Eritrea and Ethiopia.

Tsorona Market Place destroyed by the war

Tsorona Semi-urban center, after rehabilitation and reconstruction

Apart from the damage caused by the exchange of bomb shells, there was a deliberate destruction by the invading forces usung dynamite on some of the remaining infrastructure. The targets included the Water Reservoir, electric poles for the town, submersible water pumps at the source, covered market place etc. The roof cover of about 4,000 dwelling units were deliberately dismantled by some elements of the invading army and a few civilians from far away villages inside Ethopia. At times walls were scrapped to take the electric wiring inside. Hence, the project had many components and the UNDP focused its resources to rehabilitate and reconstruct the social and economic infrastructure. There were many visits to Tsorona by donor groups. In the case of UNDP assisted recovery programmes in Tsorona, the Dutch and Italian Governments and the UNDP were the principal donors. During the inauguration of the opening of the Covered Market Place, that created opportunities for one hundred and fifty women headed households, to reclaim their former livelihoods, the BBC and VOA were invited together with the local media.

The Eritrean Government and media most of the time have presented the recovery efforts as products of the hard work of the government and local authorities. Neither the name of the donor that provided the resources nor the UNDP that was executing the project were mentioned. Yet the donors have always complained and rightly so that their constituents back home need to see some mention of their contribution in the national media so that the diplomats in the country could ask for more. Yet the local authorities prepared elaborate receptions and gifts to the representatives of the donors and the UNDP.

That was compensating for the lack of coverage at the national level with the appreciation expressed at the local level. At an the opening ceremony, the Ambassador of the Netherlands was called the Queen of Tsorona.

Moreover, the town council has also designated the main square in Tsorona as "The Hague Square".

The Netherlands provided substantial amount of funding for the development of the square so that it reflects the great name it was bearing since The Hague was not only the capital city of the Netherlands but it was also the Headquarters of the World Court, the Ethiopian/Eritrean Border Arbitration Tribunal and the International Criminal Court (ICC). It was a smart move by the town adminstration.

The BBC reporter that was covering the event wanted to interview one of the Recovery team. We told him that it was better he interviews the Governor of the Southern Region or the Dutch Ambassador who was one of the key donors ,or the Minister of Construction who was attending the opening cermony. He said he will, but he would also like to interview one of us, since we were behind the successful implementation of the programme in Tsorona. We promised him that we will give him another opportuinity for a comprehensive interview on recovery that will include not only Tsorona but other places like Om Hager, Gerenfit, Tessenei, Goluj etc. He was not convinced but he did not press since he noted that we were not prepared to be interviewed.

Debriefing session with the Governor of Gash Barka region in Barentu town

Joint meeting with the Governor of Gash Barka, UNDP and Donor

Similarly, the Voice of America Tigrinya Reporter stationed in Asmara also requested us to grant him an interview. We gave him an identical reply. When we returned to Asmara, the Voice of America reporter was persistent in his quest and came to the UNDP Office in Asmara and asked the UNDP Resident Representative (RR), if we could be interviewed. We were informed by the RR that "it would be in the interest of the UNDP Eritrea to get some coverage and it was good for our annual reports as well" he added. We again tried to explain to him that there to be a context to the interview and we promised to call him when we go to Gash Barka for a field trip.

You may wonder why all the hedging. Because we have observed and learned the hard way that the local authorities would be furious for someone from the Recovery team to be interviewed about an explanation on the objectives of the projects, in greater detail, for both the national and international audiences, a task that they were most suitable for the job. We felt, at the time, that the forefeiting of publicity for the programme was a small price to pay, since the vulnerable war affected populations and communities will continue to benefit, without interference by the local authorities.

On another occasion, we prepared an elaborate programme for inaugurating a community centre in Gerenfit resettlement area. The local media were present and dispatched their report promptly to Asmara for broadcasting the next day. The coverage initially included in a video news-clip presentation, the Minister of National Devlopment, the UNDP Resident Represntative, the Ambassador representing the donor and the Recovery Technical staff. The broadcast for the day started with Tigre language followed by Arabic and finally in the Tigrigna progrmme. Every time the news item was covered, over a course of few hours, it was watered down until at the end, only a clip of the Minister was seen giving directives, without showing in the news the representatives of the UNDP, donor and other technical staff.

On another occasion, the Author was passing through the Ministry of Transport and Communication and met near the gate the Head of the Planning Department. We were introduced by a mutual friend while the Author was assisting the Ministry, on a pro bono basis, on the review of the Transport Sector Study financed by the European Commission. Thereafter, when we meet accidently on the street from time to time, we generally exchange views on a number of non-political issues for few minutes as the Author proceeds to fetch his car from a nearby garage.

In the course of our brief chat, there was an old man, an ex-fighter, who guards the office of the Ministry who was evesdropping. The Planning head, who was an ex-fighter himself, asked him if he had watched the one hour programme on Eritrean TV, the previous night on the rehabilitation/ reconstruction efforts taking place in and around Tsorona town. The guard said he did. The Planning head in the Minstry, told him that the Author was behind the project but the Eritrean TV did not mention his name or that of the United Nations Development Programme that financed it. The guard somberly replied, "From when was it that the EPLF singles out a name to give it credit". Hence, he added "do not be surprised, we are only continuing what we brought from the field and the experience of the days of struggle still prevails".

The brief encounters the Author had with this person were pleasant and educational. He was a straight talker and very engaging in his arguments on a number of technical issues. He always advised the Author not to be discouraged by some situations in the course of his work with the Recovery Programme, when encountering his government counterparts. The author was grateful for his advice.

In contrast, a similar situation in another occasion was observed, but with a different outcome. We have learned that the best way of protecting our programme was to avoid the press as much as possible, unless it was absolutely necessary. Bringing to ourself the attention of the media was counterproductive. If we had a low profile, it was better for the success of the programme we were executing.

Consequently, we have avoided the media as you would avoid a plague for the sake of the success of the recovery programmes. This paid handsomely for at the end of the three and half years, 35 schools were built, over ten thousand houses rehabilitated, etc. The cooperation of the local authorities and the government officials at the national level was superb. There was no element of competition. We were ready to go along with this arrangement. We were not there to make a name for our selves.

Training the already well trained

The experience of the Mine Action Programme in Eritrea and the contribution of one of the teams could be cited. A team of experts were trying to train manpower for Mine Action to assist the GoSE in its humanitarian demining efforts. In this particular field visit to a specific area, they ended up training already experienced hands.

This is a story of a veteran Ex- EPLF Fighter, who was demobilized and recruited in one of the UNDP Mine Action Projects. Members of the UNDP Senior Management were visiting one of the Demining Areas in Debub region. The Project Team was demonstrating to us, how the demining operations were conducted. There was an eight person team carring out a humanitarian deming exercice in an area about two square meters at a time, and the precautions they took in the process. There was an ambulance with its driver ready for action, a supervisor, a first-aid health professional, etc. It was very elaborate and closely followed international standard procedures.

In the meantime, as we were walking with one of the deminers in the demining operation (Ex-fighter), he mentioned that he was working on this particular site to earn a decent living. All these precautions during peace time are interesting but are academic and wasteful, he said. We pretend, he added, that we are learning from the instructors in order to earn a living. If we are to clear the land mines and unexploded ordinances at the present rate, it would take half a century, he added.

One of our Recovery Team members asked him what he has learned from the exercise. If we are to be guided by the international standards adopted by the United Nations, he said, and if we are to demine two square meters, using eight professionals at a time, it seems the experts will be with us for several decades to come, he said.

A team consisting of eight deminers

It seems he was demobilized in the hope of joining the de-mining team that offered better pay and working conditions. He knew more than his instructors. He narrated to the Recovery Team member visiting the site, how at night when they were having an operation against the Dergue Forces; he was able to clear 82 land mines in preparation for a surprise attack. Since this was a surprise attack, you can not use flashlights, he said, or any other light to assist you to locate the mines. Otherwise the element of surprise will be lost. The de-mining operation, therefore, was conducted at night and he had to feel the mines only with his hands.

This apparently was what sometimes made the Eritrean Government to be impatient. The argument of the Eritrean counterparts was that if it is going to take us long to clear the mines and UXOs, it was most likely, that we will have casualties from among the population. He said, however, we can finish the whole de-mining operation in two to three years and we may have few casualties. Some members of the International Community were upset with these remarks. They don't care about life, etc. they started to say among themselves. The Government countered by saying "what could the Experts show for the millions of dollars that they have already mobilized other than keeping themselves and their cronies employed".

They operated like a labour union. When they gang up against you, you have no resort but to throw them out of the country, they said. They have a well-oiled machinery to twist every thing you say, the government counterparts complained, and their patrons are too willing to listen to what they have to say.

A year later the Eritrean De-mining Authority (EDA) after they received instructions from the Government expelled initially the Halo Trust and three other de-mining NGOs and later closed the whole mine action Programme supported by donors/aid.

In our view, there was miscommunication on both sides. On the UN side mostly out of not being sensitive and on the Government side out of the perception that they knew more than the experts that came to help. The UN side of course controlled the purse and they always close ranks when confronted by Government counterparts. Generally speaking the experts are fine, some better than others.

4.6 Government and Regional Counterparts

The UNDP led Recovery Programme in Eritrea would not have been possible without the full support of the Eritrean Government Counter Parts. First and foremost the three Administrators of the three most conflict affected regions, Debub, Gash Barka and Southern Red Sea. The Administrator of Gash Barka was an affable person and pretty much committed to help his region.

He is quick to grasp the issues very well and makes quick decisions. Once he was committed to a programme, he delivers, if it was within his purvue. We had developed mutual trust and were able to achieve many things, despite the odds stacked against the speedy implementation of some projects.

The structure for decision making of the recovery programme was explained earlier. The Chairman of the Steering Committee was the Minister of National development, Dr. Woldai Futur.

Woldai was a former World Bank employee and experienced in his chosen profession. He was cool and cordial. He always asked penetrating questions before he approving the programmes and his role was to see to it that whatever interventions we make are within the overall frame work of the national development. He was fast in arriving at decisions and he never went back on an agreed position and stuck to it firmly to the end. There was no wobbling and he did not buckle under pressure from his colleagues in the implemntation of the Recovery Programmes. He was unrelenting in his support.

Woldai was also represented at some of our meetings by Prof. Abraham Kidane, a long time tenured professor in an American University in the West Coast of the United States. He was knowledgeable and easy to work with. He was also analytical and gave the programme his full support at crucial moments. He played an important high profile role in the preparation of the ill fated Integrated Recovery Programme (IRP). During the absence of Woldai a high delegation from the UNHCR that was taking the lead on resource mobilization, came to Asmara and he was firm in his resolve to maintain the integrity of the proposal despite futile attempts to politicize the process and down size the programme considerably.

Another notable partner was the Chairman of the Project Appraisal Committee, Mr. Kidane Tsige, the then Director General, Ministry of Local Government (MoLG). Kidane was an experienced professional with a post graduate degree from an American University. He was thorough in his knowledge of the various aspects of the programmes. He was a straight talker and not mince his words. He was pleasant to work with and always willing to go to the field to verify and monitor the progress of the implemenation of the recovery programmes. He was flexible in his approach, seeking solutions all the time, when the situation demands it.

The Deputy Commissioner of ERREC, Mr. Teklemichael Woldegiorgis, commonly known as Rosso, was in a class of his own. He was very conscientious of his role and very committed to the welfare of the people in and outside of camps that needed help. He was a good spokesman for ERREC, although there were always other political appointees over his head, to give the political direction. He did the bulk of the work of ERREC in relation to donors and the UN system. He was thorough and a born diplomat. He knew how to extricate ERREC from difficult confrontations with the donor community and partners. He played the apologist role of ERREC for the sake of keeping the funds flowing for the benefit of the affected populations. We had excellent working relations and were always willing to extend a helping hand when the going got tough.

The other two members that we had close working relationships were Mr. Mehreateab Fessehaye, Director General, ERREC and Ambassador Gebremichael (Lilo), the Executive Director of the Emergency Reconstruction Programme (ERP). They were both members of the Appraisal Committee. Mehreateab had a Post Graduate degree from an American University and Lilo the Manager of the (ERP), a 288 Million Dollar Project, was also a former Ambassador to the EU and a holder of a Post Gradute degree.

Mehreateab was also an experienced military fighter with deep scars in his body resulting from wounds he suffered when Massawa was liberated. He was very committed to his work and pleasant to work with.

Lilo was made a member to see to it that there were complementaries with the UNDP led Recovery programmes and the ERP. He was cordial, humble and sophisticated in his demeanour.

In general, as far as the recovery programmes were concerned these high-ranking government officials were well suited to the task and in most cases had far more knowledge and experience than their counterparts in the donor communities and UN that monitored the various programmes. Without their good will and help nothing substantial would have been achieved. It would have been full of confrontations on every intervention and no result to show at the end of the exercise. The price of not competing for attention in the media has also paid off handsomely.

Capacity Building

The provision of budget for capacity building in the various Programmes was made, as the initial experience of project identification, design and overall planning for rehabilitation, reconstruction and reintegration activities revealed that there was lack of capacity at the regional level to carry out well-planned, integrated, area-based recovery interventions. Furthermore, the regional administrations, especially in the most war-affected areas, such as Gash Barka, Debub and Southern Red Sea, faced an overwhelming challenge to track and coordinate the recovery interventions in their territories.

The pilot project for capacity building was a result of consultations between Ministry of Local Government (MoLG) at central and regional levels, ERREC and UNDP. The project was implemented in Gash Barka, Debub and Southern Red Sea regions for 700 staff from regional and sub-regional administration. The project provided technical assistance and training to the regional administrations to set up, manage and independently sustain a GIS database, done in coordination with UN, OCHA and ERREC. It also supported the planning of needed human resources, the institutional set-up and training for the implementation of data collection for GIS as well as improvement of project management.

The greatest drawback was the continuous reshuffling of staff. They were transferred from sector to sector and from one region to another. We all took it in our stride, because any capacity built was not wasted, although it would have had more impact in the region and sector they were trained. There were ample provisions for the procurement of hardware and software, equipping the offices and training of the recovery staff in the regions. In few instances there were also targeted study visits to countries who have demonstrated good results in their efforts at rehabilitation and reconstruction activiies

There was a time when a large contingent of diplomats were to visit Gash Barka. We arranged two UNMEE helicopters to carry the donors and diplomats to visit some recovery project sites. Some of the donors were scheduled to come from Nairobi and beyond to take advantage of the arrangements. It was meant to be a field visit for sensitizing the donors about the needs of the region. The trip was organized by OCHA Eritrea. Apparently there was a break in communication with the then OCHA Head in Asmara and the Governor of the region was not kept abreast with the latest schedule of activities. The group was to be led by Simon Nhongo the then Resident Representative of the UNDP and UN Resident Humanitarian Coordinator. A day earlier the Governor called OCHA and informed them that the visit was cancelled. There was panic everywhere. We happened to be in Barentu at the time and Simon Nhongo called to update us on the diplomatic slap. We immediately went to see the Governor in his office. He received us cordially and we raised the problem carefully. In light of the preparations he needed to make and the advance security detail to be employed as a precautionary measure to be taken by relevant agencies of the Government, he had a right to insist that he be given enough lead time.

Although the areas to be visited were safe and secure at the time, one has to still deploy the necessary security personnel to protect the visitors from any unforeseen incident.We explained to him that there was no malice on the part of the organizers and it was sheer incompetence that kept him in the dark. We promised him that we shall go to the root of the problem when we got back to Asmara and there will be no repeat of the situation if such a field trip was going to be organized by the UN Resident Humanitarian Coordinator and UNDP Resident Representative. He agreed reluctantly and the field visit proceeded on schedule. If there was no mutual trust there would not have been any further visits and the embarrassment of the UN authorities for such a blunder would have been unbearable. Once a decision was made there was generally no recourse for review or change. We gave him credit for the flexibility he had shown since the decision was not only by him alone but by other relevant entities that he reports to as well.

There were also at times other unpleasant encounters. On one occasion the Governor, was apparently informed of the inadequacy of the water to be supplied by the bore hole based water system in Gerenfit resettlement area designed to cater to the needs of 12,000 rural expellees from Ethiopia. The issue was quickly resolved but it left a scar on our relationship. When the expellees were moved from Shelab camp to Gerenft there were elaborate plans in place. ERREC was in charge of the transportation while UNDP monitored the move and footed the bill. The construction of a health station and the erection of temporary school facilities were in place by the PoWER programme. Yet there was someone, a local cadre, who was constantly agitating together with a notorious settler and an owner of a Truck Water Tanker who was idle at the time.

During the first three days of the move, there were unusual lines on the Public Water distribution centers (points) of about fourty people at a time. There was fear among the expellees that there will not be enough water available which at the time was not true. Every household had at least three or more jerricans (20 liters capacity) of water in their tents. ERREC's Deputy Commissioner and the Author were informed that there was a shortage of water and a baby died of thirst during the weekend. We immediately rented and dispatched a water tanker to go to Gerenfit to supplement the water, by hauling water from nearby areas with plenty of water. This was an extra insurance although it was found later to be unnecessary, because the news was false. Indeed a baby had died not because of thirst since there was plenty of water; the baby died because of natural sickness contracted when he was at the Shelab camp. The child mortality in camps was the same for the country as a whole.

People are bound to die of natural causes in a population of 12,000 people. We understood later from the expellees that the false alarm was instigated by the water tanker owner. The situation returned quickly to normancy. During this period the number of schools rehabilitated or newly constructed, the number of heath facilities built, the number of bore holes drilled and the number of roof kits distributed were phenomena.

The other partner we had was the then Governor of Debub region. The Governor was a graduate from a Russian University and always known for his measured response. He was analytical and always helpful. He was at times not as fast to make decisions but fast enough, considering the situation in the region, to achieve all the goals for the recovery programmes that we have designed with the government and local authorities.

4.7 Special Focus on NGOs as Implementing Partners

International NGOs are often key actors in post-conflict situations. UN agencies (UNDP, UNICEF, UNHCR, and WFP among others) have a track record of working with NGOs as do a number of bilateral donors. NGOs in many cases have a strong commitment to working in remote outposts and a growing competence to help UNDP reinforce local authorities and institutions.

A preliminary pre-qualification of NGOs was carried out prior to the full start of the programme to expedite implementation. Further, to speed up project appraisal and monitoring, a simplified project document format was prepared and disseminated to interested NGOs and local authorities. Appraisal guidelines were also developed to facilitate project review at various levels.

In most cases NGO skills have proven helpful and instrumental also in Eritrea in the transition from relief activities to recovery programmes. This statement of course was limited to those who have expertise beyond delivering of emergency food supplies, shelter kits etc. There were also NGOs who were ill equipped to undertake recovery projects and these were a cause of increased tension between the government authorities and NGOs that sometimes resulted in expulsions from the country.

The Recovery Programme as a whole took some unique initiatives in the choice of its projects to work with the Government, especially at the local level, to build capacities for sustainable national reconstruction and to strengthen national capacity for coordination and management by linking relief activities to sustainable long-term development.

The Programme has facilitated the introduction of Government-endorsed implementing partners for community interventions, as a stop gap solution for a limited period when Government-NGO relations were difficult. The Recovery Team at UNDP maintained an ongoing dialogue with NGO implementing partners, guiding design and implementation goals, and bringing the different components into an integrated framework.

The Recovery Programme initially partnered with 12 international and 3 national NGOs to implement projects. The Programme Steering Committee selected the NGOs.

The Italian NGOs at the time included in the partnership for implementation were APS, CESVI, COSV, CRIC, GVC, INTERSOS, ISCOS Marche, MANITESE and MOVIMONDO. Other non-Italian, international NGOs were Concern, OXFAM and Refugee Trust. The national NGOs were Eritrean Solidarity and Cooperation Association (ESCA), Eritrean War Disabled Fighters'Association and HABEN. Many of the projects have also been implemented by Government Ministries, like the Ministry of Local Government in Gash Barka, Debub and Southern Red Sea regions, ERREC, Ministries of Health and Education as well as the Ministry of Labour and Human Welfare.

Implementation through NGOs and Government Ministries has been in line with the Country Cooperation Framework (CCF) prioritizing UNDP support to decentralization and area-based development, as many of the implementing partners have concentrated their efforts in a particular geographical area or sub-zone. CESVI and MOVIMONDO have both concentrated on shelter and on rehabilitation of social infrastructure in the Goluj sub-region while COSV implemented several projects on improving the social infrastructure in Molki sub-region. Both sub-regions are in Gash Barka and Debub.

MANITESE concentrated on projects in the area of sustainable livelihoods, both in the Mekete IDP camp and its surroundings as well as in Sosona and Koita villages in Gash Barka. MANITESE has, in particular, proven that it has experience and capacity for working with community issues and women's participation. A mission from UNHCS (Habitat) expressed approval of the CRIC methodology for community participation and self-help construction. Refugee Trust also had two projects in Adi Quala (Debub region) where they implemented an integrated recovery project along with a water supply project with high community participation.

In Areza (Debub region) APS implemented two projects for the rehabilitation of social infrastructure. Other NGO partners implemented one project in Adi Keyih and several in different IDP camps, like Metera (Senafe), Zula and Soira (Adi Keyih) and in Deda camp (Mai Aini), all in Debub region. Oxfam also implemented one project in the Shelab expellee emergency camp in Gash Barka.

In addition, some of the NGOs have been able to raise complementary funding on their own for additional activities or for their projects. For example, COSV secured additional voluntary funding for the extension of a school and MOVIMONDO, which overall performed very well, arranged volunteer dental service for the community it was working with in Tesseney town in Gash Barka region.

The Regional/Sub Regional authorities in Debub, Gash Barka and Southern Red Sea regions, carried out projects in the rehabilitation of houses and social infrastructure as well as cash-for-work programmes. In Debub region the rehabilitation took place mostly in the Senafe and Tsorona sub regions. In addition, the Eritrean NGO ESCA undertook distribution of kerosene in those areas to allevaiate the shortage of fire-wood and mitigate the possibility of accelerated deforestation.

Introducing the Moringa Tree in Gash Barka region

Eritrean Mine Action Programme (EMAP)

During 2001-2002 UNDP assisted the Government of Eritrea to set up the Eritrean Mine Action Programme (EMAP). The assistance provided (initially was $100,000), acted as seed funding to set up and start the EMAP, to build capacities of the Eritrean Mine Action Agency as well as to strengthen the Ministry of Labour and Human Welfare to assist disabled persons caused by mines. The contribution then jumped to about 10 Million USD through additional support provided by the UNDP, EU, the Netherlands, Canada and the United Kingdom.

CHAPTER FIVE

5. OVERVIEW OF THE UNDP RECOVERY PROGRAMMES IN ERITREA AND LESSONS LEARNED (1992-2012)

"The true measure of the success of the United Nations is not how much we promise, but how much we deliver for those who need us most".

Ban Ki-moon, Acceptance Speech to the General Assembly upon election as Secretary General for his first term

5.1 Pre-Referendum (Post-Liberation) Projects (PRP) 1992-1993

The involvement of the UNDP in recovery programmes precdes the independence of Eritrea as a sovereign state. After the country was liberated in 1991, but before the internationally observed referendum in 1993, the Transitional Government of Eritrea requested the UNDP if it could support some highly needed emergency related interventions. The UNDP responded positively and a Capcity and Institution Building project to the tune of 6 million USD was quickly designed and implemented during the period 1992-1993.

Consequently, a UNDP Liason Office was established in Asmara in 1992 with an initial operating budget of USD 6 Million allocated from the indicative planning figure (IPF) for the period 1992-1993 to meet the immediate emergency needs of the Provisional Government to be used in Capacity and Institutional Building in the aftermath of the war of liberation.

5.1.1 Pre-Referendum (Post-Liberation) Projects: Lessons Learned

UNDP demonstrated its flexibility in accommodating the emergency needs of Eritrea which was then liberated after 30 years of war but was not yet an independent nation.

5.2 Programme for Refugee Reintegration and Rehabilitation of Resettlement Areas in Eritrea (PROFERI)

As mentioned earlier, Eritrea was liberated in May 1991 inheriting a destroyed and neglected social and economic infrastructure as a result of the 30 year war of liberation. It became an independent state in May 2003 following an internationally supervised referendum. During the 30-year war, about 500,000 Eritreans, mainly from the lowland provinces fled into neighboring Sudan. Since the end of the war, about 110,000 people have spontaneously returned, placing severe pressures on very limited social and economic facilities and resources. Immediately after liberation, the Government expressed its commitment to repatriate all of its citizens who had fled the country because of the war. Government's strategy has been to ensure that the repatriation process was organized and orderly, and that the returnees are fully rehabilitated and reintegrated into the communities from which they fled or resettled in other areas which may give them new opportunities.

Therefore, one of the major tasks that faced the country after liberation had been the repatriation, reintegration and rehabilitation of these refugees. However, given a devastated economy and physical infrastructure, the consequential task of repatriating and reintegrating the large numbers of refugees was beyond the economic and human resources of the newly established Eritrean state, and necessitated collaborative international action.

Hence, in order to begin the organized repatriation of refugees, the Eritrean government worked with United Nations (UN) agencies to design the 'Programme for Refugee Reintegration and Rehabilitation of Resettlement Areas in Eritrea' (PROFERI). PROFERI was designed to repatriate, resettle, rehabilitate and reintegrate primarily Eritrean refugees living in the Sudan. The project envisages the provision of basic social services, in such sectors as health, education and water. It was also designed to enable the returnees to lead a productive new life in their home country.

Against this background, in 1993 the Government requested various UN agencies to assist in securing resources to finance a Programme for Refugee Reintegration and the Rehabilitation of Resettlement Areas in Eritrea (PROFERI), which would facilitate the return of the refugees. A pledging conference was organized and held in Geneva in July 1993. Given the low level of pledging, the Government decided to scale down the program and began implementation of a pilot phase to repatriate some 25,000 refugees.

The pilot started in November 1994. Nine sites were selected in Gash province (at the time, there were eight provinces in Eritrea, namely: Hamassien, Akelguzai, Seraye, Anseba, Semhar, Sahle, Setit and Denkel) to accommodate an average of 500 families each, based on ease of access, availability of water, the availability of agricultural and range land, the willingness of communities to accept returnees, as well as the willingness of returnees to return to the site. Accordingly, facilities such as shelter (tukuls as well as emergency tents), water, temporary health and education facilities were put in place. A team of independent local and international consultants positively evaluated the pilot program in April 1995.

THE UNDP PORTION OF THE PROFERI PROGRAMME (PHASE-ONE)

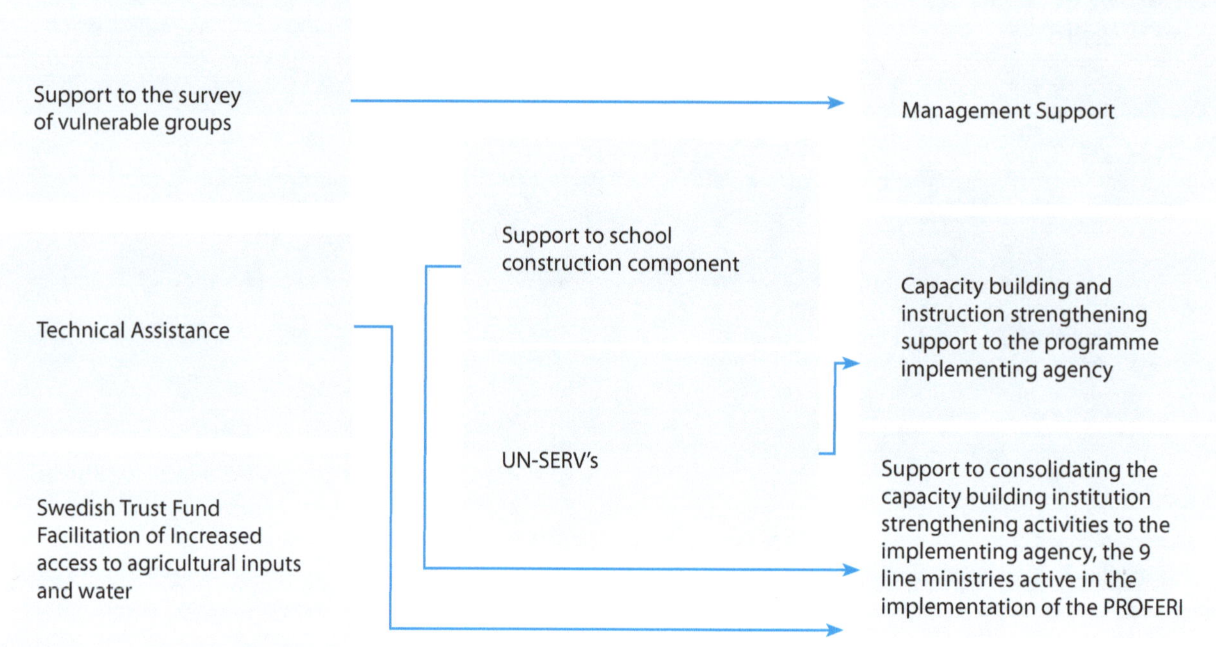

As it has been stated above, the objective of PROFERI was the repatriation and reintegration of some 100,000 refugees who were expected to return from Sudan. This was supposed to be the first phase of a broader intervention, which will lead to the repatriation of all the refugees, who were willing to come back from Sudan.

The UNDP portion of the PROFERI Phase One Programme included technical assistance, management support, capacity building and support to returnees with agricultural inputs (such as seeds, restocking), school, health and water facilities. The UNDP has extended support worth of US$9,305,873 to PROFERI programme in capacity building through construction of 15 schools in four regions namely: Gash-Barka (8), Northern Red Sea (4), Maekel (3) and Anseba (1) and training of 47 staff of the Eritrean Refugee and Rehabilitation Commission (ERREC). Furthermore, it included provision of livestock; construction of ponds, boreholes and hand dug wells to insure potable water for the settlers and their livestock (Refer annex 1).

UNDP package of assistance in the PROFERI programme consisted of:[4]

(i) *USD 60,583 as technical assistance for the preparatory process of the programme including the formulation of the programme document.*

(ii) *Management support of USD100,000, which provided assistance for the Operational Plan of the PROFERI and a coordinator for one year.*

(iii) *Capacity building and institution strengthening support of USD 1,063,290 to the programme-implementing agency.*

(iv) *Support in consolidating the capacity building/institution strengthening activities to the programme implementing agency, the nine (9) Line Ministries active in the implementation of the PROFERI as well as the construction of the fourteen (14) schools. The total assistance for this activity was USD 4,572,000.*

(v) *Support to the Survey of Vulnerable Groups of USD 63,290.00 to study and assess the level and magnitude of vulnerability in Eritrea. A preliminary report on the number of vulnerable households in the country has been produced and submitted to the government for review. Once the remaining phases of the household interviews and data analysis were complete, the study provided the basis for a comprehensive poverty strategy which would be a response to Paragraphs 26(b) – Formulation/ Strengthening the Implementation of National Poverty Eradication Plans; 26(d) – Elaborating at the National Level, the Measurements, Criteria and indicators for determining the extent and distribution of absolute poverty (of the WSSD Programme of Action) as spelled out in the UNDP Administrator's Direct Line No.6 – Poverty Eradication and Copenhagen follow-up.*

(vi) *UNDP also managed USD 2,054,795 Swedish Trust Fund earmarked for the PROFERI programme. This activity was intended for the facilitation of increased access to agricultural inputs and provision of water facilities for the Eritrean returned refugees.*

(vii) *In the case of institutional capacity development, a UNDP-funded Chief Technical Advisor (CTA) provided both ERREC and UNDP policy on PROFERI, and an Assistant CTA and ninety-seven (97) national UNV-SERVs fielded with ERREC, supported programme implementation and operations.*

ACHIEVEMENTS UNDP COMPONENTS

- Out of the 100,000 targeted only 25,000 were repatriated due to budget constraints at the time.
- 15 schools in four regions were constructed.
- 47 staff of the Eritrean Refugee and rehabilitation commission (ERREC) were trained in management, finance, programme and project planning, monitoring and evaluation and logistics and procurement.
- ERREC in turn conducted local-level building skills training for 4,606 persons in book keeping financial/business management, electrical work, carpentry, masonry, plumbing, metal work and secretarial science.
- Nine Eritreans specializing in such areas as water supply statistics, legal services, health services, logistics auditing and procurement were recruited under UNV programme.

5.2.1 PROFERI Programme: Lessons Learned

- At the inception of the Programme of Reintegration and Rehabilitation of Resettlement Areas in Eritrea (PROFERI), the transitional Government of Eritrea had limited knowledge and experience on the working procedures of international, multilateral and bilateral aid agencies, as well as working with large scale rehabilitation and development programmes. Hence, the wishes of the Government were at times, in direct conflict with the rigid rules and practices of international agencies.

- Although the government had some exposure, especially working with NGOs, in the areas under its control during the years of liberation, as a new emerging country it has faced complex and unfamiliar policies and procedures. Therefore, it would have been helpful to Eritrea as it transited from Guerilla war management style to statehood to provide its mid-level leaders an early training and set-up simple follow-up mechanisms. Moreover, in multi-donor and multi-sector programme/projects like PROFERI, the responsibilities for donor coordination and resource mobilization of the Government and UNDP could have had better results if they were clearly defined and agreed upon at the outset.

- The international development agencies, in order to meet the Government's expectations require imaginative responses based on carefully coordinated flexibilities so that their procedural rules and regulations do not hinder change and success in the development process. Besides, the Government of Eritrea is required to organize the need for practical flexibility, to find common ground and a point of convergence where balance can be found for its partnership with the international development communities for effective cooperation in its development process. The most important lesson learned from the implementation of the PROFERI is that partnership and flexibility are essential and indispensable ingredients to international development cooperation.

- The external technical assistance, as is the case in the PROFERI, was mandate driven, the target group being returning refugees from the Sudan. The preferred mode would have been a comprehensive national framework with an integrated approach, which would then provide the basis for an appropriate institutional set-up encompassing all categories of support measures from relief to development.
- The PROFERI tried to accomplish too much too soon and over-estimated the absorptive capacity of an emerging state after a thirty year war of liberation. A more modest set of clearly defined capacity building and institution strengthening measures at the outset would have been desirable for a programme of eleven major components.
- An attempt was made to identify at the designing stage the relevant but relatively young line Ministries and agencies and to involve them directly in finalizing the programme and project design. Moreover, at the planning and design stage there were rarely involvements of beneficiary returnees as they were still in emergency camps in the Sudan.
- The PROFERI programme has demonstrated clearly that the implementation of the components, in our view, would have been more efficient and effective, if the regional and sub-regional administrations were put in the driver's seat. However, decentralization could only succeed if adequate capacity and institution building proceeded or had accompanied it.
- The implementation of the PROFERI revealed that the mobilization of the energies and resources of the rural poor themselves emerges as the key factor in increasing both their productivity and their self-reliance and such mobilization requires the formation, adaptation and strengthening of community structures.
- According to the report of the Post-Facto Evaluation of the PROFERI programme, there was a need to obtain a socio-economic profile of the would-be returnees (refugees) and identify at an early stage their wish of final destination, the training they wish to undertake and the profession they plan to pursue. Moreover, consultation with the inhabitants of the nearby host villages to sort out problems of land, water and grazing area were not undertaken.
- The concept of reintegration of the returnees was based on the wrong assumption that because of their rural background returnees would want to go back to the country-side and therefore agricultural settlement would be best suited to accommodate them. Most of the returnees have stayed in Sudan for more than two decades and they may have lost their farming techniques or might have acquired new skills outside agriculture where they would like to resume their livelihood. Furthermore, women headed households comprised about 40% of the returnee households and could not benefit by the provision of land because of lack of labor. Therefore, opting for diversified activities in the different sectors of the economy for a sustainable livelihood was vital for the success of such programs.

Live stock

- The provision of livestock as a form of support to sustainable livelihoods tends to be more complex than providing other inputs such as seeds or tools. This is due to the different species, which recipients might select, and for each species, variations in breed and sex, which are appropriate for different uses, management practices, or environment. Purchase of livestock from neighboring countries raises questions of disease control and veterinary care has to be arranged for animals provided to returning refugees.
- During the design of the PROFERI project, contact with Eritreans living in refugee camps in Sudan had been minimal. Consequently, very little was known about the sites where people wished to resettle (and if their preferences matched the nine official resettlement sites) or returnees' expectations in terms of preferred means of livelihood. The lack of returnee participation in the programme prompted a reassessment of the livestock input, with a focus on the suitability and relevance of the livestock packages. The need to review the provision of livestock to returning refugees was heightened when more people than anticipated chose to return to lowland areas, particularly in the then Gash Setit province, now Gash Barka in the south-west of the country.
- Work in refugee camps in Sudan showed that some Eritrean refugees did own animals although it was also noted that accurate data on livestock numbers was difficult to obtain for cultural reasons and fear of taxation (Kibreab, 1987). However, no information was collected on the existing livestock assets of returning refugees. Consequently, it was not possible to determine whether returning refugees' choices were affected by their current livestock.
- All returnee households were to receive animals regardless of their preferred means of livelihood. Consequently, people who wished to engage in non-agricultural activities may have selected animals which could be sold immediately for a reasonable price or donkeys and camels which could be used for income generation purposes.
- The livestock package of PROFERI needs to be seen as provision of assets rather than restocking where the classical restocking program attempts to provide viable herd and targets very carefully those who wish to lead a properly agro-pastoral or pastoral lifestyle. Restocking is usually defined by NGOs as the supply of a minimum viable herd (e.g around 30 small ruminants and a donkey) to destitute pastoralists in order to enable a rapid return to self-sufficiency and use of grazing.
- The livestock component of PROFERI illustrated how the participation of beneficiaries, even at a superficial level, could have led to more appropriate and beneficial livestock inputs.
- PROFERI revealed that for a restocking component to be successful, it needs to be implemented as far as possible by the community, sometime after the refugees have arrived, at a time when animals are in reasonable condition, when availability of forage is ascertained, when returnees and MoA staff have time to attend to the animals and should progress slowly not to upset markets.

Moreover, restocking activity should also be avoided when there is drought.

- Most animals had perished because of being poor quality, lack of adaptation to the climate and many beneficiaries had no or little knowledge in animal husbandry and were short of family labour, or had no means to hire herders and therefore were unable to look after the animals they received.
- Also the number of animals given to the beneficiaries was too small (8-11 goats/sheep or one camel or two heads of cattle), far below the customarily defined viable herd size (30-70 heads) in the area. The consequence of this was that even those refugee households that returned and who have long standing experience in animal husbandry could not make use of their traditional knowledge because they did not consider it worthwhile to allocate full time family labour to look after a small number of animals. In the settlement areas, livestock owners engage in seasonal long distance migration, designed partly to take advantage of variation in the environment and partly to let the nearby grazing areas rest. The returnee households could not afford to do likewise, because to deploy their family labor in this way had greater opportunity cost related to other forms of economic activities such as wage labour, than herding a small number of animals on a full time basis.
- Supply driven planning process is generally speaking found to be a defective process and leads to wastage of resources. The lack of concrete information on returnees to devise demand driven plans resulted in the wrong identification of location of resettlement areas and wasteful use of resources. The selected villages were Adi-Bidho (Fanko), Goluj, Adi-Seidna, Duluk, Keru, Halhal, Etaro and Kamchewa. Among these villages the returnees have accepted only Adi-Bidho and Goluj, where the actual number of returnee households located in these villages surpassed the planned figure. The number of returnees in the other villages was insignificant. Hence, it is important to ascertain the wish of the remaining refugees returning from the Sudan regarding their preferred site of resettlement, type of training, livestock preferences and other related issues.
- During the implementation the PROFERI, it became apparent that every technical cooperation activity for area based development should be analyzed from the point of view of the participation and involvement of the rural community and the effect on different groups within the rural community, particularly the vulnerable groups such as women and children within these groups.
- The implementation of the PROFERI also revealed that different social groups within the same community are likely to face different constraints and define priorities accordingly. Flexibility is, therefore, imperative regarding the sequence of steps or the relative emphasis given to interventions in different regions depending on the specific problems and capacities of the communities involved and on the flexibility of the intervention proposed.
- The PROFERI has defied the traditional precepts of technical cooperation which is to facilitate the introduction and local application of new technologies by making such cooperation people-centered activity aimed at creating the enabling conditions for sustainable livelihoods. About 80% of all PROFERI expenditures were made directly at the local level and concentrated on those activities, aimed at improving the living conditions of the rural poor while at the same time, laying the foundation for sustainable human development.
- In the settlement/resettlement sites a uniform model had been worked out instead of different models based on regional differences such as the availability of land and its suitability for farming. For instance, the initial program modality designed for Red Sea coastal zone model was spate irrigation with the provision of inputs and livestock. However, during implementation the intervention took little account of these guidelines and was the same irrespective of returnees' experience, gender and environment.
- The possibility of conflict between returning refugees and those who stayed behind "***stayees***" if the former benefit alone at the expense of the latter should be underscored. Most of the refugees who came from the Sudan were from the low lands of Eritrea, hence they were returning in most instances and resettled in new areas in and around the Goluj semi-urban areas. It was soon realized that resettlement sites and the provision of cultivable land for returnees, if possible, should not be at the expense of those who had stayed behind. Hence, meticulous efforts were needed to provide that returnees should also be encouraged to settle outside the formally allocated resettlement areas, possibly return to their villages of origin, so as to minimize the conflict that would possibly arise from competition for land in the western lowlands of Eritrea. Therefore, all involved parties, that is, the refugee communities as well as the local communities that are to receive the returnees must participate in the planning process.
- The returning refugees should have been differentiated whether they were returning to their original villages or were to be resettled in new areas. In many instances the original villages have been devastated and would need to be rehabilitated. In the case of new areas, it would be imperative to have new infrastructure (school and health facilities, shelter, new farming implements where applicable, and household level packages). If they were to be integrated to existing communities, the infrastructure has to be bolstered, e.g. more class rooms, new boreholes etc.
- in spite of all the constraints mentioned above, the Pilot phase of PROFERI was by and large very successful, although the subsequent phase was not planned fast enough. Instead the country was engulfed in a new conflict – the border war with its neighbor Ethiopia.

5. 3 Pre- Post War Emergency Recovery Programme (PRE-PoWER)

Soon after independence, tension between Ethiopia and Eritrea emerged and broke into a border war in 1998. The border war of 1998-2000 and years of persistent drought had severe impacts on Eritrea. Consequently, over 1.1 million people were displaced primarily, from the regions of Gash-Barka, Debub and Southern Red Sea from their homes to safer areas within

Eritrea. These and the communities who hosted the Internally Displaced Persons (IDPs) camps have suffered from shortage of natural resources as well as inaccessibility of adequate social services such as schooling and health care.

The peace agreement that was negotiated in December 2000 had resulted in the establishment of Temporary Security Zones (TSZ) and the presence of a UN peacekeeping mission to Eritrea and Ethiopia (UNMEE). This enhanced a period of relative peace and allowed most of the IDPs to return to their former homes.

Hence, in 2001 some of the 208,000 IDPs who were in emergency camps for almost a year have started to move home in or around the Temporary Security Zone (a 25 Kilometers buffer zone inside Eritrea that separated the two armies) where the UN peace-keeping force has been deployed). However, it was clear that these returning IDPs and refugees and the hosting communities continued to need a broad range of humanitarian assistance including both food and non-food aid. Those returning to their original villages found their home areas badly war-damaged and needed help to rebuild their lives and re-establish themselves in their home communities.

Because of the border war, there was heavy damage to housing and infrastructure in the war affected areas of Eritrea, which produce 70% of the country's food. The situation was further complicated by the fact that the majority of returnee households were female-headed and that there was an absence of male support in construction and developing livelihoods.

Initially the Government of the Netherlands and USAID promptly acted on the emergency situation, by joining UNDP to provide assistance to the IDPs. The Government of the Netherlands provided close to USD 1.2 million through UNDP for the purchase and distribution of tents and household items for IDPs. USAID contributed USD 900,000 for charter flights to bring in blankets and plastic sheets as well as locally procured kitchen utensils for the IDPs.

At the same time (June 2000) the Italian Government approached UNDP to arrange for the provision of emergency assistance to war-affected victims, expressing an interest in trying out a modality of using primarily NGOs to deliver the assistance. This actually became the basis for a larger Italian-funded programme that followed. The Italians made an initial contribution of USD 1.45 million to the UNDP "Trust Fund for Crisis, Post-Conflict and Recovery Situations", administered by the Bureau for Crisis Prevention and Recovery of UNDP, for Eritrea. This project assisted the local authorities in IDPs camps to respond to the increased demand for social services.

PRE-POWER PROGRAMME

PROGRAMME COMPONENTS 1999-2000

- Provision of medical staff and drugs; rehabilitation of the resource and supply depleted hospitals
- Supply additional quantities of supplementary food and non-food items (such as tents, kerosene) to the border-where affected IDPs were living in emergency camps.
- Drilling wells and constructing reservoirs as well as restoring the water systems of the hosting towns
- Introduce educational and hygiene environmental activities related to proper use of water, fire and energy resources and improve sanitation in the camps
- BUDGET : 1,648,811 (UNDP Italy and USAID)

A Pre-PoWER programme was conceived to address the prevalent adverse socio-economic condition of the war-ravaged communities of the nation. That was the focus of the Pre-PoWER programme. It was an emergency assistance programme to war victims that tried to respond to the immediate and urgent needs of the IDPs/Expellees in camps. There were seven projects under this programme from July 2000 to May 2001 and the total budget was $1,334,461 (1,648,811) fully funded by the Italian Government, the Dutch and USAID. The UNDP had managed the fund and the implementing partners were NGOs, including CRIC, APS, CESVI, MANITESE and ESCA and the Ministry of Health. An additional activity undertaken was organizing workshops for women IDPs and supplying them with materials for small handcraft works.

The budget also had a provision for assisting returning IDPs other than those mentioned above. The funds were to be used mainly for activities in the above sectors implemented by international NGOs, jointly selected by UNDP and the Italian Cooperation, and for payment of airlifts as agreed with the Italian Cooperation. The project was important in trying out the modality of working through NGOs, a modality then adapted for the PoWER programme. The project was directly executed by UNDP, which entered into an agreement with a number of specialized NGOs to implement specific components of the project. Five NGOs, four Italian and one Eritrean, were selected to implement the projects.

The projects were formulated promptly to meet the emergency needs of the IDPs and host populations, mainly in Debub and Northern Red Sea Zones. In Debub, the influx of IDPs put a lot of pressure on the water supply resources of the hosting towns and communities. The project helped to improve the water supply systems in several areas in Debub by drilling new wells and by restoring the water supply system in Areza town. In addition, some essential non-food items were distributed to around 20,000 IDPs from the Senafe area as well as kerosene for 30,000 families in Senafe and Tsorona areas, as little firewood was available and it was not possible to collect it due to the risk of land mines.

The Mekete camp in the Af'abet sub-region in the Northern Red Sea Region hosted a large number of IDPs. The camp required immediate assistance in providing social services, especially in the areas of health, nutrition and sanitation. The project assisted through provision of medical staff and drugs as well as by supplying additional quantities of supplementary food. Further on, it provided sanitation and hygiene education for the camp population, organized workshops on income-generating activities for the women in the camp, and ensured that children could follow their primary education. The Af'abet town hospital faced an increased case load, which the project helped to alleviate through rehabilitation of the hospital and provision of technical assistance with particular emphasis on the obstetric and surgical emergency care.

The activities to improve the infrastructure of the Mekane Hiwot Hospital in Asmara were delayed beyond the planned project duration but were implemented in 2002.

Finally, in line with the provisions in the project document, some of the funds were used to pay for air cargo of relief supplies donated by NGOs in Italy and the Italian Cooperation.

5.3. 1 Pre- PoWER – Lessons Learned

- Under the Pre- Post War Emergency Recovery (Pre-PoWER) programme one best practice that needs to be highlighted was the way the emergency camps were set up. During the border war over 1.1-1.6 million people were displaced and emergency camps were setup. The IDPs/Expellees were organized in the emergency camps (some of which contained more than 20,000 persons each) by clustering their tents in accordance with their original villages. This allowed the villagers to assist each other and have a secure environment. Their village/kebabi and sub region administrators were also living among them.
- As the years went by, this arrangement was bearing valuable fruits. Women headed households (over 60%) and girls were living among the people whom they know well and they included their brothers, uncles, aunts, cousins etc., which gave them added security.

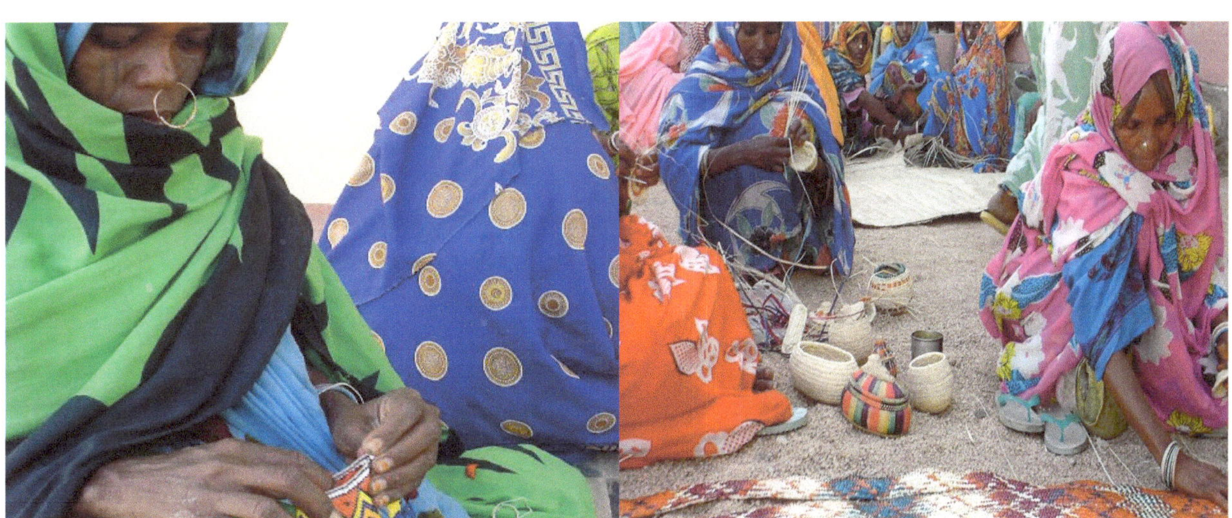

Straw weaving training for women at Afabet camp

Hand loom training for women at Afabet camp

They were well protected from predators and people in authority including NGOs engaged in emergency programmes. To our knowledge there were no reported cases of abuse, sexual harassment or other undesirable experiences in the camps.

Adi Keshi camp, Temporary Emergency School, Gash Barka region

When the UN Under-secretary General for children in armed conflict, Olaro Otunnu, visited the Adi Keshi camp in Gash Barka, he was amazed and impressed at the arrangement and publicly stated at the end of his trip that this was unique and could be cited as best practice that should be replicated in other countries with IDP camps. Moreover, he also promised to report to the then Secretary General, Kofi Annan what he has observed as best practice to be followed internationally.

5.4 Post-war Emergency Recovery Programme (PoWER I and II)

Following the end of the Pre-PoWER programme, the Government of Italy made a further contribution of USD 16 million to the UNDP "Trust Fund for Crisis, Post-Conflict and Recovery Situations", and using those funds to further respond to the challenges of the emergency situation, the UNDP Post-War Emergency Rehabilitation (PoWER) Programme was quickly conceived and signed on 13 November 2000. The overall objective of UNDP's assistance was to contribute to the national rehabilitation and reintegration of displaced and war-affected populations, to build capacities for sustainable national reconstruction and to strengthen national capacity for coordination and management by linking relief activities to sustainable long-term development.

The Italian funds contributed to the PoWER programme have been used to identify and implement emergency and rehabilitation projects amounting to USD 14.9 million over a period of one and a half years. To maximize the impact of the programme, UNDP contributes its own resources as seed funding and mobilizes resources from other interested donors. In this way, UNDP attracted funding from the Government of the Netherlands with which it has been able to execute the rehabilitation of over 5,400 housing units in Debub and Gash Barka, costing USD 2,339,148.

In accordance with UNDP's global restructuring process, the UNDP Country Office (CO) in Eritrea started a restructuring process in 2001 to better respond to the needs of the country. Its response to the emergency situation in Eritrea was matched by a change in the country office's administrative structure. As a result of a re-profiling exercise in the CO, UNDP reorganized the office and merged the emergency and rehabilitation programmes, including PoWER, into a new "Recovery Team" led by a Senior Advisor on Recovery.

The Post War Emergency Recovery (PoWER) Programme was, therefore, intended to link relief and development so as to facilitate the transition from emergency relief to sustainable rehabilitation and to support the resumption of economic and social development. During its first six months of operation, the programme was intended to concentrate on meeting urgent needs while concurrently underpinning the promotion of sustainable and integrated recovery activities in the return and resettlement area as well as rehabilitation of social infrastructure, agricultural production and human capital. During the remaining period of the project the focus has been on contributing to the long process of rehabilitation and development, in addition to meeting emergency needs that may arise.

The projects under this programme were implemented through an area-based development approach in accordance with the objectives of the first Country Cooperation Framework (CCF) signed between the Government of Eritrea and UNDP, which prioritizes UNDP support to decentralization and area-based development. The recovery projects were developed through a participatory process involving both the affected populations and the local government authorities. This has resulted in a series of integrated projects prepared by local community organizations, line ministries, and NGOs for their implementation.

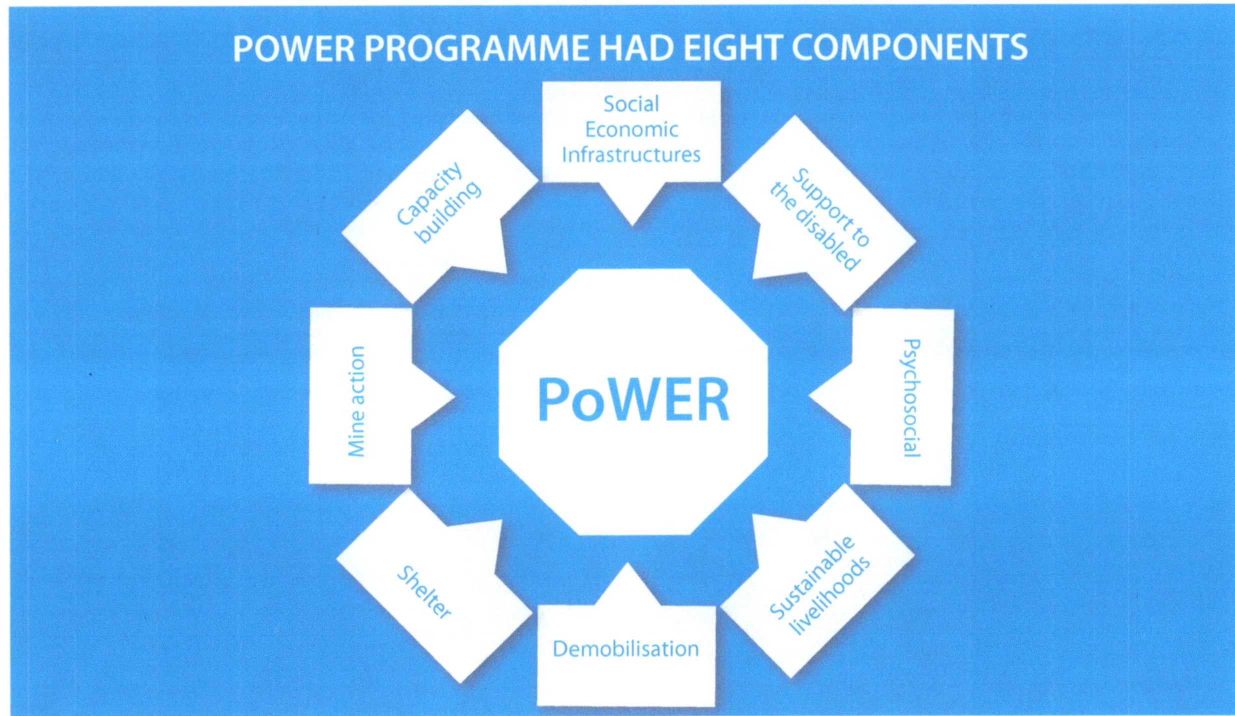

5.4.1 PoWER I – First Phase

A rapid joint assessment of the needs of IDPs by the Government of Eritrea (GoE), UNDP and Cooperazione Italiana (CI) in July 2000 laid the basis for an initial donation by the Italian Government that allowed the establishment of a UNDP transition recovery initiative. This provided the setting for further contributions to UNDP's relevant trust fund from the Italian Government and later from the Dutch and American Governments and resulted in the creation of the Post-War Emergency Rehabilitation Programme (PoWER I).

The first phase of PoWER nominally ran from November 1st 2000 until December 31, 2001. It was concerned with utilizing the USD16 million provided by the Italian Government and USD 2.4 million provided by the Dutch Government for the rehabilitation and reintegration of displaced and war-affected people, the building of national reconstruction capacity and the national capacity for coordination and management. The basis for PoWER I modality of operation was to link relief to sustainable long-term development.

UNDP was involved in the successful return of IDPs and expellees in Debub, Gash-Barka and Southern Red Sea regions through projects worth over USD 20 million under the PoWER Programme, for the rehabilitation and reconstruction of houses, schools, health facilities, water supply, promotion of sustainable livelihoods and de-mining activities.

Transportation

This activity included the dignified and safe transportation of the IDPs in both regions of Gash-Barka and Debub to their places of origin. Under PoWER I programme, about 200,000 IDPs benefited by the transportation facilities and the budget spent for this purpose was USD 450,000 and the implementing partner was the Eritrean Relief and Refugee Commission (ERREC).

Shelter

The shelter component of the PoWER programme included the construction of new houses, rehabilitation of destroyed houses, construction and rehabilitation of public facilities such as market areas. Under the programme, there were nine projects: five in Gash-Barka, three in Debub and one in Southern Red Sea region. Accordingly, 173 permanent new houses and 10, 950 emergency shelters were constructed and 1,400 houses, which were damaged by the war, were rehabilitated with a total expenditures of USD5,894,371.

Health

Under the health component of the PoWER I programme, 18 projects with a budget of USD2,881,735.61 had been undertaken. The activities included:

- construction of new health stations
- rehabilitation of hospitals, MCH clinic and health centers
- provision of health and sanitation facilities in emergency camps
- dissemination of PHC services
- procurement and supply of drugs and medical equipment; provision of orthopedic appliances
- provision of technical assistance such as anesthetist
- on job training for medical staff

Education

The education component of the PoWER I programme consisted of construction of new schools, rehabilitation of the damaged schools and restocking schools with supplies and facilities. It also included training component for youth and women. There were 15 projects in this programme with nine in Gash-Barka, three in Debub, two in Northern Red Sea and one in Southern Red Sea totally worth USD 3,685,695. Particularly, the projects also included; moving the existing makeshift classrooms from Shelab emergency camp sheltering expellees to Gerenfit resettlement sites; rehabilitation of the elementary and middle schools in Mai-Dima, the elementary school in Dabre and the elementary and junior school in Mai-M'ne including the provision of furniture, school materials; rehabilitation of two schools in Goluj and Gergef including the supply of furniture, school materials and teaching items; rehabilitation of seven schools including the supply of furniture, school materials and teaching items; and the rehabilitation of the Tsorona Junior and Secondary school. By rehabilitating/ constructing the latter schools, it gave chance especially to girls who would otherwise not be able to go to Adi-keyih and Dekemhare urban centers to continue their education by renting housing far from their families.

Furthermore, a project to build four new classrooms in Endagaber and a dormitory (four bedrooms) for teachers in Mai-Dogalle as well as supplying furniture, educational and teaching material was implemented under this programme. COSV rehabilitated the school in Endagaber but the returning

IDPs increased the number of enrollments by 500 additional pupils and therefore new spaces were needed. The construction of a new primary school in Koita benefited two of the historically disadvantaged groups of the Eritrean population namely; Kunama and Nara by making access to primary education possible for small children in Koita.

Rehabilitated Om Hajer Arabic School, Gash Barka

Besides, a direct execution by the MoLG Gash-Barka region, through the engineering and programme management department, a package of 12 schools in the region has been constructed. UNDP PMU has designed the project document together with the Gash-Barka administration and under the supervision of the planning department of the Ministry of Education (MoE). The cost estimation was based on the bill of quantities prepared by the Regional administration engineering department. Similarly, in Debub region there was a direct execution modality project implemented by the local government, through the engineering and programme management department, of a package of seven schools in the sub-region of Senafe and Tsorona. UNDP PMU has designed the project together with the Debub administration and with the supervision of the planning department of the MoE.

Middle School in Om Hajer destroyed during the border war

Middle School reconstructed in Om Hajer

Moreover, the Ministry of Education was granted the funds to re-supply about ten junior and three senior secondary schools to replace their damaged school library books and supplementary reading materials, and also for the provision of education supplies for the total of 80,000 students affected by the border war.

Water and Sanitation

Under the PoWER I programme, the water and sanitation component had 14 projects that address the emergent needs of the IDPs in the camps as well as permanent needs in their return villages with a total budget of USD2,509,317. The activities undertaken by these projects were improving the water and sanitation facilities in the villages surrounding the IDPs' camps; provision of sanitation facilities, hygiene promotion and distribution of water storage equipment; construction of bathing areas and latrines in the camps; rehabilitation of water systems; construction of boreholes and fitting them with motorized pumps; rehabilitation of hand dug wells; construction of distribution pipelines, construction of reservoir and public fountains; and replacement of hydro-metrological instruments.

Sustainable Livelihood

PoWER I programme not only attempted to respond to the emergency needs but also contributed in the restoration of sustainable livelihoods for the war-affected communities of Gash-Barka and Debub regions through 14 projects that focused on income generating activities with the budget of USD 6,020,639. The activities undertaken under the sustainable livelihoods component were various and included the following:

- Opening of accessible land, distribution of farm animals, seeds and agriculture tools
- Distribution of beehives and training on bee-keeping

- Manufacturing of Beehives for distribution in Senafe sub region, Debub
- Restocking, such as distribution of goats
- Poultry farming targeting women headed households; distribution of chicks and chicks' feed, provision of construction materials for the cage, and training the beneficiaries
- Training women in home economics, basic agriculture, sewing, hand looming and providing assistance to establish small businesses

- Enabling the communities to generate income through engaging them in productive labor through cash for work. Thereby, the output of such things as the construction of foot-path, maintenance of feeder roads, harvesting runoff water and rehabilitating the eroded land have had a direct positive impact in agriculture which was the main stay of their livelihood.
- Rehabilitation of war-damaged Farmers Training Center
- Rehabilitation of a market place, bakery and establishment of a mill.

5.4.2 PoWER I I – Second Phase

The fluidity and unpredictability of the emergency situation called for a flexible programme so that programme funds could be used—provided the situation dictated and in consultation with all concerned—in areas outside the original plans. Indeed, during actual implementation some of the funds were used for areas not foreseen in setting the objectives for the programme or in the original budget.

The Second Phase of the programme continued to target the following beneficiaries: war-affected households, displaced people in camps, host communities and returning refugees. Female-headed households received special focus. In the case of the inhabitants of Om Hajer in Western Eritrea, for example, some of the IDPs were displaced three times in the short span of three decades. The first was during the reign of Emperor Haile Selassie where the town was completely obliterated. This wanton destruction was repeated again by elements of the Mengistu Hailemariam regime. The latest destruction that struck the town and its inhabitants was as a result of the border war with Ethiopia. During the last episode some of these IDPs were also turned refugees. They were forced to flee to the Sudan for a second time after they returned to Om Hajer from three decades of misery in the Sudan. Hence, the recovery programme was complex, the needs great and the resources limited. The main components of the programme were:

Rehabilitation and reconstruction of houses; rehabilitation, and in some cases, reconstruction of social infrastructure including water and sanitation, health and education; promotion of sustainable livelihoods through support to agriculture and to increasing employment opportunities through income-generating activities in agricultural and non-agricultural activities in rural areas; and support to coordination of the emergency and reconstruction response.

Particular attention was paid to addressing gender concerns, including support to the special needs of women and youth.

Before launching the PoWER Programme, the UNDP recovery programmes consisted of: 3 projects funded by the UNDP in the Post Liberation years, 13 PROFERI projects funded by the UNDP, 7 pre-PoWER projects funded by the Italian Government under another window; 64 projects approved by PoWER and funded by the Italian Trust Fund; 4 projects funded by the Dutch Government;

a project on Technical Assistance for the social and economic reintegration of demobilized soldiers funded by USAID; project on the capacity building of the Mine Action funded by (Norway, Dutch, EU, UK and Canada); 1 UNDP project for the re-settlement of rural expellees from Ethiopia; 8 projects under the joint programme phase one funded by (UNDP, Norway, Netherlands, USAID, UNICEF, Italy, WFP and the Government) and 20 projects under the expanded joint programme funded by (UNDP, Norway, Netherlands, USAID, CERF, EC, UNICEF, UNHCR and UNFPA) and projects were funded by UNDP, Norway and EC under the Transition and Early Recovery Programme.

After the PoWER programme was approved, it has rehabilitated/reconstructed 37 schools, relocated and constructed 31 makeshift class rooms and 18 new class rooms and 18 teachers' rooms and supplied them with school furniture and materials. A new primary school was also constructed. It also stocked the libraries of 10 junior and 3 high schools with books and other reading materials.

The construction of a new health station(1); rehabilitation of health centers (15); rehabilitation of hospitals(2), MCH clinic and health centers; health and sanitation facilities in camps; dissemination of PHC services; procurement and supply of drugs and medical equipment; provision of orthopedic appliances; provision of technical assistance such as anesthetist and on job training for medical staff. 173 permanent new houses and 10, 950 emergency shelters were constructed and 1,400 houses and a market area which were damaged by the war were rehabilitated; drilled 12 boreholes and constructed two hand-dug wells benefiting 12 villages. It has supported a national safety net through a cash-for-work programme to over 125,000 individuals. The programme has provided assistance and NFI to several IDP camps, and implements in three areas integrated community-based projects that improve the living conditions in those communities and successfully provide sustainable livelihoods through skills training and income-generating activities for all community members, especially women.

Community Elementary School in Debub

Resettlement and integration of expellees

During the border conflict between Ethiopia and Eritrea (1998-2000), the Ethiopian Government expelled 75,000 Eritreans and Ethiopians of Eritrean origin. Almost a quarter of these expellees were agro pastoralist farmers and the majority of them came from Northern Ethiopia, just across the border from Eritrea. One of the main alleged reasons for their expulsion was that the Ethiopian Government feared that they were more sympathetic to their place of origin, Eritrea and hence could filter intelligence information to them across the border. Inhabitants of whole villages were expelled and many of the expellees had to leave behind some of their family members, and all their belongings, arriving in Eritrea empty-handed. Many expellees were initially sheltered in temporary emergency camps until a permanent solution was found for them.

In 1999 UNDP approved a project with the Government of Eritrea for the rehabilitation of the war-affected populations in the Gash-Barka region. In particular, the project was expected to settle and integrate 12,000 rural farmers who were forcibly expelled from Ethiopia and had chosen to settle in Gash Barka. The project also provided assistance to 1,623 hosting households.

Before the UNDP project could be implemented, the Government of Eritrea was expected to allocate land to each settler-expellee, provide water and health facilities, counseling and administrative support and be responsible for the smooth and successful implementation of the project through its regional government structures. When these conditions were in place, it was expected that the project could start in full. UNDP was committed to provide assistance in the areas of agriculture, water supply and other basic social services. In particular, it would purchase agricultural inputs, machinery and livestock, provide for diversion of canals and construction of ponds and water troughs, upgrade existing education, health and water resource facilities, and train resource personnel and trainees.

However, the project faced delays in its implementation, mainly due to the border conflict with Ethiopia. The expellees could not be settled in the planned areas as those areas were directly affected by the war. The Government was not able to identify alternative settlement areas for all the expellees. Some changes were made to the project to accommodate the delay; for example the duration of the project has been extended. Eventually, the Government worked in close collaboration with UNDP, ERREC and HABEN, a national NGO, in finding sustainable solutions in Gerenfit, a newly identified resettlement area, in Gash Barka region for the expellee population.

In early 2002 five sites in the Gerenfit area were identified where the rural expellees can be settled. They were to be moved to these sites once the site layout had been designed and the availability secured. Eventually, a new Health Station was to be constructed and temporary schools erected. The community was also to be assisted with the distribution of farming tolls, seeds, ploughing services and oxen. The government issued to each household two hectares of fertile land.

First Harvest in Gerenfit

Shelter

The two-year Eritrea-Ethiopia border conflict had a significant foot print on the destruction of social and economic infrastructure especially in the shelter sector. The most affected zones were the border regions of Debub and Gash Barka. Destruction and damage to housing in those regions was reported to be extensive.

According to information collected from sub-regional administrators, 52,000 houses (units) were seriously damaged: 41,600 totally destroyed 30,528 in Debub and 11,072 Gash Barka) and 10,400 partially affected (2,165 Debub and 8,235 in Gash Barka[22]. The return of IDPs and returning refugees caused an imminent need to start rehabilitation and reconstruction of the houses. Without shelter the returnees were unable to begin rebuilding their livelihoods.

EVOLUTION OF THE SHELTER PROGRAMME

- Emergency (tent and wooden poles)
- Ronda Structure (Royalties)
- Agudo Structure semi permanent (Tesinma-UNDP)
- Expandable farmer's house Gerenfit pilot project
- Shelter Kits distribution -plus and minus
- Empowering People/Cash Assistance

Altogether, the Recovery Programme has provided funding for the construction of specially designed 173 housing units, rehabilitation of about 7,600 housing units, and rehabilitation of the market area in Omhajer and distribution of 1,471 agudo structures of which 271 have been upgraded to a more permanent structure. The project to build additional especially designed 73 houses was also implemented.

22 Programme for Emergency and Rehabilitation in War-Affected Areas in Eritrea, Shelter Component. Ministry of Local Government, UNCHS (Habitat), and Italian Cooperation. October 2000.

The first projects in the shelter sector started with constructing new houses for the most vulnerable members of the target communities in Goluj and Tesseney sub-regions, both in Gash Barka. In these areas the Recovery Programme also supported activities in health and education. Both sub-regions were seriously affected by the conflict, for example in Goluj sub-zone 11,169 houses were totally or partially destroyed, which corresponds to 78% of the entire stock of dwellings (14,900). In general, in Gash Barka 44% of the dwellings had sustained some kind of damage, according to a sample survey of 36 villages conducted in April-May 2001.

These projects included the building of 60 specially designed fairly large houses with three rooms with a prototype to be approved by the Steering Committee of the Recovery Programme. The designs were to be revised to incorporate any recommendations resulting from a parallel programme of research and development in housing implemented with technical advice from Habitat. The projects were also expected to link the reconstruction activities to the development of local productive economic activities, to maximize the beneficiaries' participation through self-help programmes and to carry out tests to improve and introduce new building components (for example roofing). The latter was linked to a workshop organized in Tesseney in August 2001 on outcomes of the research done by one of the implementing NGOs, CESVI, and Habitat on construction materials, new technologies and soil testing, and the case studies of low-cost housing in Eritrea.

The prototype constructed by CESVI was found to be satisfactory and it proceeded with building 30 houses each in Goluj and in Tesseney. In addition, CESVI implemented a project in Omhajer for the rehabilitation of 400 houses and the market area. All the works were completed by April 2002.

400 Houses destroyed by war in Omhajer – Gash Barka

In July 2001 the return of IDPs into their villages in the Tesseney area created a new emergent need to distribute emergency shelters for them. The programme decided to distribute Agudo rather than Ronda structures as soon as possible. The delivery of 1,200 Agudo structures took place immediately in August 2001. The local authorities selected the 1,200 beneficiary households, which consisted of many female or child headed families, elders and disabled. Assembling the Agudo structures turned out to be difficult for some of them, and the implementing NGO arranged teams to remain in the villages to assist in mounting the structures.

Agudo structures

Early in the programme, a company from Geneva came to collect royalties for the use of the Ronda metal structure design to build emergency tents. We were ready to comply with international norms and abide by intellectual property rights in the emergency sector.

We were, however, surprised to note that it is the details of the metal frames that were patented. Conceivably the hut is a native African Architecture and could not be patented by any group.

Hence, we decided to be creative and make our own designs. The agudo structure, was therefore, created as an emergency shelter produced in the country, specifically in Dekemhare, a town 40 kilometers south of Asmara..

It was a joint effort of the UNDP Recovery Unit and Tesinma manufacturing industry. It contained a metal frame that can be upgraded to a semi-permanent structure, by constructing a 20-30 cm wall to an anchoring mechanism to protect it from wind-shear and providing local materials to cover the frame.

While the foreign designed structure used to cost, at one time, about 1,500 USD per family unit, the new UNDP/Tesinnma design was a fraction of the cost about 180 USD per unit. The cover was to be of local material such as mat, tarpaulins and skin hides. Thousands were manufactured and many were erected in Debai Sima, Southern Red sea region

Assistance was also given to the IDPs in Debai-Sima and Musa-Ali in Southern Red Sea Region. The Recovery Team assessed the situation in the area and contacted the IDPs as well as local elders and authorities. The IDPs needed emergency shelter, NFI, and rehabilitation of school and water reservoirs. For the emergency shelter 271 families received one Agudo structure each, and a mat to cover it. After mounting the Agudo structure, the households were assisted in improving the structure by building a wall up to the height of 40cm. The project was implemented by the Ministry of Local Government Southern Red Sea Region with the support of ERREC and Eritrean Catholic Secretariat.

In June 2001 the Sectoral Working Group (SWG) on Shelter and Non-Food Items reported that at least 5,000 families of returning IDPs in Debub and at least 3,000 families of returning IDPs in Gash Barka were in need of an immediate shelter.

Agudo Metal Structure – Debai Sima, Southern Red Sea region

The SWG decided that the best way to provide permanent shelter would be, in those areas where it is practical, to rehabilitate houses that were partially destroyed by the war. A suitable package for rehabilitating housing units in these areas consisted fo the provision of corrugated iron sheets, rafters, purlins and materials for doors and windows. The branch offices of the Ministry of Local Government (MoLG) in Debub and Gash Barka were selected to implement the rehabilitation of the housing units, which is in accordance with one of the overall objectives of the Recovery Programme to strengthen the capacities at the Regional level to handle and deliver rehabilitation works and other recovery activities.

Rehabilitation of the damaged houses in Tsorona sub-regiona in Debub started in earnest on 31 July 2001 with the target of rehabilitating around 3,000 houses in sub-region Tsorona and 1,000 houses in sub-region Senafe through the provision of a roofing kit, doors and windows. UNDP procured the materials directly and all these materials were delivered to the project site. Local village committees, comprised of 7 members including 3 women, identified the houses to be rehabilitated.

The implementation carried out directly by the MoLG in Debub had successfully rehabilitated the planned number of houses by the end of November 2001. Funds from the Government of the Netherlands were utilized for the project. Furthermore, ERREC also assisted with in-kind provision of 17,300 corrugated iron sheets.

The rehabilitation of an additional 1,000 housing units in the Tsorona and Senafe regions was funded through the regular PoWER budget at the end of 2001. These housing units were completed in February 2002.

In Gash Barka the Ministry of Local Government Technical Unit was responsible for rehabilitating more than 2,400 partially damaged housing units in the war-affected areas using the same roofing kit as in Debub. UNDP procured all of the roofing materials through international bidding and delivered them to the project site. The project started in November 2001 and was almost completed by June 2002.

Traditional Agudo Structure

Stone wall with soil mortar

PoWER supported another shelter project in Adi Quala sub-region in Debub, in Geza and Medabia villages. The overall objective of the operation was to support the reconstruction process by providing building materials and technical support to the war-affected communities in order to reconstruct 113 completely destroyed houses. At the start of the project many of the returnees of the two villages were living in emergency shelters (tents and plastic sheets used as temporary roofing material). The houses were to be built by combining a low-cost construction intervention with good technical input, incorporating the lessons learned from the CESVI project on low-cost housing. The project mobilized the beneficiaries to participate in the construction, as well as to implement a bottom-up approach in sanitation and other issues. The project started in January 2002 and was completed in June 2003.

Non-Food-Items (NFI)

PoWER had one project for the distribution of NFI. UNDP procured the items and ERREC distributed them to the beneficiaries in the war-affected areas in Debub, Gash Barka and Southern Red Sea Regions. The items distributed included kitchen sets for 8,000 households, blankets for 80,000, bed sheets for 40,000 and clothes for 30,000 beneficiaries as well as soap for 248,348 beneficiaries.

Assistance provided by the UNDP Recovery Programme to IDPs/Expellees Sheltered in Emergency camps

The Recovery Programme has provided assistance to several IDP camps. Under PoWER funding, it has provided emergency assistance for IDPs from Senafe and surrounding areas that were hosted in the Buya camp in the Northern Red Sea Region and in Zula and Soira camps in Adi Keyih sub-region in Debub. It has supported the improvement of shelter, health and sanitation conditions in the Deda camp in Mai Aini sub-region in Debub. At the Mekete camp in Afabet, Northern Red Sea Region where assistance was provided already under the 1st phase, the work continued to improve the water, sanitation and social services for the IDPs. Furthermore, it arranged training and home economic courses for women and supported sports activities for students in the surrounding areas of the camp. The Shelab camp, which hosted rural expellees from Ethiopia, has benefited from a Public Health Programme. Finally, the 271 IDP families who were stranded in Assab neighborhoods were also assisted to resettle in Debai-Sima IDP settlement areas.

Buya, Zula and Soira IDPs emergency camps in Debub region

Many of the IDPs from the Senafe area were hosted in the Buya, Zula and Soira emergency camps. Previously the Recovery Programme had already distributed non-food-items for IDPs from Senafe, but there was a need for further assistance. The new project was set up to provide essential NFIs and to improve sanitation and health facilities in the three camps. As the situation of IDPs and their movements was changing all the time, the project had to make adjustments to its plan of activities. For example, Buya camp was closed by the time the project was approved in January 2001, and no activities were implemented at that camp. Furthermore, the coordination between the different organizations working with IDPs was not always very good and there was sometimes confusion around who had implemented or was going to implement what. GVC, the implementing NGO, however, operated well in this environment and was able to quickly change its operations when needed.

At the end, activities to maintain the water facilities, to organize hygiene promotion and to distribute non-food-items were undertaken in the two camps in Adi Keyih.

The Deda IDPs emergency camp in Debub Zone

The improvement of shelter, health and sanitation conditions in the Deda camp was to take place through NFI distribution (blankets, plastic mats, kitchen sets, impregnated mosquito nets, hygienic items), and through support to the elementary and secondary school as well as to the Deda Camp Health Post. The implementing NGO achieved most of the objectives. Due to the imminent return of the beneficiary population to their place of origin, the Recovery Programme did not foresee continuation of assistance to the camp. It planned, instead, to follow-up the developments of the population movements and assist in the resettlement of the families.

The Mekete IDPs emergency camp in Northern Red Sea Zone

The project to improve the water, sanitation and social services for the IDPs in Mekete Camp in Af'abet was a continuation of the activities carried out by the NGO Manitese at the camp during the first phase of the Italian funding. The new project was designed to improve the administration of the existing water system in the camp, to impart professional training programmes for some women in the camp, to integrate sports and recreational activities into the school activities and to continue play groups for children. It was also expected to provide support to the regular and adult education programmes as well as the health services at the camp, in particular the administration of the supplementary feeding centres.

The activities were implemented according to schedule and the NGO was one of the closest to the communities. All the missions visiting the camp praised especially the training activities for women and the management of social services as well as the hygiene promotion in the camp. Due to the activities in the supplementary feeding centres the indicators for malnutrition of children under 5 at the camp were among the lowest in the country.

The local branch of the Ministry of Agriculture requested that the home economics activities be extended to the host community while the Af'abet branch of the National Union of Eritrean Women requested that the courses on traditional handicraft production also be provided for women outside the camp.

The Recovery Programme had also already requested Manitese to investigate the potential for these projects to benefit the host community. Accordingly, courses on home economics and traditional handicrafts for women as well as sports activities for school children were organized for the host community in Af'abet.

The Shelab emergency camp in Gash Barka region

Shelab camp, located in a semi-arid area, hosted families who were mostly rural expellees from Ethiopia. They moved to this camp in late 2000 from Jejah emergency camp where they arrived in 1999. Although very basic needs such as water and public health care were provided and some NFI were distributed by different agencies, the population lived in very harsh conditions. For the majority of the population, the hopes to be permanently resettled and given suitable land for self-sustainment were not materialized before the summer of 2002.

Family Pit Latrines in Shelab Emergency camp for Expellees

The camp received further assistance through a project implemented by OXFAM GB. The project responded to emergency needs to upgrade the water and sanitation conditions. It consisted of the provision of sanitation facilities, hygiene promotion and provision of household items with which to maintain personal hygiene, distribution of water storage equipment, construction of bathing areas, and the building of around 164 family latrines. An important aspect of the project was that the host-community was also included in the project planning and implementation. They received the same assistance as the camp population. Oxfam also succeeded in mobilizing the beneficiaries to participate in the project implementation themselves. For example, the beneficiaries did most of the excavation for the latrines, which has led to community ownership of the results. After the project there has been a marked decrease in diarrheal diseases.

IDPs return to their original village in Debai-Sima in Southern Red Sea

The project at Debai-Sima IDPs settlement aimed to rehabilitate 79 family water reservoirs, drill one borehole and complete the construction of a building to be used as a school in addition to the distribution and upgrading of the Agudo structures as described at the Shelter section above. In June 2002 the Agudo structures were already distributed and upgraded and many of the family water reservoirs rehabilitated, but the other activities took time to fully implement.

Transportation of IDPs/Expellees

The transportation of the IDPs was not foreseen originally in the early draft of the Recovery Programme, but when ERREC needed assistance in providing transport services the Programme was able to accommodate this emergent need.

Transport of IDPs to their original villages

PoWER Programme funds have been used to assist ERREC in paying retroactively some private transportation companies, whose services were used during the third phase of the border war with Ethiopia when fleeing IDPs had to be transported to safe areas as well as some back to their home areas when it was peaceful. As soon as the Temporary Security Zone was established, approximately 300,000 IDPs (about 50,000 families) who were in emergency camps wanted to return to their original homes immediately and without delay. They wanted to start to rebuild their lives and to take advantage of the rainy season for cultivation. The PoWER programme assisted ERREC in providing the transportation for this category of people to return to their homes. Moreover, the PoWER programme was funding the transportation of IDPs in the Southern Red Sea Region as well.

The Road was rehabilitated so that IDPs could safely be transported to Ambesete Geleba

Moreover, the Eritrean Relief and Refugee Commission (ERREC) organized the transportation of about 180,000 IDPs to return to their homes, while larger numbers returned at their own initiative. The remaining 57,000 IDPs were returned or resettled by the Regional Administrations of Debub and Gash Barka. At the time of writing this manuscript, there are about 1,333 households who are currently sheltered in Adi Tsetser and are still not able to return to their homes due to the presence of mines, or the proximity to or location of their villages in areas under Ethiopian administration close to the southern boundary of the Temporary Security Zone.

Social Infrastructure

The activities under this heading include rehabilitation and reconstruction of the infrastructure for health, education and water sources/services.

Health Facilities and Infrastructure

In Eritrea the border war further exacerbated the already poor health service situation. Existing health services were inadequate to meet the health needs of the war-affected populations and the returning IDPs/Expellees. The influx, however limited it may seem, of returning refugees from Sudan put further pressure on the health structures. The health services in the war-affected areas were seriously disrupted by destruction and damage to the physical facilities as well as by the looting of medical equipment and furnishings. An assessment by the Ministry of Health (MoH) of facilities in the war and drought affected areas in Gash Barka and Debub showed that 3 hospitals, 12 health centres and 32 health stations were damaged or destroyed during the border conflict. Furthermore, there was an acute shortage of trained manpower and essential drugs.

In light of the above the Recovery Programme has supported the rehabilitation of 9 health stations, 4 health centres and provided technical assistance and supplies to 3 hospitals in the two regions in addition to the provision of technical assistance to the hospital in Af'abet in the Northern Red Sea Region. The Programme has also provided the pharmacies of the Ministry of Health in Debub and Gash Barka with drugs worth USD 700,000.

One of the first projects approved to improve health services was the rehabilitation of the Molki health centre in Gash Barka Region. The Molki health centre was completely looted during the war, losing all their furniture, electrical appliances, equipment and drugs. When the health staff returned to the village, they found the health centre had no facilities. ERREC and the local government representative identified the need for rehabilitation. The Recovery Programme succeeded in rehabilitating the health centre and in addition provided drugs, training of health personnel and an information campaign on health. After the intervention, the health centre has been able to offer both preventive and curative services and is in better condition than before the conflict.

The same NGO, COSV, under the supervision of the programme continued working in the Molki sub-region in order to strengthen the existing health system in Gash Barka through focusing their intervention on the Public Health Care facilities in Molki sub-region and the Agordet referral regional hospital. The project concentrated on providing technical assistance through expatriate experts. COSV also implemented projects in the education sector in the same area.

Areza sub-region in Debub also received assistance from the Recovery Programme in the health sector. The Italian NGO APS implemented a project to rehabilitate 1 health centre and 3 health stations in Areza, in addition to rehabilitating some schools in the same areas. The project also trained Traditional Birth Attendants and malaria agents. APS continued working the Areza, in particular strengthening the Mother and Child Health Care services in the sub-region as well as the gynecological/obstetrical services in the Dekemhare referral hospital. This project was proposed on the basis of a field assessment which revealed that only a very limited percentage of women receive ante-natal care and even fewer are attended to by a health professional during delivery. The project targeted the whole continuum of Mother and Child Health Care (MCHC) from the Traditional Birth Attendants all the way to the regional hospital. An expatriate expert, who also arranged on-the-job training in the hospital, provided technical assistance.

The third geographical area that benefited from the interventions of the Recovery Programme was Goluj sub-region in Gash Barka. Efforts were first directed towards the structural and functional rehabilitation of the health centre in Goluj and the health stations in Gergef and Tebeldia, as well as the reactivation of the emergency obstetric and surgical departments of Tesseney referral hospital. Assistance included the supply of drugs and medical equipment, technical assistance, and an IEC campaign on preventive community health. The authorities in Gash Barka as well as the medical staff in the hospital identified the need for the further improvement of the Tesseney hospital, and later support was given to the other departments of the Tesseney hospital. Furthermore, strengthening the potential and the quality of the comprehensive health services offered to the population by the Tesseney hospital was a priority in Gash Barka for the Ministry of Health.

PoWER continued funding activities in Gash Barka through MOVIMONDO, which implemented a project on health and sanitation support for returning refugees from Sudan.

The Recovery Programme had not foreseen providing assistance exclusively to the returning refugees, but as the settlement areas for the returnees were facing a serious emergency in terms of lack of health and education facilities, the programme was able to adjust to meet their needs. In general, most of the improvements for the infrastructures under the Recovery Programme were benefiting not only the returning IDPs but also the host communities and returning refugees. The project activities included refurbishing and installation of two health stations in Omhajer and Gerset, provision of drugs, support to Goluj health centre staff and improvements in the sanitation. Further, MOVIMONDO implemented an emergency rehabilitation project to make the health centre in Omhajer functional, including supply of drugs and medical equipment. This project was a part of an integrated recovery programme for different sectors in Omhajer, in which PoWER was also funding the rehabilitation of schools as well as of 400 housing units and some public buildings including an Administration building.

Rehabilitation of Adminstration Building in Om Hajer

Rehabilitated Market Place in Om Hajer

Rehabilitated Market Place in Om Hajer

In February 2002 the Ministry of Health approached the PoWER programme for assistance in supplying hospital furniture and equipment. At the height of the third phase of the border war of May 2000, when the Ethiopian army advanced deep into the Eritrean territory, the MoH responded by deploying extra manpower and other medical resources depleting the supplies of hospitals in Asmara. After the cessation of fighting and peace talks, a return to normal routine activities resumed. But because of the shortage of supplies, the desired level of health services could not be maintained. The PoWER programme agreed to, and replenished the needed supplies.

Education facilities and infrastructure

In the education sector, a total of 15 sub regions in Debub and Gash Barka areas were directly affected by the conflict with Ethiopia. The academic year 1999-2000 was disrupted. According to the Regional Administration, an estimated 30% of the 249 schools and education facilities, school supplies and furniture were destroyed or heavily damaged in Gash Barka and Debub. Over 1,000 classrooms in primary and secondary schools sustained severe to minor damages to physical structures and furnishings. Around 140,000 students were disrupted from their schooling, and more than 60,000 school age children were hosted in camps at the beginning of 2001. The displacement of people led to pressure on host communities and increased the teacher/student ratio from 50 to 70.

After the conflict there was an acute shortage of school space, furniture and teaching/learning materials. Education continued under trees or in makeshift classrooms—temporary structures made of wooden poles and locally made straw mats and/or wooden poles and corrugated sheets. Such structures are not suitable for a good learning/teaching atmosphere, and are exposed and vulnerable to wind and cold, which can cause health hazards to the school children. Difficulties in accessing potable water and sanitation facilities affected the health status of children. Furthermore, some of the children had witnessed human rights violations, or had possibly been targets of assaults. There was an immediate need to return them to a normal and stable environment.

As of June 2002 the Recovery Programme in the education sector had funded the rehabilitation of 34 schools altogether of which work in 8 were still ongoing. Most of these schools have been supplied with furniture as well as educational and teaching materials. In one area four new classrooms and the teachers' dormitory were also constructed. Finally, the programme has assisted in providing tens of thousands of students with learning materials and textbooks at the start of the academic year 2001-2, as well as books and reference materials for more than a dozen middle school and secondary school libraries in the affected areas.

Goluj sub-region in Gash Barka was one of the most affected by the conflict. The first project approved by PoWER in the education sector aimed at rehabilitating schools and teachers' housing in Goluj and Gergef villages in the Goluj sub-region. The project also included the supply of furniture, school materials and teaching items as well as improvement of the water supply in the Gergef village and school.

In the Molki sub-region in Gash Barka, which was seriously affected by the conflict, the PoWER funded a project in order to meet the student enrollment at school with proper facilities and education materials. The project aimed at providing equal access to education materials and infrastructure, enforcing the level of motivation among teachers, improving the sanitation environment and building a relaxing and peaceful atmosphere in the school.

These were achieved by rehabilitating and refurbishing 8 schools, supplying education and teaching materials as well as textbooks, rehabilitating the living conditions of teachers and re-establishing sport-facilities for the students.

The activities in Molki sub-region continued through a project aimed at building four new classrooms in Endagaber and a dormitory of four bedrooms for teachers in Maidhogalle as well as supplying furniture, educational and teaching materials.

The implementing NGO, COSV had already rehabilitated the school in Endagaber but the returning IDPs increased the number of enrollment by 500 additional pupils and therefore additional space was needed. Maidhogalle, where COSV had also already rehabilitated and furnished schools, the living conditions in the village were rough and the teachers were occupying part of the classrooms to live in.

COSV faced several implementation problems especially during the first project due to the shortage of skilled labour, the absence of raw materials and water and the inaccessibility of Molki. Nevertheless, it succeeded in achieving its objectives and even added some activities for the second phase by using funds it had been able to secure from other sources and voluntary donations.

The Recovery Programme established several activities in the Areza sub-region in Debub. In the education sector it achieved the rehabilitation of the elementary and middle schools in Mai Dima, the elementary school in Dabre and the elementary and junior school in Mai M'ne.

The project included the provision of furniture and teaching-learning materials for 4,500 students and 70 teachers as well as the arrangement of recreational activities for the students. APS has shown flexibility in adapting to requests from local authorities and communities.

The Ministries of Local Government in Gash Barka and Debub got involved in the rehabilitation of schools. In Gash Barka, the Recovery Programme designed the project together with the Gash Barka administration under the supervision of the Planning Department of the Ministry of Education.

The project was implemented through the Engineering and Programme Management Department of the regional administration and included the rehabilitation of 12 schools in the region benefitting 7,539 students.

The administrators in Senafe, Debub region reported a pressing need for the children in that area to attend school, as many of them had missed a lot of school time. However, many of the school buildings were damaged or destroyed and lacked school materials. Therefore, the project supported 1,710 school-aged children from the Senafe and Tsorona areas by setting up temporary boarding facilities in order to facilitate their attendance throughout the school term 2001-2002.

Funds for the project were transferred from a planned project to address the psychosocial needs of separated children through the establishment of Child Friendly Centres in the IDP camps, a project that became obsolete when most people, including children, left the camps to return to their homes.

The Debub Region Engineering Department implemented the rehabilitation of 7 schools in the Senafe and Tsorona sub-regions. This project was also designed jointly by the Recovery Programme and the Debub regional administration with the supervision of the Ministry of Education Planning Department. The project was still ongoing in June 2002, with the children going to school in makeshift shelters.

The Ministry of Education requested emergency assistance in 2001 to provide school children with the necessary supplies and learning materials and to replace the lost and damaged property of schools affected by the war.

The Recovery Programme assisted by providing funding to acquire learning materials and textbooks for 80,000 students. In addition 12 middle schools and three secondary school libraries were provided with books and reference materials.

Water and Sanitation

Supply of adequate and safe water was and is a major problem in Eritrea, with over 70% of the country receiving less than 400mm of annual rainfall normally. The water supply problem was not limited to inadequate sources of water but was equally constrained by lack of storage, distribution/collection and cleaning facilities.

The insufficient water available in the wells is not clean and safe for drinking, since both animals and humans use the same sources. There is also a lack of tanker trucks to bring water to communities in emergency need. Almost all areas in the regions that were invaded or occupied by the Ethiopian army experienced damage and contamination of their water

Public Fountain in Ambesete Geleba - Debub region

supply systems. Therefore, the problem of the water supply is not only limited to the places where the IDPs were temporarily hosted but was a major problem when people returned to their homes of origin.

During this period the achievements of the Recovery Programme in the water sector were:

- Construction of a pipeline from the borehole at Hamboka IDPs camp to the Metera village to provide water for the villagers as well as for the camp
- Construction of two protected wells in Adi Quala to provide water for five villages
- One borehole drilled in the Debai Sima IDP camp during the first phase of the Italian funding
- Construction of structural pipelines for 10 boreholes and drilling of 3 new boreholes in Gash Barka
- Strengthening the management capacity of the Assab Water Resources Department (Southern Red Sea Region) and drilling of three new boreholes
- Construction of four hand-pumps and a new borehole in Sosona and Koita in Gash Barka through an integrated development project
- Four boreholes constructed for the rural expellees from Ethiopia in Gerenfit resettlement area in Gash Barka region.

The projects approved in the water sector were targeted to help with the water supply in IDP camps, their surrounding villages and other targeted villages in Debub and Gash Barka. The first of the projects aimed at improving the water and sanitation facilities in the villages surrounding the IDPs camp in Deda, Mai Aini sub-region in Debub, to reduce social tension between IDPs and hosting communities.

Unfortunately, the contractors for the drilling and civil works were not actively monitored, and the project encountered several difficulties. At the end it was decided to close the project due to the problems with the contractors.

The initial problems of the water sector may have been caused partly by the lack of technical expertise in the water sector within the Recovery Team, which was also expressed by the Project Appraisal Committee in June 2001. During the first six months of the implementation of the PoWER programme and during the first phase (August- November 2000) the design, implementation and assessment were not properly carried out.

The Italian Cooperation proposed to put their technical water expert at the disposal of the Recovery Programme to become their advisor on all ongoing and future water activities. The proposal was approved, and since then the expert had reviewed all the water and sanitation proposals and visited the prospective sites of water projects. During the second half of the PoWER, a technical specialist with experience in water sector was recruited to join the Recovery Team.

The objective of a subsequent project was to provide the population of Hamboka IDPs camp and Metera village, Senafe sub-region in Debub with a sufficient quantity of potable water. A pipeline was connected from the borehole at the camp to Metera village, enabling the villagers to use the water source after the IDPs have been able to go home. The project also established also a Water Committee for the maintenance of the water pump and generator.

The water supply and pipeline project in Adi Quala sub-region in Debub aimed at constructing two protected wells to provide sufficient and safe water to five villages with a total population of 2,625. The need for the wells was acute as many households were walking up to 10 kilometers to fetch water while others relied on contaminated water from unprotected water holes.

In 1999 ECHO and the Lutheran World Federation had started a project for the provision of clean and adequate water supply for war affected communities in Gash Barka. The project was disrupted in 2000 because of the war and could not be resumed due to unavailability of funding. The project had also met with drilling problems due to inadequate technical assessment at the beginning of the project. At the request of the Government and ECHO, the Recovery Programme agreed to complete the project.

It was aimed at supplying 10 communities with clean and adequate water. Existing boreholes were to be fitted with motorized pumps and the civil work were to continue while other new boreholes were drilled. The project was implemented in two phases: during the first phase three boreholes were drilled and structural pipelines built for seven existing boreholes. Pipeline work for the three new boreholes were done in the second phase after the availability of water had been secured.

To ensure technical quality, the Recovery Programme engaged an independent water engineer to review the project and make recommendations in addition to the experts it had available for reviewing its water projects. The Ministry of Local Government in Gash Barka implements the project, but UNDP procured the pumps and generators.

In Assab the water supply system was wasting huge resources because of a combination of 40% leakage, old structures that were built during the Italian occupation and poor management. In addition, most of the 15 boreholes out of 18 in Harsile that provide water to the town faced high salt sedimentation due to over usage, the water table was going down and three of them needed to be replaced. PoWER supported the drilling of three boreholes in cooperation with the Water Resources Department. The project also aimed at improving the management capacity of the Assab Water Resources Department and at maximizing the efficiency of the water system by reducing leakage and by maintaining current water pipes and related accessories. Moreover, the PoWER programme also funded the replacement of some critical pipelines and valves at intersections. These were achieved through the help of a Consultant, who provided us with advisor services and appropriate designs.

Sustainable Livelihoods

In 2000 it was estimated that 35% of the cultivatable land remained fallow and the harvest on cultivated land was not good due to late and inadequate rainfall. Extensive looting had resulted in a substantial loss of assets in farming households. Losses in the two regions (Gash Barka and Debub) included thousands of cattle, camels, horses, mules and donkeys, and millions of small ruminants (sheep and goats) and poultry[23], which represented an important pillar of family food security and source of income for farming households.

In addition, an extensive loss of assets, farm implements and cereals was also recorded. Persons not engaged in farming, such as traders and craftsmen lost implements of their trades as well as entire inventories.

Agriculture

The Debub region comprises only 7% of the area of the country but produces 27% of the crops. In addition a large majority of people in that area were at the time dedicated to animal production. During the war a great number of the productive establishments, public services and agricultural structures were damaged. Large quantities of animals (55% of the cattle and a large number of chickens and goats) were looted, as well as veterinarian equipment. Due to lack of forage and feed and the damage done to the veterinary centre, the remaining animals were in danger. The Ministry of Agriculture identified the need for a project to restock animals in the war-affected areas. The PoWER programme through the GVC, an Italian NGO, helped to design the project and implemented it jointly with the Ministry of Agriculture in the Adi Keyih, Adi Quala, Senafe and Tsorona areas.

The project provided 2,000 households each with a flock of 25 chickens and a shade/cage to protect them from predators. Most vulnerable households were targeted, like returnees and female-headed households. The households were expected to use the chickens for income-generating activities, namely the sale of eggs and possibly reproduction of the flock. The GVC supported the MoA training activities for the beneficiaries on animal keeping, basic veterinarian services and management of small-scale economic activity. The project also distributed animal feed and drugs.

23 Programme for Emergency and Rehabilitation in War-Affected Areas in Eritrea, Shelter Component. Ministry of Local Government, UNCHS (Habitat), and Italian Cooperation. October 2000.

A veterinary expert provided support to the agricultural department in Debub to fulfill activities beyond the GVC project.

Cash-for-Work programme

The Ministry of Local Government branch offices in Debub and Gash Barka both implemented a cash-for-work project in their respective regions. The interventions were planned primarily in the areas of soil and water conservation works, maintenance of feeder roads, and some activities in forestry as well as well/canal cleaning. The project provided cash for the labour engaged in public works and created competencies in the construction and management of such works.

The project was also an income-generating programme and had an impact in improving the livelihood of the war-affected populations in Gash Barka and Debub. It helped to efficiently deliver effective social, economic and administrative services. The project benefitted a large number of people and produced assets that have a direct and positive impact on the sustainable livelihood of the communities in particular, and on the improvement of the environment in general.

The project took place in 14 sub-regions in Gash Barka and in 12 sub-regions in Debub, in 368 villages altogether. There were 125,000 beneficiaries, most of them women. The project provided not only a means of livelihood for them but acted in general as an initiative for further work in the area

Socio-Economic Development in Sosona and Koita in Gash Barka

The Sosona and Koita districts in sub-region Barentu were inhabited by the indigenous people of the area, Kunama (followers of the Orthodox Church) and Nara (Muslim), who both still live and produce in a traditional way. During the conflict they did not flee to the camps but remained within their territory and came back to their homes a few days after the occupying forces pulled back. The economic and social situation in these areas was not very developed even before the conflict but became even worse after it. There was destruction and loss of property including animals, tools, and stored grain as well as domestic objects.

A project was designed to support food production and social and economic development in Sosona and Koita by: providing tractor hire service for ploughing accessible terrain; distributing farm animals, farming tools, and seeds; initiating some women in poultry farming by giving them training and 25 chickens each (for food and income); constructing and rehabilitating the water supply system; and constructing a mill.

Beneficiaries of the project were farmers and in particular female-headed households. The PoWER programme through the services of Manitese, an Italian NGO, started intervention with only a limited number of villages. After the successful implementation of the 1st phase, more villagers were ready and willing to cooperate to improve their social service facilities, and it was agreed to launch another project.

The new project was aimed at providing the two areas and its surroundings with a health facility that will meet the needs of 7,500 people, improving the water supply through drilling two more boreholes in order to meet the needs of an additional 1,650 people, and finally, providing Koita sub region with a primary school.

The two projects fulfilled more development needs than emergency rehabilitation. The construction of the school and health centre improved the situation compared to what it was before the conflict. The Kunama and Nara ethnic groups needed additional support in preserving their identity; this was partially achieved through education, as the Government policy stipulates, in their own respective languages. The project was an integrated approach to upgrading social services by the NGO Manitese, which has shown a high sense of responsibility in assisting war-affected communities to recover in the Gash Barka region. Moreover, Manitese continued the activities of the first phase project with funding from elsewhere other than the PoWER programme. It had also started working on community development projects and on women's training with funding from other sources.

Integrated relief and recovery programme in Adi Quala in Debub Region

This project of the PoWER programme, implemented by Refugee Trust in six villages in Adi Quala Sub region, started with relief and concluded with improved income for 3,300 of the targeted female-headed beneficiary households. In its relief efforts the project distributed essential household items like utensils, blankets and clothing. In rehabilitation efforts, the project provided educational equipments; conducted psychosocial support activities; re-established and improved agricultural activities through provision of tools, seeds and livestock; and promoted sustainable community-based employment and income-generation through a scheme of micro-grant assistance and technical support. The project also had high involvement from the Ministry of Agriculture branch office in Debub region.

The project was planned and implemented with high community participation. The income-generation and grant-in-kind components created 400 new jobs for female headed households. The jobs created for women were mostly in poultry, sheep and goat farming but also in pottery, dressmaking, bakeries and grain retail selling.

During the implementation it was also discovered that the area had severe problems with its water supply. The Refugee Trust proposed another project for the area to improve their water services, which was approved and financed by the PoWER programme.

The rural recovery programme in Adi Keyih in Debub Region

The rural recovery programme financed by PoWER and implemented by CONCERN (international NGO) in five administrative areas namely: Qohaito plateau in Adi Keyih Sub region was also directed first toward the emergency needs of the communities before phasing into rehabilitation. The emergency relief phase in March 2001 distributed seeds and tools to 4,000 households to support the planting season. The rehabilitation phase was aimed at reducing dependency on food aid, improving access to markets and basic services and increasing capacity of the communities and local administration to address food security needs.

Reduced dependency on food aid was achieved by enabling 400 households in the area to keep bees, which provide honey for consumption and sale or exchange for other goods. Improved access to markets and basic services for 2,000 households was achieved by reconstruction of footpaths (62kms).

The capacity of the local staff to address food security needs of the community was partially achieved through improved agriculture support services, enhanced community awareness and increased understanding and promotion of sustainable community food security initiatives. The project also witnessed the formation of community associations working by mid-2002.

The beneficiaries belong to a traditional Saho (Muslim) community, which maintain a strong code of conduct. It was initially very difficult to work on gender issues with the community as gender dictates several areas of work and female-headed households depend on relatives and neighbours to work their land.

Support to Disabled and Land Mine Victims

More than 100,000 people in Eritrea are suffering from various disabilities. More than 40,000 of these are estimated to need orthopedic appliances. PoWER had approved a project implemented by COSV, which proposed to establish a mobile orthopedic unit to reach the disabled in Gash Barka and Anseba regions as well as to support the Keren workshop for orthopedic appliances. The objective was to benefit the disabled who do not receive assistance from any other source. The activity was part of the MoLHW long-term strategic plan.

The Barentu Bakery, Supermarket, Snack bar and Stores enterprises of the Eritrean War Disabled Fighters' Association (EWDFA) was also geared at creating jobs, raising social interaction and morale of disabled ex-fighters with the ultimate aim of enabling them to rely on themselves by being owners of small business. The Barentu Bakery was completed by the EWDFA in November 1997 but was then destroyed in May 2000 during the Border War. The association aimed to reconstruct the bakery and restore its activities.

The bakery was expected to have a net income of USD 7,000 per month that will be utilized for the repayment of the loan to the Association, which will reinvest the capital in other similar activities with an ultimate aim of creating new employment opportunities to other disabled members. The beneficiaries of the project were directly the 11 employees of the Bakery, and indirectly the 10,000 members of EWDFA and the population surrounding the Bakery who will have access to fresh bread.

Capacity Building

The provision for capacity building in the PoWER Programme budget was made as the initial experience of project identification, design and overall planning for rehabilitation, reconstruction and reintegration activities revealed that there was a need to build capacity at the regional level to carry out well-planned, integrated, area-based recovery interventions. Furthermore, the regional administrations, especially in the most war-affected areas, such as Gash Barka and Debub, faced an overwhelming challenge to track and coordinate the recovery interventions on their territories.

The pilot project for capacity building was a result of consultations between MoLG at central and regional level, ERREC and UNDP. The project was implemented in Gash Barka, Debub and Southern Red Sea regions for 700 staff from regional and sub-regional administration. It aimed to support the regions through organizing a variety of training courses to the staff to upgrade their capacity to deal with daily management tasks and assisting in the planning and the administration of those activities.

The project provided technical assistance and training to the regional administrations to set up, manage and independently sustain a GIS database, done in coordination with OCHA and ERREC. It also supported the planning of needed human resources, the institutional set-up and training for the implementation of data collection for GIS as well as the improvement of project management.

Early Interventions on Mine action component

During 2001-2002 UNDP assisted the Government of Eritrea to set up the Eritrean Mine Action Programme (EMAP). The assistance provided (altogether $100,000), acted as seed funding to set up and start the EMAP, to build capacities of the Eritrean Mine Action Agency as well as to strengthen the Ministry of Labour and Human Welfare to assist disabled due mines.

Presently, the EMAP is finalized and most of the funding for the activities comes from the EU, the Netherlands, Canada and the United Kingdom.

Excerpts from the Evaluation Report on the way the programme was managed.

SUMMARY OF PROJECTS COMPLETED UNDER THE UNDP/PMU PoWER PROGRAMME BY YEAR

Description	Year				
	2001	2002	2003	2004	Total
1. Health Facilities	12	2	7	-	21
2. Water Supply	6	9	11	-	26
3. Schools	12	12	14	1	39
4. Shelter	4,700	2,500	3,000	4,500	14,700
5. Sustainable Livelihood Projects	3	2	2	2	9
6. Capacity Building	-	1	1	-	2
7. Mine Action	-	4	-	-	4

PoWER Management

The Project Management Unit (PMU) has been staffed by a group of highly motivated and well-chosen individuals. The quality of their work was high. The speed with which they established the programme was quite remarkable. They rapidly established mechanisms which translated funds into activities which brought immediate and direct benefit to beneficiaries.

A frequent comment from NGOs and government at all levels concerned the timely and flexible nature of the PoWER programme. Its ability to quickly respond to priority issues has proved to be particularly valuable in the emergency phase. Its flexibility was reflected in the PMU's willingness to accept short proposals with strong ideas and to arrange for the quick disbursement of funds.

The role of the PMU in implementation, while not a focus in the TOR, should not be overlooked. Four principal features were identified. i) Their procurement capacity was of particular benefit to NGOs and government agencies alike. It short circuited what had the potential to be a problematic activity and enabled implementers to more rapidly deliver. ii) Their support in assisting local government draw up plans and project proposals was outstanding. In addition to expediting the delivery of assistance it formed an important capacity building function, one of the 'soft' forms of intervention which are notoriously difficult to capture and quantify. iii) The PMU spent considerable time and energy in helping almost all the NGOs produce financial reports. iv) NGOs frequently reported that the PMU was always ready to send staff to assist when difficulties arose during the course of implementation. No other donor was able to provide such a comprehensive and rapid response to problems being experienced by NGOs.

While PMU financial reporting was good, the process of narrative reporting in the initial period was for the most part poor. The NGOs provided few interim reports. End of project reports were very rare, as were evaluations. While PMU staff were assiduous in travelling to the field to deal with problems and providing field trip reports describing their findings, these do not represent an adequate means of capturing what was taking place. Government partners were exceedingly poor in producing narrative interim and end of project reports. Given the substantial sums which have been disbursed to them, this is a matter of concern".[5]

POST WAR EMERGENCY RECOVERY PROGRAMME (POWER)

RESULTS ACHIEVED:

- 170,000 IDP were provided with transportation to return to their original villages
- 14,700 houses were built/rehabilitated
- 39 schools were reconstructed/rehabilitated
- 26 water supply schemes were constructed
- 2 hospitals and 21 health centres/stations were reconstructed/rehabilitated and
- 3000 households were provided with agricultural tools/seeds or livestock and 9 sustainable livelihoods projects completed
- 4 mine action points were undertaken

***For further details on the activities of the PoWER programme refer to annex** 3.*

6.4.1 PoWER PROGRAMME: lessons learned

- At the outset, the Post War Emergency Recovery (PoWER) Programme was designed to be an emergency intervention with developmental approaches. That is, essential emergency steps were taken stage by stage in consideration of the development opportunities lost by the war. It also incorporated the essential elements and tenets that would help the overall development of social and physical infrastructures while solving the immediate problems that arose due to the war.
- Project identification was mainly done by the implementing partners in close collaboration with and guided by local communities represented through their community leaders and advised by experts in the sub region administrations heads of branch offices of line ministries. There was some screening mechanism for the community to set the right priority and clear the proposal that is presented as a relevant and effective means of addressing the needs.
- In the PoWER Programme the resettlement of the rural expellees from Northern Ethiopia, in Gerenfit was successful because of the relationship that was first established with the host community The local people were assured that they could share schools, health centers and water provided for the resettled community.
- In the PoWER Programme a significant number of the implementing partners were international and national NGOs. One of the negative experiences was that the international NGOs had relatively high overhead costs. The Government's initial reaction to this fact was to reduce and ultimately expel all international NGOs. There were also other political considerations that the Government was not willing to state.
- While some local Government agencies may have comparative advantages due to local staff, local knowledge and existing capacity, very few International NGOs had international "best practice" in their niche sectors. Moreover, in the immediate aftermath of the war emergency interventions, local Government did not have full capacity to deliver major assistance, and NGOs, despite relatively high overhead cost, were the only ones who had institutional means to raise international funds to provide early emergency/recovery requirements to affected populations.
- Partnerships have been created with the Ministry of Local Government at regional and sub regional levels through which cash for work, shelter and social infrastructure

activities have been implemented. This strategy was highly effective in delivering, rapid low cost and sustainable outputs for cash for work, shelter repair and the maintenance of schools and health centers. However, a significant weakness of local government bodies, like their counterparts in the NGO community, was their failure to provide timely reports on project progress. Generally speaking, no end of project reports were presented to the main stakeholders. One regional governor stated that "for me a one page report is enough while the donors are demanding a lot more pages, which does not have an added value". He added, however, that "the financial reports should always be there". In contrast NGOs were relatively better at reporting.

- With the exception of few party organized local civil society organizations and parastatals, such as the Eritrean War Disabled Fighters' Association (EWDFA), National Confederation of Eritrean Workers (NCEW), National Union of Eritrean Women (NUEW), HABEN, ESCA and the National Union of Eritrean Youth and Students (NUEYS), PoWER did not develop significant partnerships with local civil society other than those mentioned above. On the positive side the PoWER programme contracted local consultants for all designs related to water, village site layouts and shelter prototype developments.
- It was soon realized that while NGOs may have comparative advantages in the delivery of emergency assistance, long-term sustainability required developing local government capacity. The PoWER programme gave as a matter of priority adequate attention to enhance the capacity of regional and local authorities and involved NGOs who have a development focus and expertise only.
- There was considerable diversity in the capacity and approaches of NGOs which was observed in the variable nature of project outcomes. Beyond discussions in coordination meetings and technical support activities, there was little evidence that skill and knowledge sharing was taking place across the aid community. Some of the more established NGOs have a repository of knowledge and experience that could have been shared to the benefit of all but this was not capitalized on. It was realized that greater information sharing between implementing partners on project implementation practice, particularly cooperation among NGOs to permit sharing of information and ideas about approach, methodology, needs, location and so on could have been beneficial.
- The Government of the State of Eritrea, immediately after independence, has come with the arrangement of regulating future NGO activities in Eritrea and the work of the Eritrean Relief and Rehabilitation Agency (ERRA). ERRA was designated as a supervising body in order to facilitate the smooth operation of the activities of international and local NGOs. Furthermore, the Government stipulated that NGO activities will be confined to relief and rehabilitation work. In late 1996, the Government further imposed severe restrictions on Non-Governmental Organizations (NGOs) operating in Eritrea. Thenceforth NGOs would be permitted to operate only in the education and health sectors, and expatriate personnel would be required to pay income tax at a rate of 38%.
- Many NGOs expressed concern that the restrictions would prevent them from continuing their work in Eritrea. In early 1998 several key Western NGOs withdrew from the country. Nevertheless, during 1999 the Eritrean Government invited back selected NGOs in an attempt to alleviate the humanitarian consequences of the border war with Ethiopia, and significant US, Dutch and Italian emergency assistance was forthcoming during 2000-2002.
- Moreover, the expulsion of mine-clearing NGOs in August 2002 and June 2003 appeared to be a further manifestation of Eritrea's deteriorating relationship with donors and NGOs. In an attempt to boost self-reliance and to reduce its dependency on the international community which it feels to be too lenient towards Ethiopia's rejection of the Ethiopia-Eritrea Border Commission's (EEBC's) 2002 border ruling, the Eritrean government has since mid-2005 been curtailing the activities of international agencies active in the country.
- On 11 May 2005, the Eritrean government announced new regulations governing the operation of nongovernmental organizations. The proclamation required imported relief items – including food – to be taxed and NGOs to have at least $2 million at their disposal in the country, while registering annually with the government. The Ministry of Labour and Human Welfare (MoLHW, which absorbed ERREC in its structure) became responsible for food aid and relief activities, as well as the registration and supervision of NGOs (Proclamation 145/2005: Gazette of Eritrean Law, 11 May 2005).
- More time is required to involve the local authorities and communities in the design and planning process. Hence, in few instances local communities were not consulted due to shortage of time. Furthermore, most projects were located in remote, isolated and mine infested border areas, which made it difficult to get the logistics on time due to lack of transportation and communication links. Mobile telephone service was not available then.
- Although there is a trade-off between a quick response to urgent needs and a carefully planned reconstruction process that allows for consultation, participation and capacity development, it is necessary to opt for the latter in order to ensure the effective use of resources, to ensure that recovery mirrors the actual demands of the affected communities and to develop capacity in the long term.

Consultation with representatives of beneficiaries and elders of the community

- The process of monitoring and reporting contributes towards understanding the nature of project outcomes. This is important in the context of recovery programmes that aspire to link relief-emergency to development objectives. The project controls in the PoWER programme dedicated a considerable amount of effort to financial reporting. This was done deliberately to assure Donors that every single cent was accounted for.
- UNDP was responsible for the execution of the PoWER programme under the modality of Direct Execution (DEX). To this effect, UNDP has formed a Programme Management Unit (PMU) that functioned to streamline and coordinate all activities of this programme. The project implementation procedures prepared by the PMU clearly articulated the requirement of mid-term and final reports on projects for monitoring and evaluation purposes. However, the implementing agencies were weak in preparing and submitting periodic narrative reports.
- Government partners were exceedingly poor in producing narrative interim and end of project reports. While PMU financial reporting was good, the process of narrative reporting for the most part was poor. The NGOs provided few interim reports. End of project reports were very rare, as were evaluations. However, the PMU staffs were assiduous in traveling to the field to deal with problems during the course of implementation.
- Furthermore, regional authorities were involved in the planning, design, implementing and monitoring of the recovery process. Involving local governments at all stages of the process was also an effective way to develop capacity.
- Whenever there are fewer resources, people will compete for them. Periodic appraisals have helped to ensure that the maximum amount of assistance goes to those with the greatest need.
- The General Framework of the PoWER programme was worked out at the outset. It was, however, PMU policy to start with what you have at hand rather than wait until all the resources needed were mobilized. The programme was in full swing when additional resources were secured from the Italian Government. For the sake of financial accountability of the two separate but complementary contributions, it was found to be prudent to divide it into two phases.
- The PoWER Programme was to be a bridging Programme, until such time that a more substantive Programme was to follow it. The WB sponsored Emergency Reconstruction Programme (ERP), but it took time to design the components and start of implementation was further delayed.
- The issue of statistics to be raised in Gerenfit the figure was 8,700 expellees, but later the figure jumped to 11,000 since people came from faraway places to take advantage of the packages including land and shelter kits.
- Buying of 23 project cars to avoid exorbitant rental costs incurred by implementing partners including NGOs had a notable success.
- International procurement of materials and equipment was excellent. This will be elaborated upon later

5.5 *The Integrated Recovery Programme (IRP)*

The impetus for the preparation of the IRP came from gaps in needs not addressed by existing programmes, and from the collective recognition by the Government and its development partners that in the face of the persistent succession of emergencies, the short-changing of the recovery assistance to the War-affected Population (WAP) is likely to persist unless it is deliberately addressed/countered. IRP was designed to be an exit strategy from emergency humanitarian assistance, particularly food aid. Although continued lifesaving programmes need to be addressed with urgency, funding the IRP was the ultimate salvation from dependency on food aid.

Gash Barka illustrates best the challenges inherent in the recovery process in regards to the populations directly affected by the war. Gash Barka sustained most of the damage and destruction caused during the border war, estimated as high as USD 565 million, about 74% of which is in Gash Barka[24]. At the time of the launching of the study it had registered consistently some of the highest rates of malnutrition in the country. In 2003, as many as 28% or nearly one out of every three children under five, in some areas of Gash Barka, were acutely malnourished[25]. At the same time, Gash Barka has been the destination of choice for returnees from Sudan and rural expellees from Ethiopia. It was estimated that one out of every four residents in Gash Barka will be a returnee or an expellee by the time UNHCR's repatriation programme was completed and rural expellees resettled.

ICC/ERREC figures show that the total value of projects related to emergency and recovery in the country as a whole as of November 2001 (we do not have figures for later years) was USD 228 million and that humanitarian assistance took the lion's share of 61%, followed by relief-to-development activities at 26% and recovery efforts at 13%. No figures were obtained specifically for Gash Barka region but it is likely to follow a similar trend. Most interventions were short-term in nature due to short planning and the budgeting cycles followed by many humanitarian agencies.

According to the UNDP Study cited below, this poses a challenge in terms of support to long-term development activities, particularly assistance for the successful reintegration of expellees and returnees. This adds to and compounds a number of other constraints being faced in the reintegration of returnees and expellees in Gash Barka[26]. Apart from its imbalance, this allocation of resources means the existence of a large gap in recovery resource requirement.

The UNDAF 2002-2006 noted the myriad of ongoing and planned programmes have in general a vertical approach to implementation, (i.e., rarely integrated with other programmes). This resulted in gaps between the various programmes. The IRP was designed to fill these gaps such as the Emergency Recovery Programme (ERP), the Demobilization and Reintegration Programme (DRP) etc. As such, the IRP was a sub-set of what should be a wider national recovery programme for Eritrea.

24 Consequences of Ethiopia's invasion of Eritrea, University of Asmara Group, page 15

25 MoH/UNICEF, Nutrition Survey Report, June 2003

26 Sustainable Livelihoods Study, UNDP, Sept. 2002, page 14-15

The justification for an integrated recovery programme dedicated to the IRP target population came from considerations, which taken together make the IRP an efficient and effective means of addressing the recovery needs of the War Affected Populations (WAP) namely:

- The scale of the problem in terms of the size of the population affected. (Over 20% of the population of the country was affected)
- The degree of vulnerability of the target group, which was beyond the "normal" poverty problem. Homelessness, landlessness, and destroyed social coping systems were the typical problems confronting the-would be IRP direct beneficiaries. These are problems that are typical of the extremely poor – those consuming less than 1,800 calories per day who made up 37% of the then population of Eritrea) at the time
- The geographic concentration of the affected population. 70% of the returnee population have been resettled in 3 sub-regions in Gash Barka[27]. As a result, returnees represent 30% of the population in two of these sub-regions (Tessenei and Goluj). On the one hand, this means a sharp increase in the burden on the social service infrastructure and the natural resource base. On the other hand it offered a natural context for targeted and highly focused area-based type programming. The potential environmental impact was magnified further when considered against the fact that Gash Barka is one of the breadbaskets of the country.

Hence, the IRP was a time-bound three-year Recovery Programme, envisaged under the UN Development Assistance Framework (UNDAF) and developed through the joint Government-UNDAF Thematic Group on Recovery, which aims to fill the gap, and effect in an integrated manner the transition from relief to development of the four war affected target groups; Returnees, Internally Displaced People, Expellees and Host Communities in three war affected regions of Eritrea. As mentioned earlier, the IRP was meant to build on the short lived 4Rs paradigm, which encompassed; repatriation, reintegration, rehabilitation and reconstruction interventions for returnees (refugees), IDPs and expellees, as well as for affected host communities

Goals, outcomes and expected results

The specific goal of the IRP was to ensure the sustainable socio-economic reintegration and rehabilitation of those displaced populations and their host communities through an area- and community-based approach. The following outcomes/results are expected from the IRP interventions:

- Greater social cohesiveness between host communities, returnees and expellees.
- Enhanced capacities of communities to manage their social and economic lives.
- Improved access to, and quality of, social and economic infrastructure (schools, health, water supplies, and roads); expanded market access and trade leading to better conditions of living for communities and greater economic development.

27 ibid, page 11

- Enhanced food security, better and more diversified livelihoods and reduced vulnerabilities to economic and climatic shocks.
- Beneficiary communities will have been fully re-integrated and are net contributors to the economic and social development of their communities and the country at large.
- Dependence on food aid and other forms of emergency and humanitarian assistance will have been substantially reduced and/or eliminated among the beneficiary population.
- The stock of physical, financial, natural and human capital and assets among target beneficiaries will have been improved and vulnerabilities to natural and economic shocks will have been reduced.
- Improved food security and natural resource conservation will result from the adoption of sustainable agricultural practices by the target communities.

Target populations

The table below shows planning figures for the IRP target populations as of June 2004.

Targeted Recovery Programme Population by Category and Numbers

Population Category	Already Returned/ Resettled	Remaining for Resettlement	Total Target Population for IRP
IDPs	185,569	58,180	58,180
Expellees	12,000	7,700	19,770
Returnees	118,000	33,000*	151,000
Host Population	-	-	526,585
Total		98,880	**755,535**

a. Refugees repatriating from Sudan: Over 110,000 Eritrean refugees have returned home since UNHCR-supported repatriation operations began in July 2,000; the vast majority of them to the western Eritrean region of Gash Barka. It was estimated at the time that an additional 60,000 would choose voluntary repatriation.

b. Rural Expellees from Ethiopia: In May 2003, 12,000 rural expellees from Ethiopia were resettled in Gerenfit, Gash Barka, (8,570 of which were expellees from Shelab camp). An additional 7,700 remained in the temporary camps of Adi Keshi, Korokon, Kotobia and Mai Alba.

Transportation of IDPs from Kotobia to Tebeldia – Gash Baraka

Transportation of properties of IDPs from Kotobia to Tebeldia – Gash Baraka

c. Internally Displaced Persons:

An estimated 47,500 IDPs were residing in camps in Gash Barka, Debub and Northern Red Sea. In addition, there were 10,680 IDPs living with host communities in Gash Barka and Southern Red Sea. The return of these 58,180 IDPs who came from areas in the Temporary Security Zone (TSZ) was delayed for a number of reasons including the lack of resources for demining, social and economic infrastructure, shelter and the perceived lack of security by some camp dwellers due to concerns related to the close proximity of Ethiopian troops across the border.

d. Host Communities:

Communities that were receiving significant numbers of expellees and returnees had very limited absorption capacity, having themselves experienced destruction from the war. Their social and economic infrastructure, basic services and natural resource base were under heavy pressure and unable to cope with the sudden arrival of new populations.

The task of reintegrating populations displaced by war was enormous. Entire towns, and the social and economic systems that allow them to function, needed to be built anew. The populations themselves were afflicted by an intense sense of dislocation. Returnees have been out of the country for decades, the majority were not even born in Eritrea. IDPs have spent years in camps and were returning to destroyed homes and communities that they barely recognized. Expellees were trying to start new lives after being dispossessed of all belongings and forcibly evicted from their homes. Trust needs to be built and community structures strengthened.

IRP – Sectors and projected activities:

The successful reintegration of the war-affected populations requires the restoration of sustainable livelihoods, and social services such as water, health and education systems. New land for agriculture must be cleared and seeds provided for planting; linkages must be established to markets including feeder roads, and income-earning opportunities and services must be provided. It is only when these services are in place and functioning, that the long-term reintegration of the WAP can be considered to be sustainable.

The following are brief sector descriptions of activities that were to take place under the IRP. A fuller description has been provided in the Annexes to the main IRP document.[28]

28 Integrated Recovery Programme – 2004-2007

MAIN COMPONENTS IRP

- **Sustainable Livelihoods** (Microfinance, Economic Infrastructure, Community Development, Income Generation Skills Training and Agriculture)
- **Health**
- **Water and Sanitation**
- **Education**
- **Roads and Shelter**
- **Programme Support Costs**

TOTAL BUDGET PROPOSED: USD 124,559,388.00

Sustainable Livelihoods: While the provision of social and economic infrastructure is an urgent necessity, recovery efforts will only be successful if large numbers of the target population can pursue livelihoods on their own and become self-supporting and autonomous. The IRP helped build sustainable livelihoods the provision of micro-finance (to improve household incomes and raise standards of living), improving economic infrastructure (to facilitate better market access), promotion of Income Generating Activities (to build skills and enhance opportunities for gainful employment) and support agricultural production activities (to help households attain food security). Building sustainable livelihoods therefore not only reduced the need for relief and reduce dependence, but it also directly contributed to the economic revitalization of Eritrea and contribute to long-term development prospects.

Health: The overall goal of the Health Recover Programme was to create access to and demand for quality primary health care services and to ensure nutritional security for IDP, returnee, expellee and host community populations in three war and drought affected Regions including Gash Barka, Debub, and Southern Red Sea.

The program aimed to reduce morbidity, mortality and malnutrition and promote wellness among the most vulnerable segments of the target population, primarily children under five years of age, pregnant and lactating women and the elderly. The Health Recovery Program Core Components are:

- Reconstruction of Primary Health Care Infrastructure & Quality Service Delivery
- Increased Coverage of Sustainable Community Health Care System
- Nutrition Security and Growth Protection among Vulnerable Groups

Water/Sanitation: The provision of safe water supplies will be achieved through the repair and rehabilitation of existing schemes as well as the construction of new schemes. New construction will focus on development of groundwater sources through more efficient and cost-effective drilling technologies. Long-term sustainability will be ensured through the establishment, training and support to community-based water and sanitation committees (comprising half men and half women) coupled with the provision of essential spare parts and tools to communities and the back up of government support and monitoring from both the regional and central levels.

Sanitation will focus on the development and provision of standard latrines for schools (with separate facilities for girls and boys) and health centers, as well as hygiene training for teachers and promotion of improved personal hygiene practices such as hand and face washing for the targeted communities.

In addition, low-cost, affordable models of latrines and slabs will be developed and slabs provided as incentives to those households prepared to dig their own latrines to provide a superstructure. Community-based contractors will be trained in latrine construction, which can also serve as an income generating activity.

Education: Interventions in the education sector enables reintegrating IDPs, returnees and expellees, and their host communities to fully participate in, and benefit from the Ministry of Education's long-term development plans. Specific activities in this regard include the construction and supply of new schools, teacher recruitment and training, training of school PTAs, capacity building in the Ministry of Education, and expansion of adult education services.

Shelter and roads: The IRP shelter sub-component aims at providing suitable shelter to the most needy, which could be progressively built into a more sustainable and permanent dwelling. Environmental considerations and sustainability of settlements would be a priority in the provision of shelter. Key components of the shelter sub-component will include mobilizing communities in the construction and maintenance of shelters; increasing the involvement of private sector; involving key stakeholders, NGOs, village councils, and government officials. Implementation will have a major component of well-defined capacity building measures, through training and credits to set up production units (doors, windows, frames, blocks, bricks etc.), with equal opportunities for men and women so as to have a long-term economic impact. In the short term, the shelter sector would provide employment and income generating opportunities and in the long run it would result in the development of small businesses and contractors for the construction industry.

As a major component of the Integrated Recovery Programme some rural access roads will be constructed/ rehabilitated with the aim of creating all-weather access to communities, access to markets for livelihoods and improved connectivity between villages and towns reducing travel time and costs. Mindful of the limited institutional capacity of the line ministries and regional authorities in the field of construction and maintenance and lack of skilled labour force, the community participation and increased involvement of the private sector and NGOs are essential. It is expected that all activities of the IRP will be implemented with freely contracted and paid labour.

The Integrated Recovery Programme (IRP) provides an overarching framework for institutional collaboration in the implementation of programmes for returnees, IDPs, expellees and affected host populations. Its aim is to ensure the sustainable socio-economic reintegration and rehabilitation of these displaced populations and their host communities through an area and community-based approach. As such, it represents an integrated framework of sectorial recovery activities, which will prepare these areas and populations to be effectively included in the reconstruction and longer-term development processes. The programme is spread over three years (2004-2006). The IRP 2004 is designed to complement the CAP 2004. It focuses on specific projects that enhance the recovery effort where the CAP 2004 leaves off.

Eritrea was one of the pilot "4Rs" countries (Eritrea, Sri Lanka, Afghanistan and Sierra Leone) dealing with complex recovery involving displaced populations being developed and implemented jointly by the UN agencies, IFIs and bilateral development agencies. Lessons learned from pilot operations would help develop systematic rules of engagement. The guiding principles and critical success factors for this integrated approach were: a) ownership of the process by the Government; b) integrated planning process at the country level by the UN Country Team and the World Bank; c) strong institutional cooperation and commitment to support timely and at decisive moments, the needs and efforts of country teams to bridge essential gaps in transition strategies; d) participation of the plethora of actors who form part of the development community - UN agencies bilateral and multilateral institutions. While there were constraints that had to be overcome to successfully implement the Integrated Recovery Programme, there were positive trends to capitalize on: Government commitment to durable solutions for the target population, the indomitable enthusiasm and determination of the Eritrean people to rebuild their country; the cessation of hostilities and upcoming border demarcation, UN commitment to joint programming; and numerous ongoing and planned programmes from which to learn and build upon.

It has been agreed early in the process that the IRP being a three-year programme, the resource mobilization should be focused on the first year (IRP 2004). The projects to be selected should serve as complementary to those in the CAP 2004 which were life saving interventions. IRP programs comply with the government's decentralization plans and fit into the government's mid-term basic social safety nets and poverty reduction strategy (I-PRSP). IRP will:

- In a holistic, integrated and convergent manner, provide time-limited services, capacity building and infrastructure identified as gaps in other current or planned programmes to facilitate the target populations' abilities to sustain themselves and their communities and to develop their community's economic self-reliance; and
- Contribute to rehabilitation of the 3 regions identified by the government as principle growth areas for the country thus supporting the overall economy of Eritrea, creating conditions for long-term economic development locally and providing a model for an Eritrea-wide recovery program.

Moreover, the projects and activities in the IRP 2004 were therefore:

- performance-based;
- area/community-based approach fostering sustainable livelihoods through community development and training;
- gender-sensitive;
- addressing gaps in other programs;
- limited to those activities which involve rehabilitation, repair or reconstruction of basic social and economic infrastructure, facilities and services required to ensure the sustainable socio-economic reintegration of the target populations;

- compatible and consistent with local/national reconstruction and development priorities and strategies; be implementable within 3 years;
- financially sustainable and not require external subsidies for continual operation in surrounding communities not affected by the war or the return of refugees, as the reference for applicable standards while at the same time considering innovative technologies (solar, energy saving stoves, etc.) that would have a long-term positive impact on the environment and economy;
- low cost and efficient; building on existing institutions and programs (integrated);
- ensuring economies of scale for procurement and for staff in different UN agencies.

5.6 Social and Economic Reintegration of Demobilized Soldiers (SERDS)

In November 2000, following the deployment of the UNMEE peacekeeping force and prompted by significant progress in the peace process, GOE announced its intention to launch a demobilization and reintegration program, building on the previous GOE program, international experiences and best practice. GOE subsequently requested the international donor community, led by the World Bank, to provide technical and financial assistance for the preparation and implementation of the program. GOE plans to reduce its army by two thirds and demobilize 200,000 troops within a two-year time frame.

The troops to be demobilized consist of remobilized ex-fighters, people serving in the mandatory National Service programme, and soldiers from the regular armed forces. To lead this effort, GoSE established a National Commission for the Demobilization and Reintegration Programme (NCDRP) by a proclamation issued in April 2001, in order to oversee the Emergency Demobilization and Reintegration Programme (EDRP).
The NCDRP was directed by a Commissioner based in Asmara who oversaw the operations of the headquarters office, and who supervised the various regional offices.
The headquarters was organized into two main departments for programming, which includes units for reintegration, information and sensitization, MIS and M&E; and finance and administration which includes procurement Units for public relations and internal auditing provide additional support to the Commissioner and his Deputy. Regional offices were more streamlined but organized similarly. The Commission was in the early phase of establishing itself; staff recruitment was on-going, management systems were being developed and put into operations and four regional offices were opened. Technical assistance was provided in the areas of financial management, management information systems design and installation, and reintegration strategy – and later: rural development. DRP strategy and components

The Demobilization and Re-integration Programme was formulated in a series of events in 2001, including a workshop on planning and re-integration programme in Selam Hotel, Asmara from 21-23rd August in 2001 that the Author participated in.

The overall objective for the programme was the following:

- Demobilized Soldiers (DS) were re-integrated into their communities and the economy

The immediate objective was:

- To create an enabling environment where DS have access to:
  a) Counseling and rehabilitation services to facilitate re-entry to family and community life;
  b) The economic opportunities within the macro-economic framework and initiatives of the GoSE

These objectives were distinct, but also related and interacting with each other. The project thus basically consisted of two components: (i) social re-integration and (ii) economic re-integration. With their supporting sub-components the central structure of the programme looked like this:

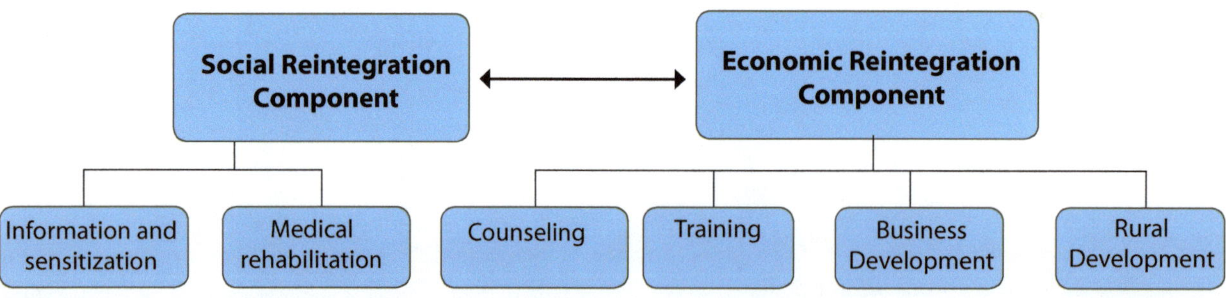

Rural development was thus supposed to be part of the economic re-integration process. It had Training and Business Development Services (including financial services) as the other two sub-components. And their objective were:

- To develop the financial self-sufficiency of a demobilized soldier's household through productive and gainful (self) employment.
- The economic reintegration services provided to be demand driven and opportunities that demobilized soldiers chose to access.

This objective presented two of the component's key approaches:

(i) Being demand driven and

(ii) Focusing on the self-sufficiency of the DS's household. In terms of programme targeting the objective for economic re-integration, this indicates that there was a dual focus on: a) the demobilized soldier, and b) the demobilized soldier's household. Initially it was a facilitation – rather than interventionist programme, which was expected to provides '***opportunities that demobilized soldiers chose to access***'.

Another basic approach, which lays out the strategy of the rural development sub-component, was its dual focus on rural reconstruction and development.

Technical Assistance Programme (TAP)

Within the scope of the above objectives, a Technical Assistance Programme was initiated in July 2002 and consultancies were commissioned in accordance with the terms of reference contained in the Technical Assistance Plan developed by UNDP under the umbrella of the Recovery Programme in April 2002. The original purpose of the TAP was to plan and facilitate the efficient implementation and management of the NCDRP training activities related to social and economic reintegration interventions. It involves the provision of Technical Assistance, Strategic Planning, Operational Advice and Capacity Building of staff and implementing partners.

The objectives of the plan were to:

- Strengthen the capacity of NCDRP at both central and regional levels through short and medium term technical assistance;
- Build capacity of local staff through twinning arrangements with this technical assistance;
- Develop a plan to strengthen the capacity of implementing partners.

The TAP came to a close in December 2003, but was subsequently extended to the end of March 2005. The USAID funds (amounting to USD 563,765) covered the extensive technical assistance programme executed by the UNDP in partnership with the NCDRP.

Demobilization Status

The NCDRP has demobilized during the period mentioned earlier a total of 103,550 (51.8 % of the total target of 200,000) soldiers in the pilot demobilization phase and subsequent phases of the programme.

This constituted 98.19% of the targeted cumulative (Phase I: 65,200 and Phase II: 38,350 to the end of March 2005 of the demobilization programme. Statistics generated by the NCDRP reveal that 26.33 % of the groups were female. The statistics also reflect that 10.6% of the demobilized soldiers (DS) were employees of parastatal/public organizations; 43.10% were engaged in farming; 16.5% have returned to their original business and 21.8% were engaged in small trading, or employed in general services, as daily labourers and the like.

The bulk of the DS (59.6%) have returned to the community where they were located before the war, 79.5% were either employed or self-employed in the private sector (farming, petty trade, small business, etc.) and 99.77% have received their TSN payment.

As a group, the level of demand for services required was expected to be relatively low although the disabled group shows a marked inclination towards starting up new businesses, in many cases, of perceived diminished suitability for formal jobs. It was expected that reintegration opportunities and services be available for soldiers discharged within the first quarter of 2004. Although they have been demobilized, the reintegration opportunities have yet to be provided.

NCDRP priorities

The following were considered to be the priorities of the NCDRP:

- Capacity building of staff although the capacity of the NCDRP has been sufficiently developed, the lack of implementation and operational experience of the NCDRP posed initial problems. For example, regional staff (although they may have an overview of the objectives and programmes of the NCDR) did not have the detailed knowledge to provide specific information to the DS on opportunities available.
- NCDRP staff, particularly at the Regional level, needed to be trained and instructed in the generation of the opportunities at the Regional level by soliciting and developing sub-projects and processing them through the procedures outlined in the operations manual. Regional staff began the process of generating the localized opportunities with training providers – particularly in respect of attachments.

- Calls for projects
- The public call for proposals was made. Where public calls for proposals were indicated, the NCDRP must make those calls and process proposals as per the operations manual. Where proposals are submitted on specific interventions and services; the NCDR must process these proposals; and then award contracts to successful proposers.
- Project preparation
- Although the operating systems for implementation have been developed and were contained in the Operations Manual, detailed systems within the regional offices were not put in place on time. These systems meant to be the specific systems used to make the services and opportunities available to the DS themselves.
- Memoranda of understanding
- The various relationships that have to be developed with implementing partners must be followed up and Memorandum of Understanding (MoUs) signed where relevant. The NCDRP must actively and vigorously pursue these relationships – especially in respect of implementing partners who have been lax in responding or are dithering in their decision making regarding engagement on NCDRP projects. Strict deadlines must be set for the signing of the memorandums of understanding.

The budget estimate for the whole programme was 50 million USD, with the following breakdown:

Social Reintegration Component:	***8,110,000***
Information and sensitization sub-component:	670,000
Counselling sub-component:	5,385,000
Medical rehabilitation sub-component	2,055,000
Economic Reintegration Component:	***41,890,000***
Training sub-component:	19,790,000
Business development sub-component:	10,100,000
Rural development sub-component:	12,000,000

The border war between Eritrea and Ethiopia was unique in a sense that it was the only recent armed conflict in Africa fought by regular armies on both sides, according to the rules of conventional interstate war and not involving civilians as combatants. Furthermore, there was not much disintegration between the soldiers and the society at large. Consequently, the social reintegration of the demobilized soldiers in Eritrea is not as challenging as in other African countries.

The planning and implementation of demobilization programmes calls for a high degree of co-ordination and flexibility. It has often proven expedient to entrust a single institution in the country with the programme co-ordination; this institution should contain personnel from both civilian and military backgrounds. In addition, the institution should include individuals who are well-trained and sensitized to the needs and perspectives of vulnerable groups (children, young adults, women, the elderly and disabled). This should be ensured at all levels, with special focus on the local level, in order to have a positive effect.

As mentioned earlier, the institution in charge of the demobilization and reintegration is the National Commission of Demobilization and Reintegration Programme (NCDRP) which was legally established for this purpose in April 2001 and has a definite structure and clearly defined responsibility. It is a coordinating structure which does not intervene in practical implementation. USAID provided technical assistance and training to the NCDRP between 2002 and 2004 through the UNDP. The World Bank has also been the lead agency in the mobilization of resources and in the planning of a number of activities.

The UNDP's support on technical assistance programme to the NCDRP had significant contribution towards laying the basis for facilitating the implementation of demobilization and reintegration programmes. The support provided was in accordance with the strategic plan of the National Commission. The consultancies undertaken focused on different forms of training and assessment of the labor market for employment opportunities.

Overall, the objectives of the TAP have been substantively achieved in that the planned consultancy assignments have been successfully carried out.

The documentation emanating from the TAP had been read and largely internalized by the NCDRP. The staff of the NCDRP had an overall understanding of the Social and Economic Reintegration components and the related implementation imperatives and was in a position to begin implementation in earnest.

The capacity of the NCDRP to implement the Social and Reintegration components had been substantially increased. The internal training of NCDRP personnel through the TAP had been extensive and, provided there is a minimal turnover or attrition of staff, the institutional capacity of the NCDRP to implement the programme at the time was considered to be sustainable

Skills transference from international to national consultants has been considerable and is sustainable. The country now has a base of national consultants who are sufficiently informed and capacitated to provide additional support during the full-fledged implementation of the programme.

Study tours, organized and financed, to Uganda, Sierra Leone and South Africa undertaken by senior NCDRP staff have provided the NCDRP with the opportunity to assess international practices and apply this, where applicable, to the Eritrean situation.

Although the consultancies have produced documentation and plans to guide the NCDRP in its implementation of the Social and Reintegration components, such plans cannot be considered final. The consultants' reports each contain recommendations and actions for NCDRP follow up. It is only once actual implementation begins that the plans will be subjected to real scrutiny and an assessment of appropriateness, relevance, viability and sustainability made. It is without doubt that amendments to strategy, methodology and detailed plans will have to be made once initial projects are prepared and taken through the planned project cycles as laid out in the operations manual.

In September 2004 the Programme Management Unit organized a conference to highlight the accomplishments of UNDP recovery efforts in Eritrea from 2000 to 2004. The Seminar included presentations by UNDP staff members and implementing partners on UNDP projects in the areas of; emergency shelter construction, social and economic rehabilitation of the infrastructure, sustainable livelihoods, mine action and the social and economic reintegration of demobilized soldiers. Workshop sessions were additionally conducted among donors, implementing partners and UNDP representatives to discuss the specific needs of each recovery area and to brainstorm regarding future directions for UNDP recovery efforts in Eritrea.

The conference took place at the then Hotel Intercontinental from September 21st to 23rd, 2004. It was organized by the Programme Management Unit of the UNDP and was attended by 75 people; this included implementing partners, government representatives, donor agencies, UNDP staff members and other relevant stakeholders.

Serha trading centre, Southern region – rehabilitation of residences and shops

6.6.1 Social and Economic Re-integration of Demobilized Soldiers: Lessons learned

- Reintegration is a process that mainly takes place in communities at the local level. It was at this level that the PoWER programme identified the needs of the target group and designed the project for Gerenfit that had great potential for successful reintegration.

Demobilization in Mendeferra, Southern region (Pilot Phase)

- In Gerenfit resettlement villages, the community included over 800 demobilized soldiers' families, Land Mine/UXO victims, women/child/elderly headed households together with the other normal expellee households. Hence, it was no surprise to find in areas of return or resettlement demobilized soldiers, mine victims and other vulnerable households.
- Whereas both demobilization and reintegration support programs emphasize the importance of self-help and community support, in reality, the participation of beneficiaries and local communities in designing programmes was nonexistent.
- This applies especially to the vital issue of land use, but also to other important questions like participation in planning and implementing local projects.
- The technical assistance programme provided to the National Commission for Demobilization and Re-integration Programme (NCDRP) under the UNDP Recovery Programme, was in accordance to the strategic plans of the commission and it primarily focused on enabling the commission to offer skills development and training programs linked to the promotion of employment, micro-enterprise support schemes and rural development activities, on the ground of information provided by the labor market and economic sector analysis.
- Training can be a medium/long-term process with an uncertain future for the trainees and with no guarantee of success. In a poor job market, training in the absence of job-creation incentives may only raise expectations and produce an educated group of unemployed. The supply of skilled labor does not create its own demand: it should be linked to employment referral or self-employment.
- In order to facilitate the co-ordination of reintegration assistance and employment opportunities for demobilized soldiers, a nationwide information system has been established. Demobilized soldiers could receive advice in branch offices in the six regional administrations of the country. A system such as this served the purposes of communication, but was also important in providing demobilized soldiers with a realistic idea of their prospects and chances on the labor market. They could assist the Government and indirectly the UNDP in keeping track of demobilized soldiers, especially those involved in reintegration programmes.
- The provision of the consultancy services was essential for the creation of a nationwide information and employment exchange system. An information system such as this can create programme-specific coherence, especially in cases where there are multiple donors operating in the field.
- However most of the outputs of the technical assistance programme was not implemented because of the shift of strategic plan of the NCDRP after its mid-term review of its program and reluctance by the donor agencies to commit fully to implement their respective pledges due to their mistrust of Government intentions. Hence, the NCDRP has adopted a community based reintegration programme where implementation was undertaken by regional authorities and relevant line ministries in line with their development programs.

- Programmess targeted only at ex-combatants or ex-soldiers and their dependents often result in resentment from non-participants. In the case of Eritrea, IDPs/Expellees and demobilized soldiers had specific packages of assistance at the household level, but a major portion of the budget was earmarked for community related facilities (school and health facilities, water schemes such as dams etc.) where everyone benefits. Hence, interventions by and large have been sound and cohesive.

- The reintegration programme adopted by the commission has targeted specific groups of the demobilized soldiers for special treatment. Given that the demobilized soldiers are all members of the armed forces, where the minimum recruitment age is 18; there are specific programmes for women, war disabled and war orphans and families who lost their loved ones. Moreover, the disabled demobilized soldiers have access to interest free loans as preferential treatment. Special emphasis was also placed on those suffering from HIV/AIDS, who were offered specific awareness and orientation sessions.

- As regards to women soldiers there have been the inclusion of measures to ensure equality and equal access to opportunities in order to maximize economic capacity and full access to all the activities being organized and the introduction of a gender perspective. The first pilot project for demobilization consisted of 4,000 women that were demobilized through grants made available by the Netherlands.

- Despite all the preparations for a concerted effort, due to the no peace no war situation, only 100,000 were demobilized of the originally expected figure of 200,000.

- By focusing on a demand-driven approach, the commission allowed the ex-soldiers to choose for themselves what route they take for employment or self-reliance. This can support and develop a change of attitude, away from thinking in terms of entitlement and the state being responsible for them, toward taking initiative in their own regard. Furthermore, the programme was to be integrated with other national training and employment programmes and this could have a multiplying effect on the whole target community.

Pilot Phase demobilization in Mendeferra, Southern region

- The consultancy provided for the Monitoring and Evaluation was the most crucial intervention in establishing a system of Monitoring and Evaluation of the programs of the NCDRP and empowering the personnel to undertake the required monitoring and evaluation of the programme.

- Skills transference from international to national consultants has been considerable and was sustainable. The NCDRP now has a base of national consultants who are sufficiently informed and capacitated to provide additional support during the next case of implementation. Furthermore, the study tours to Uganda, Sierra Leone and South Africa undertaken by senior NCDRP staff have provided the NCDRP with the opportunity to assess international practices and apply these, where applicable to the Eritrean situation.

- Although the consultancies have produced documentation and plans to guide the National Commission for Demobilization and Reintegration Programme (NCDRP) in its implementation of the Social and Economic Reintegration Components, such plans were not considered final. The consultants' reports each contain recommendations and actions for NCDRP follow up. It is only through actual implementation that the plans could have been subjected to real scrutiny and an assessment of appropriateness, relevance, viability and sustainability carried. However, due to the lack of implementation, no assessment could be made on the output of the numerous consultancy services provided by the technical assistance programme. Nevertheless, with some revisions and updating the produced documentation could be used as an important input for future reintegration programmes.
- One of the biggest challenges was mobilizing the implementing partners especially the line ministries who have been lax in responding or have dithered in their decision making regarding engagement on NCDRP projects and keeping them capacitated; timely mobilization of financial resources and adequate consultancy; and involving institutional partners in an active manner. The challenge of mobilizing the implementing partners has been overcome through allowing the line ministries to engage in the reintegration program based on their existing development programmes.

Excerpts from Independent Evaluation Report on the Eritrea Demobilization and Reintegration Project

Executive Summary

Overall programme performance and achievements

The programme design meets high international standards. It reflects the priorities of Government and the attention and technical support of the United Nations Development Programme (UNDP), the United States Agency for International Development (USAID), the World Bank and other development partners.

2.2. Emergency Demobilization and Reintegration Project The United nations Development Programme (UNDP) carried out an exploratory mission on the demobilization and reintegration of soldiers in October 2000 and provided initial financial support to the Government during the preparatory planning process. Building on these efforts, in November 2000, the Government called on the World Bank to provide technical and financial support for the preparation of a comprehensive demobilization and reintegration programme, in collaboration with UNDP and other development partners. The World Bank and UNDP led two multidonor missions to Eritrea in January and June 2001, respectively, which helped the Government develop the EDRP. The programme targets 200,000 soldiers and its estimated cost is approximately USD197 million

Programme Performance and Achievements[6]

Programme Design

The evaluation team concluded that measured against the above internationally recognized principles, the EDRP programme ***design*** was of ***high*** standard. It reflects the priorities of the Government and the attention and technical support of UNDP, USAID, the World Bank and other development partners during the programme preparation phase. The design put emphasis on development reintegration, national capacity building and coherence with national poverty reduction strategies. This is in accordance with Eritrean policies and international practice, prioritizing broad community-based poverty reduction programmes delivered through line ministries and national institutions.

Technical Assistance Program

USAID and UNDP have funded an extensive TAP: to tune of USD 580,000 and USD 200,000, respectively. However, these funds had been depleted by the time of the Independent Evaluation. In all, 20 consulting reports were commissioned, concentrating primarily on reintegration planning, along with some capacity building. Topics covered in these reports include: training design and apprenticeships; regeneration of skills development centres; rural development; social reintegration; land for demobilized soldiers; labour market analysis; and sea-water farming

Development partners and NCDRP staff interviewed were all positive in their assessment of this work. The evaluation team studied selected reports (especially those with a focus on rural development and agriculture), and its general impression is that high quality and relevant work has been done. The caveat is that, as reported, EDRP reintegration activities are yet to begin. Consequently, it was not possible to evaluate how this broad preparatory work eventually will improve programme delivery. In a similar vein, the World Bank pointed out to the NCDRP that there is a need to describe how the outcomes of the TAP 'are being used by the implementing partners and/or NCDRP at central and Regional levels to jump start the process of reintegration activities'. The Independent Evaluation, therefore, can only offer the cautious observation that the TAP mechanism appears to have been important in informing the EDRP. It has generally produced excellent work with a relevance that extends beyond the EDRP-related reintegration component. This potential, though, has not been fully realized.

In light of the recommended strategic reorientation of the reintegration component, it was obvious that some of the consultancy reports deserved to be revisited. The evaluation team recommends that this be part of the work programme of the MTR. There certainly seems to be good reason to extend the TAP, should the NCDRP so request. In such an event, it would be preferable that the Terms of Reference for additional consulting work identify who are the potential users of the information/ analyses and specify how the NCDRP will monitor the effect or application of the knowledge generated. An extended or new TAP should be more geared towards doable actions and results-oriented proposals.

5.7 Mine Action Programme[29]

Overview: Eritrea has a major landmine/UXO contamination problem dating back from the struggle for independence with Ethiopia (1962-1991). Landmines were used to defend strongholds around cities and populated areas, military camps and roads; landmines were also found in rural farmlands, near water sources and along borders, primarily in areas near former battle zones.

The recent conflict between Eritrea and Ethiopia (1998 – 2000) has been a source of further landmine and unexploded ordinance contamination. Some reports indicate that more than 100,000 mines have been laid during this recent conflict.

During both wars, systematic and non-genetic disabling factors including wanton shooting, aerial bombardment, mine explosions, and physical torture have significantly increased the number of people with physical and psychosocial needs in the country. The environment remains dangerous.

Mines in frontline Trenches

Preparatory assistance: Support to Mine Action 2001-2002

On 18 June 2000, the Governments of Eritrea and Ethiopia signed a Cessation of Hostilities Agreement (CHA). In the CHA the Governments formally requested UN assistance for Mine Action activities in the contested areas.

In response to such request, the UN, sent to Eritrea and Ethiopia an Interagency Technical Mission (the Mission). The Mission recommended the establishment of a three tier National Mine Action Structure (the Structure) consisting of:

i. A policy body responsible for approving National Mine Action Plans;
ii. A National Mine Action Centre that would act as the secretariat for the policy body and would be responsible for: (i) preparing National Mine Action Plans; (ii) implementing approved National Mine Action Plans; (iii) accrediting NGO and other organizations wishing to do mine action work in Eritrea.
iii. An Operational Body made up of organizations accredited by the National Mine Action Centre to carry out mine action work in Eritrea.

Based on discussions with the Government of Eritrea, the recommendations of the Mission and UN Mine Action Policy, the Preparatory Assistance: Support to Mine Action in Eritrea was prepared. The Project document was signed by the Government of Eritrea and UNDP on 23 April 2001.

29 UNDP Final Report: Mine Action Capacity Building Programme (MACBP) 2002-2006

The key development objective of the Preparatory Assistance: Support to Mine Action was:

"To ***recreate a safe environment*** in which the needs of ***land mine victims are addressed,*** and in which ***economic and social development*** can occur free from the constraints imposed by mine and unexploded ordinance contamination."

The specific objectives of the Preparatory Assistance were:

- To assist the Government to define the National Mine Action Strategy;
- To assist the Government to develop a comprehensive National Programme for Mine Action in Eritrea
- To assist the Government to strengthen the capacity of the National Mine Action Authority [7]

The Preparatory Assistance: Support to Mine Action in Eritrea 2001-2002 was a two year Project. It provided for the recruitment of a Senior Technical Advisor (STA) to develop key mine action documents (31) including the Mine Action Capacity Building Programme (MACBP).

Due to difficulties in identifying and recruiting the STA 30 the implementation of the Preparatory Assistance did no start until mid-2001. The STA was not identified till end of 2001 and was not able to be in Eritrea till January 2002.
After consulting with the relevant stakeholders [31] it was decided to recruit a consultant for a period of 2 months to prepare the Mine Action Capacity Building Programme (MACBP).

In developing the MACBP, care was taken to ensure that those capacity building activities that had not been implemented under the umbrella of the Preparatory Assistance, would be included in the MACBP.

Mine Action Capacity Building Programme (MACBP) 2002 – 2004

It may be recalled that the Mine Action Capacity Building Programme 2002-2004 of the PoWER programme, was signed by UNDP and the Government of Eritrea on 21 March 2002.

The main objectives of the MACBP 2002-2004 were as follows:

Capacity building of :

i. **The Eritrean Mine Action Programme (EMAP), which later became the Eritrean Demining Authority more usually referred to as EDA[32];**
ii. **The Eritrean Deming Agency, which later became known as the Eritrean Demining Operations more usually referred to as EDO[33];**
iii. **The Ministry of Labour and Human Welfare (MLHW).**

30 Preparatory Assistance :Support to Mine Action in Eritrea report – April 2001 – April 2002

31 Eritrean Mine Action Programme (EMAP); the Commission for Coordination of Peace Keeping Mission the having a supervisory role of the mine action sector; UNMEE-MACC

32 Eritrean Mine Action Programme (EMAP) later the Eritrean Demining Authority (EDA) – Proclamaition123/2002

33 Eritrean Demining Agency (EDA) later the Eritrean Demining Operations (EDO)

Implementation of the Landmine Impact Survey (LIS)

The main focus of the Mine Action Capacity Building Programme (MACBP) 2002 -2004 was the development of the Eritrean Mine Action Programme (EMAP); the implementation of the Landmine Impact Survey (LIS) and the capacity building assistance to the Disability Department of the Ministry of Labour and Human Welfare (MLHW).

In regard to the Eritrean Demining Agency (later the Eritrean Demining Operations) the assistance to be provided was limited to supplement/enhance the assistance that was being provided by International Mine Action NGO's.[34]

The MACBP 2002-2004 was developed based on the assumption that there would be a number of actors playing a critical capacity building role in the Mine Action Sector in Eritrea namely; (a) United Nations Peace Keeping Mission in Ethiopia and Eritrea Mine Action Centre (UNMEE-MACC);(b) and the International Mine Action NGO's then operating in the country.

At the time of formulation of the MACBP 2002-2004 it was envisaged that UNMEE-MACC would focus its support on the Eritrean Mine Action Programme (EMAP) – later the Eritrean Demining Authority- and provide complimentary capacity building support in the following areas:

- Support and training in database management;
- Support and training in quality assurance and quality control;
- Support and training in accreditation procedures;
- Technical support on operational issues;
- Strategic planning support;
- Support to the National Training Centre (NTC) to deliver mine action training in accordance with International Mine Action Standards (IMAS).

To facilitate the interaction between UNMEE-MACC and EMAP and to maximize the use of resources, the office of the EMAP was co-located with UNMEE-MACC offices.

At the time of formulation of the MACBP 2002-2004 it was envisaged that the international mine action NGO'S would focus their support on the Eritrean Demining Agency (EDA), which later became the Eritrean Demining Operations (EDO). The areas of support were:

- Support and training of manual demining teams;
- Support and training of mechanical demining teams;
- Operational capacity building;
- Support and training of quality assurance and quality control;
- Logistical training and support.

34 NGO's and other Mine Action partners operating in Eritrea 2000-2002: (a) Halo Trust; (b)Danish Church Aid (DCA); (c) Danish Demining Group (DDG); (d)Mine Awareness Trust (MAT);(e) Landmine Survivors Network(LSN); (f) ICRC; (g) Ronco; (g) Mines Advisory Group (MAG); (h) Intersos

Following the signature of the MACBP 2002- 2004 the following events took place: (i) Proclamation 123/2002 – A Proclamation to establish the Eritrean Demining Authority (EDA) transformed the Eritrean Mine Action Programme (EMAP) into the Eritrean Demining Authority (EDA); (ii)The Eritrean Demining Authority (EDA) and was relocated from the UNMEE-MACC site to its own premises; (iii) At the same time the Eritrean Demining Agency (a National Mine Action NGO) was transformed into the Eritrean Demining Operations (EDO); and (iv) Several International Mine Action NGOs operating in the country were asked to cease operations.[35]

The Five Pillars of Mine Action

- Demining
- Mine Risk Education
- Advocacy
- Victim Assistance
- Stockpile Reduction

During the implementation of the MACBP 2002-2004: (i) the Ministry of Labour and Human Welfare (MLHW) developed a 4-year plan for victim support based on the principles of Community Based Rehabilitation; (ii) the Eritrean Demining Authority (EDA), with the assistance of UNDP, developed an Interim Eritrean National Mine Action Framework setting out the framework for how EDA and EDO would operate.

As a consequence of the above-mentioned events, the scope of UNDP's role in support of capacity building in the Mine Action Sector in Eritrea widened to include the following:

Eritrean Demining Authority (EDA)[36]

- Develop the capacity to set up and manage a national database capable of recording all available information on :(a) the threat of landmines and unexploded ordinance including Landmine Impact Survey (LIS) data; (b) mine action activities in the country; and (c) landmine victims.
- Develop the capacity to elaborate and implement an accreditation process and to perform quality assurance in accordance with International Mine Action Standards (IMAS).
- Develop the capacity to set up a monitoring system for mine action, investigation of mine/UXO incidents and post-clearance socio-economic impact assessment (PCIA).
- Develop the capacity to do strategic planning by reference to the Landmine Impact Survey (LIS) data, existing rehabilitation national development strategies and development projects.

35 Danish Church Aid (DCA); Danish Demining Group (DDG; Mine Awareness Trust (MAT); Landmine Survivors Network (LSN); Mine Action Group (MAG).
36 The State of Eritrea. National Mine Action Strategic Plan. 2011-2015

- Develop the capacity to task and co-ordinate the operations of various implementing agencies as well as to mobilize funds.
- Fully develop the curriculum and capacity of the Mine Action National Training Centre (NTC).
- Develop the capacity to draft Standard Operational Procedures (SOP) and technical and safety standards that adhere to the International Mine Action Standards (IMAS).
- Establish regional offices to oversee and fulfill roles identified in Proclamation 123/2002 – A Proclamation to establish the Eritrean Demining Authority (EDA).
- Collect data on landmine survivors and collaborate with the Ministry of Labour and Human Welfare (MLHW) in regard to Victim Support.

Eritrean Demining Operations (EDO)

- Develop the capacity to manage and conduct:
    1. Technical Survey
    2. Manual Demining
    3. Mechanical Demining
    4. Dog Demining Operations
    5. Mine Risk Education
    6. Minefield Marking
    7. Explosive Ordinance Disposal
- Collect data on landmine survivors and collaborate with the Ministry of Labour and Human Welfare (MLHW) in regard to Victim Support.

Ministry of Labour and Human Welfare (MoLHW)

- Develop reliable data on landmine survivors in Eritrea.
- Develop an integrated Victim Support database linked to the Landmine Impact Survey (LIS) using the Information Management System for Mine Action (IMSMA).
- Ensure that people with disability including landmine survivors are given equal opportunity of access to services utilizing the socio-economic model in Eritrea.
- Decentralize and build capacity in psychosocial needs through the Ministry of Health in Community Based Rehabilitation (CBR) areas.
- Build capacity and technical skill with volunteers at the community level, regional level and national level.
- Build capacity, choice and access in rehabilitation aids and equipment.

In the first instance, UNDP assisted the transition from Eritrean Mine Action Programme (EMAP) to Eritrean Demining Authority (EDA) and from the Eritrean Demining Agency to the Eritrean Demining Operations (EDO).

This included relocation of premises, inventory of demining and other equipment of EDO as well as purchasing of equipment to render the offices of the EDA and the EDO functional.

Revision of the Mine Action Capacity Building Programme (MACBP) 2002-2004

In response to the widening scope of UNDP's role in capacity building in the Mine Action in Eritrea, the Mine Action Capacity Building Programme (MACBP) 2002-2004 was revised. The revision of the MACBP was a two-step process:

> ***Extensive Budget Revision*** – sought to adjust priorities and incorporate additional as well as ongoing requirements with available funds. Both the Government and UNDP signed this document in July 2003
>
> ***Extensive Programme Revision (Revised Mine Action Capacity Building Programme)*** – sought to incorporate all the additional requirements of the Eritrean Demining Authority (EDA), the Eritrean Demining Operations (EDO) and the Ministry of Labour and Human Welfare (MoLHW). Originally the document was prepared for the period 2003 –2005. The document was prepared in June 2003 and at that time was unfunded.

In May 2004, the remaining International Mine Action NGO[37] was instructed to cease operations. This event resulted in a further revision of the Mine Action Capacity Building Programme (MACBP) delaying the signature of the Programme Document.

The Revised Mine Action Capacity Building Programme together with the Consolidated Appeal (CAP) 2004 and the Mine Action Portfolio (MAP) 2004 were used to mobilize resources. Delays in the process of mobilizing resource meant that the time frame for the implementation of the Revised Mine Action Capacity Building Programme had to be adjusted to 2002 - 2006.

Revised Mine Action Capacity Building Programme (MACBP) for the remaining period 2004 – 2006 under the umbrella of the JP on IDPs/Expellees return/resettlement programme.

The Revised Mine Action Capacity Building Programme (MACBP) 2004 -2006 was signed on 06 July 2004 and became part of the JP on IDPs/Expellees return/resettlement programme.
The desired outcome of the MACBP 2004-2006 was defined by the Interim Eritrean National Mine Action Framework; as " .. an expanded national capacity for mine action."

The Key outputs of the MACBP 2004-2006 were:

Fully functioning Eritrean Demining Authority (EDA). Specifically EDA was to be assisted to:

i. Initiate, set up and implement management systems (finance, budget, accounting, logistics, procurement and contracting) to ensure effectiveness, efficiency and transparency in the management of EDA;
ii. Initiate the development of capacity to set up and manage a national database (Information Management System for Mine Action – IMSMA) to record all available information on: (a) the threat of landmines and unexploded ordinance, including Landmine Impact Survey (LIS) data; (b) mine action activities in the country; and (c) landmine victims;

37 Halo Trust. The Eritrean Demining Authority (EDA) by letter dated 22 May 2003 requested that Halo Trust cease demining operations no later than 30 June 2003

iii. Initiate the development of capacity to set up a monitoring system for mine action, including accreditation, quality assurance and investigation of mine/UXO incidents, and post clearance impact assessment (PCIA);
iv. Fully develop the capacity and curriculum of the National Training Centre (NTC);
v. Develop the capacity to draft Standard Operational Procedures (SOPs), technical and safety standards that adhere to the International Mine Action Standards (IMAS);
vi. Establish regional offices to oversee and fulfil the roles identified in Proclamation 123/2002 – A Proclamation to establish the Eritrean Demining Authority;
vii. Develop Explosive Ordinance Disposal (EOD) and Technical Survey capability;
viii. Develop the capacity to do Strategic Planning by reference to LIS data, existing rehabilitation, and development projects and national development strategies, task mine clearance operations, co-ordinate mine action activities of various implementing agencies as well as mobilize funds;
ix. Collaborate with the MoLHW in regard to Victim Support.

Fully functioning Eritrean Demining Operations (EDO); specifically EDO was to be assisted to:

i. Initiate, set up and implement management systems (finance, budget, accounting, logistics, procurement and contracting) to ensure efficiency, effectiveness and transparency in the management of EDO;
ii. Initiate the development of capacity to conduct:
   (a) Technical Survey;
   (b) Manual Mine Clearance;
   (c) Mechanical Mine Clearance;
   (d) Manual Dog Clearance Operations;
   (e) Mine Risk Education;
   (f) Minefield Marking;
   (g) Explosive Ordinance Disposal; and
   (h) Victim Support data collection.

Farming with a camel in Shilalo, after the area was cleared of land mines

Capacity Building of the Ministry of Labour and Human Welfare (MLHW). In particular the MLHW was to be assisted to:

- Improve capacity to co-ordinate activities to define an operational national policy and to improve resource mobilization;
- Improve access to services for people with disability including landmine survivors;
- Develop reliable data on landmine survivors in Eritrea;

- Develop an integrated victim support database linked to the Landmine Socio-economic Impact Survey (LIS) using the Information Management System for Mine Action (IMSMA);
- Ensure that people with disability including landmine survivors are given equal opportunity of access to services utilizing the socio-economic model in Eritrea;
- Decentralize and build capacity in psychosocial needs through the Ministry of Health in Community Based Rehabilitation (CBR) areas;

Manual landmine clearance in the vicinity of Senafe valley

- Build capacity and technical skill with volunteers at the community, regional and national level;
- Build capacity, choice and access in rehabilitation aids and equipment.

Landmine Impact Survey (LIS) (Integrate with the earlier heading on LIS.

At the same time as the Mine Action Capacity Building Programme(MACBP) 2002-2006 was revised to reflect the expanded scope UNDP's support, UNDP started to assist the national authorities with the transition: (i) The Eritrean Mine Action Programme (EMAP) to the Eritrean Demining Authority (EDA); (ii) the Eritrean Demining Agency to the Eritrean Demining Operation (EDO). The assistance included assistance to relocate premises, inventory of demining and other equipment of EDO and purchasing of equipment to render the offices of both EDA and EDO functional.

Resource mobilization efforts also increased. Despite the goodwill of donors there were delays in the process of resource mobilization. The delay was partly due to the fact that a number of key donors were still reacting to the request by the Eritrean Government that a number of International Mine Action NGO leave.

Consequently the time frame for the implementation of the Mine Action Capacity Building Programme (MACBP) was adjusted to 2002 to 2006.

The adjustment of the remaining time frame (2004- 2006), for the implementation of the MACBP, also took into account the difficulty that the Programme already had in identifying and recruiting qualified national staff that had completed all the necessary requirements of the National Service.

The staffing issue had affected the implementation of the Landmine Impact Survey (LIS) and continued to affect the capacity development of the Eritrean Demining Authority (EDA). In the case of EDA at the date of suspension of the Programme [38] key post had not been filled.[39]

The key partners of the Revised Mine Action Capacity Building Programme (MACBP) 2004-2006 were:

Eritrean Solidarity and Co-operation Association (ESCA) ESCA was contracted by UNDP to engage National Staff required for execution of the Landmine Impact Survey (LIS), to administer those contracts and to act as the disbursing agent for expenses related to travel, living subsidies and operating costs.

UNICEF - In accordance with its mandate within the UN system, UNICEF provided to the Eritrean Demining Authority (EDA) and the Eritrean Demining Operations (EDO) support in the area of Mine Risk Education (MRE).

UNOPS - In close co-ordination with the Senior Technical Advisor MACBP, UNOPS implemented specific aspects of the Mine Action Capacity Building Programme that required specialized demining technical expertise.

UNMEE - continued to provide co-operation and support in maintaining the National Mine Action database as well as providing access to UNMEE assets for humanitarian mine action when possible and emergency medical evacuation (CASEVAC).

Ronco - an International Mine Action Organization – continued to work in Eritrea as bilateral partner. Eritrean Demining Operation (EDO) Manual Clearance Teams and Ronco Dog Clearance Teams worked in partnership

Completion of the Landmine Impact Survey (LIS)

Data collection for the LIS was completed by April 2004. The LIS report receive International Accreditation and was accepted by the Eritrean Demining Authority (EDA) in October 2004.

In mid-2004, Price Waterhouse Cooper, through the mechanism of the Ulysses programme[40] carried out a study: "Landmines in Eritrea, the socio-economic impact, prioritization on the basis of community visits"

The Price Waterhouse Cooper study linked up with the Landmine Impact Survey (LIS) to assess the socio-economic impact of landmines. The study also assessed the socio-economic benefits of mine action prioritization and the integration of mine action with national development programmes (priorities). The Study also linked up with ongoing work for the preparation of the National Mine Action Strategic Plan 2005-2009.

The report advocated for an integrated approach to mine action and expressed concern about the fact that in the three key national development policy documents[41], available at the time, there was little mention of mine action.

Technical Appraisal of MACBP 2004-2006

At the 2003 annual donor meeting, it was agreed to carry out a Technical Appraisal of the MACBP 2002- 2004. Such an appraisal was to provide a midterm appreciation of the Programme's direction as set by the Government, UNDP and the donors, and ascertain if the overall objectives and future directions of the Programme were within the National Development Plan and thus inform all stakeholders on the appropriateness or otherwise of the Mine Action Capacity Building Programme (MACBP) 2002 -2004.

The Technical Review of the MACBP took place over a period of 21 days starting on 19 July 2004, and was carried out by an independent team consisting of 4 persons – each person tasked with reviewing a separate aspect of the Programme namely: (i) institutional and legal framework; (ii) socio-economic impact; (iii) technical clearance and mine risk education; and (iv) victim support.

The composition and the expertise of the Appraisal Team were balanced so that both the technical and the socio-economic aspects of the Programme could be addressed. The Appraisal team consisted of an economic expert from NORAD, nominated by the Norwegian Government, a mine clearance/ capacity building expert; a victim support expert and an independent national economics expert. The victim support expert acted as the team leader.

The scope of the Technical Appraisal was to assess whether the Mine Action Capacity Building Programme (MACBP) 2002- 2006 was [42]:

38 October 2005

39 Regional Office Managers; Post Clearance Impact Assessment Team Leaders; Information Management Systems for Mine Action (IMSMA) Office; Personnel Officer; Logistics Officer; Procurement Officer; Vehicle /Generator Mechanic; National Training Centre (NTC) Instructors; NTC Logistics manager

40 Ulysses Programme was a Price Waterhouse Cooper leadership programme that envisages the cooperation of the accounting firm with UN Agencies and NGO in development project through out the world.

41 Interim Poverty Reduction Strategy; Integrated Recovery Programme; Food Security Strategy

42 Mine Action Capacity Building Programme (MACBP) 2002 – 2006 Final Report

Fully integrated in the National policies and adequately supporting other recovery initiatives: (i) economic development; (ii) poverty reduction; (iii) food security; (iv) recovery and reconstruction.

Addressing target populations and fully integrating into existing services.
Identifying and quantifying the mine action activities required in clearance, marking, and survivor victim assistance.

Providing the Government with the right tools to ensure that mine action activities will be fully responsive and integrated into the National priorities taking into account activities by other UN agencies and International NGO's.

Proposing adequate resources and is achievable taking into account the country's workforce, capacity development retirements and donor support.
Contributing to the further Millennium Development Goals through structure and focus on i) Poverty Reduction; (ii) Equal access; (iii) Education for all; (iv) Gender; (v) Food security etc.

The key findings of the Appraisal were that the MACBP 2002- 2004:

- Played a crucial role in developing the national capacity for humanitarian mine action for Eritrea.
- Implementation of capacity building activities was organizationally and economically sound.
- The achievement of the Programme as at the date of the Appraisal demonstrated its effectiveness for building mine action capacity in Eritrea in a very short time.
- The Programme proceeded in accordance with agreed frameworks and was developing in a direction that according to the Appraisal Team would have enhanced sustainable development for the people of Eritrea.
- Had achieved much in very little time, with paucity of resources, and that its role was crucial to the further growth of a national mine action capacity in Eritrea.

The Appraisal Team emphasized the importance of the development of the institutional structure of the Eritrean Deming Authority (EDA) and the Eritrean Demining Operations (EDO). In particular the Team highlighted the importance of an institution such as the Eritrean Demining Authority (EDA) to have sufficient capacity to influence national policy and to integrate mine action issues in accordance with its mandate under Proclamation 123/2002 – A Proclamation to Establish a Mine Action Authority. [43]

Echoing the concerns expressed in the Price Waterhouse Cooper study, the Appraisal Team also highlighted the fact that:

"Review of key documents reveals that mine action is hardly mentioned in any document, and that when it is mentioned it is only mentioned in terms of demining. While the Consolidated Appeals Process (CAP) is the only document that has clear emphasis and focus on this field other documents like the IPRSP44 only mentions mine action in relation to the decrease in agricultural output in 2000"45

Post Clearance Impact Assessment – Millennium Development Goals

One of the recommendations of the Technical Appraisal Team, was that the MACBP 2002 - 2006, should monitor not only the short term outputs produced, but should also monitor if the activities /outputs of the Programme lead to useful outcomes and have a lasting impact on the lives of mine affected communities. That is the MACBP 2002-2006 should put in place a mechanism for measuring the contribution of mine action to the attainment of the Millennium Development Goals. This type of monitoring is usually done through a Post clearance Impact Assessment.

Integrated Community based Mine Action Model

Based on lessons learnt during the implementation of the Mine Action Capacity Building Programme (MACBP) 2002-2004, taking into account the general concerns of ensuring sustainable impacts of mine action and measuring the impact of mine action activities in Eritrea, the Integrated (Community Based) Mine Action Model was developed.

The Integrated (Community Based) Mine Action Model was designed to ensure that all the five pillars of mine action (i.e. survey, marking, victim support, mine risk education, and clearance) moved together. The model included the transition of Landmine Impact Survey (LIS) teams to Post Clearance – Impact Survey teams. Implementation of the Model was to start in 2005.

Suspension of Revised Mine Action Capacity Building Programme (MACBP) 2004-2006

In September 2003, Eritrea experiences its first fuel shortage. This impacted on the planned activities of the Eritrean Deming Authority (EDA) and the Eritrean Demining Operations (EDO), but, as it lasted for a few months only, EDA and EDO recovered from the overall impact. In September 2004, Eritrea experienced its second fuel shortage which lasted until June 2005. The Government of the State of Eritrea decided to take action regarding the fuel issue, to reduce consumption and eliminate abuse by implementing agencies.

In late March 2005, as part of the national effort, impounded all Government Project Registered vehicles (G Project). At this time the Eritrean Demining Authority (EDA) and the Eritrean Demining Operations (EDO) and the Ministry of Labour and Human Welfare (MLHW) were operating a fleet of 43 vehicles, of which 40 were G Proj plated (Government Project) registered vehicles. The first six vehicles to be impounded were taken on 26 March 2005 from the manual clearance teams working in Shilalo. The remaining vehicles were taken from the Eritrean Demining Authority compound on 08 April 2005.

43 Article 5 – Objective – art 5 (d) integrate demining action into the national development strategy
Article 6 - Powers, functions and Responsibilities of the Authority. Art 6 (1) (b) . prepare national plans for demining action , including long term strategic plans and annual work plan, describing all demining action actives and other strategic activities related to the national management or activities of the demining action sector an d implement all demining action activities .

44 IPRSP – Interim Poverty Reduction Strategy Paper
45 Mine Action Capacity Building Programme (MACBP) 2002 – 2006 Technical Appraisal page 15

The vehicles in question were UNDP vehicles with G Proj number plates. It should be remembered that in accordance with UNDP Procedures, EDA, EDO and the MLHW were given "right of use" of the vehicles for the purpose of the activities described in the Mine Action Capacity Building (MACBP) 2002-2006 document.

At the time of the impounding of the vehicles, UNDP held several meetings with the Government, including the Ministry of National Development, Ministry of Foreign Affairs, Eritrean Demining Authority (EDA) and Eritrean Demining Operations (EDO); to try to resolve the vehicle situation. Each time UNDP was assured by the Government authorities that the vehicles would not be misused and that EDA/EDO will have access to them.

In the meantime, without vehicles, it became impossible to continue mine clearance operations safely (i.e. in accordance with International Mine Action Standard(IMAS)), therefore the Eritrean Demining Authority (EDA) placed all Manual Clearance teams and Explosive Ordinance teams on leave. At first the teams were to report back to work on 03 May 2005, this date was changed to 18 May 2005 and then again to 15 June 2005. The decision of EDA to put all manual clearance teams on leave, pending the resolution of the issue of the vehicles/fuel, was supported by Mine Action Capacity Building Programme Technical Advisory Team. The manual clearance teams did not return to work.

In February 2005 Mr. Joe Wenkoff, Chief Technical Advisor to the Eritrean Demining Authority (EDA) and Programme Manager of the Mine Action Capacity Building Programme (MACBP) 2002-2006, left the programme to take up another appointment. In April 2005, Mr. Paul Collinson arrived as the new Chief Technical Advisor/Programme Manager.

Between January 2005 and April 2005, according to the National Mine Action Strategic Plan, three 20- person manual clearance teams and one quality assurance team were to be trained. This training did not take place and during the meeting with the Deputy General Manager of the Eritrean Demining Authority (EDA), Mr. Habtom Seghid, UNDP was informed that it might not be possible to go ahead as per the original plan (i.e. the National Mine Action Strategic Plan and Work plan for 2005).

During the month of April, discussions were held between the Eritrean Demining Authority (EDA), the Eritrean Demining Operations (EDO) and the MACBP- Technical Advisory Team on how to maintain the capacity of the existing Manual Clearance team, pending the resolution of the issue of the vehicles. The discussion focused on the possibility of the teams attending refresher and upgrading courses. UNDP through the Mine Action Capacity Building Programme (MACBP) 2002-2006 would cover the cost of the training. At the time, EDA and EDO wanted the training to be done in Shilalo (approximately 300Km from Asmara).

EDA's intention was that UNDP would hire vehicles to transport personnel to the site and support them once there. For logistical purposes (i.e. lack of vehicles, fuel, supervision, food, water, etc.) UNDP recommended to EDA and EDO that this proposed National Training Centre (NTC) in Keren be used for the purpose, as this training site had been used to train deminers in the past successfully.

Consideration was also given to the fact that, in Shilalo, it would be difficult for the Technical Advisors to monitor and supervise the training as access to these areas depended upon clearance being granted by the Government. EDA made the decision not to conduct the training in Keren and stood down all operational personnel till 18 May 2005.

In May, the Eritrean Deming Authority gave notice to UNDP that all Mine Action Capacity Building (MACBP) 2002-2006 Technical Advisor's contracts (except for Chief Technical Advisor and the Technical Advisor to the Eritrean Demining Operations (EDO)) were to be terminated by 30 June 2005. UNDP raised the issue in writing with the Ministry of National Development, the Eritrean Demining Authority (EDA) outlining the requirements for the Technical Advisors with an overview of all current international positions.

A meeting was held on 13 May 2005 with the Ministry of National Development, EDA and EDO. At that meeting it was agreed that, in principle, all international staff positions would continue until current contracts expired. Soon after that meeting, EDA informed UNDP in writing that they still required all international staff contracts to terminate on 30 June 2005, with the exception of: (a) the Operations Technical Advisor to EDA whose contract could continue until 31 August 2005, and (b) the IMSMA Technical Advisor who could stay in post until a suitable national counterpart was identified and trained.

Following a number of discussions in relation to the above events involving UNDP, the Ministry of National Development, the Eritrean Demining Authority (EDA), and the Eritrean Demining Operations (EDO), it was agreed to call a Tri-Partite Review (TPR) meeting of all Mine Action Capacity Building (MACB)) 2002-2006 stakeholders on 08 June 2005. The meeting was never held.

Considering these events, in August 2005, the planned high level UN mission on Humanitarian Issues for the Horn, led by Special Envoy of the Secretary General, Mr. Martii Ahtisaari, in addition to the humanitarian issues, was charged with seeking a resolution to the impounded vehicles situation.
Following the UN Mission on Humanitarian Issues, on 25 August 2005, there was a further meeting between the Ministry of National Development, UNDP Country Office, UNDP Bureau of Crisis Prevention and Recovery, the Mine Action Department, UNHCR, the Eritrean Demining Authority (EDA); and the Eritrean Demining Operations (EDO). At this further meeting the following issues were discussed:

- **The impounded vehicles- the Government of Eritrea was informed of the UN position according to which no new project vehicles and spare parts would be released until the issue was resolved;**
- **The Mine Action Capacity Building Programme (MACBP) 2002-2006 – generally, the UN expressed its willingness to continue supporting the Eritrean Government efforts in mine action; it was also clearly highlighted that it is unlikely that the donor community will provide resources to UNDP to support the Government if the vehicles were not returned.**

At the meeting it was agreed that the Mine Action Capacity Building Programme (MACBP) 2004-2006 would be fully audited/ evaluated including its financial and administrative practices. As part of the process, the support provided to the national mine action institution as well as the management capabilities of both the Eritrean Demining Authority (EDA) and the Eritrean Demining Operations (EDO) were to be assessed. Terms of reference were prepared.

In October 2005 the Mine Action Capacity Building Programme (MACBP) 2002-2006 was suspended. Following the suspension of the Programme draft Terms of Reference for the Audit/Evaluation were prepared for consideration of both the Government and the Donors.
The Draft Terms of Referenced envisaged a two phase process for the Audit/Evaluation namely:

Phase I - Audit
Phase II - Evaluation

As at the date of this Report, only Phase I Audit has been carried out. A Draft Audit Report was submitted to both UNDP and the Government in August 2006. Finalisation of the report is pending.

In March 2007, the Norwegian Government agreed that unspent Norwegian, MACBP 2002 -2006, funds could be "....earmarked to be used as part of the Norwegian contribution towards the implementation of the joint programme on IDP return and resettlement in Debub and Gash Barka region.."[46]

A terminal evaluation of the Mine Action Capacity Building Programme (MACBP) 2002 -2006 was successfully carried out in at the end of 2009.

The main findings included:
The Mine Action Capacity Building Programme (MACBP) 2002- 2004 and 2004-2006 was implemented, through direct execution (DEX) by UNDP.

Key Humanitarian Challenges

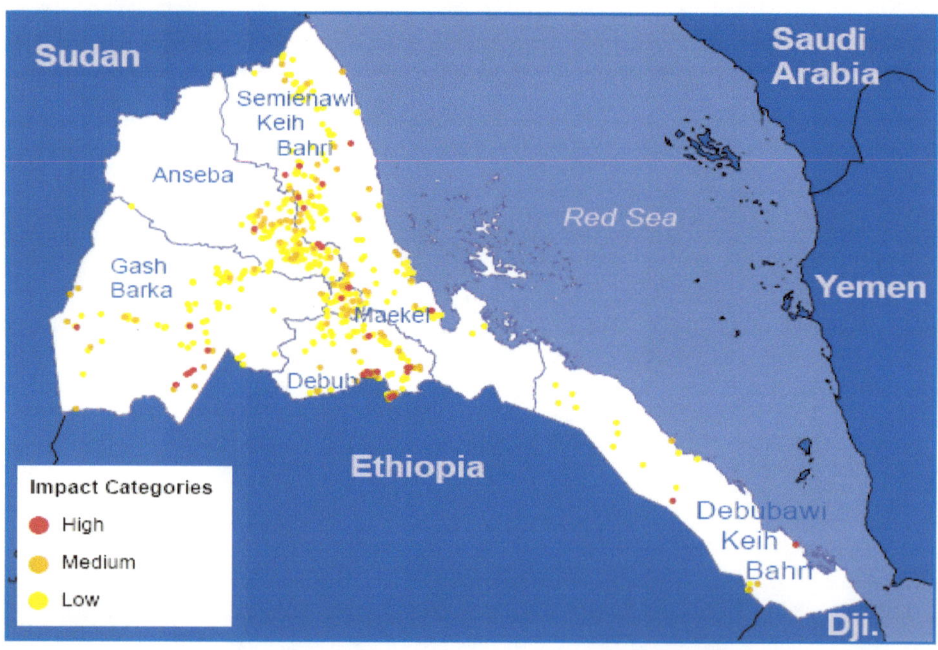

MAP 2
IIMPACT CATEGORIES OF THE 481 IMPACTED COMMUNITIES

At the start of the implementation of the Preparatory Assistance: Support to Mine Action 2001-2002, a key humanitarian challenge, was the lack of key data on the nature and extent of the landmine contamination in Eritrea; as well as lack of data on people with disability and specifically on landmine victims.

46

In 2004, the Landmine Impact Survey (LIS) Eritrea was completed. The LIS provided much needed information on the extent and the impact of landmine contamination in Eritrea. The LIS identified:

- 481 communities with landmine and /or unexploded ordinance (UXO) contamination in 55 of the 58 sub-regions[8].
- According to the LIS an estimated 655,117 people live in communities having some level of mine impact, which means that approximately 20% of the Estimated Eritrean population of 3.2 million people is living in mine impacted communities.
- 914 suspected hazard areas[9];
- Young males were the primary victims of landmines (most involved in pasture related activities);
- 20% of the places of origin of the IDP were impacted by landmines.

From June to September 2002, the Ministry of Labour and Human Welfare (MLHW) conducted a National Survey of People with Disabilities in Eritrea (NSPDE). With the raw data of the NSPDE and the information gathered by the LIS a clearer picture of the impact of landmines in Eritrea was starting to emerge. Through the assistance provided by the Mine Action Capacity Building Programme (MACBP) 2002-2006, the MLHW was working on finalizing the data analysis; linking the NSPDE with other capacity building activities of the MACBP such as Information System Management for Mine Action (IMSMA) and the Landmine Impact Survey (LIS). The work was never completed because of the suspension of the MACBP in 2005. Consequently there remains to this date a gap in mine action data for Eritrea.

The key Mine Action humanitarian challenges that remain to be addressed in Eritrea are: (a) completion of the work started on the National Survey of People with Disabilities in Eritrea (NSPDE); (b) addressing the need of 481 communities 47 identified by the LIS as being socially and economically affected by landmines .

Key Results

From the start of the Mine Action Capacity Building Programme (MACBP) in March 2002 to October 2005 (suspension), the Key Achievements of the MACBP were:

Eritrea National Mine Action Structure

Among the landmark results were:

- The submission by Eritrea of the Chapter VII (Ottawa Convention) report;
- Proclamation 123/2002 – A Proclamation to establish the Eritrean Demining Authority (EDA) published – this Proclamation sets up a legal framework for the Mine Action Sector in Eritrea.
- National Strategic Planning Teams (NSPT) and Strategic Working Teams (SWT) for mine action approved. These structures supported the implementation and finalization of the Landmine Impact Survey (LIS).
- Mine Action Technical Working Group, chaired by the Eritrean Demining Authority (EDA) started to, meet monthly. The Technical Working Group involved all relevant Mine Action organizations.
- EDA General Manager started to hold monthly mine action co-ordination meetings. First monthly mine action co-ordination meeting was held on 16.10.200348.
- National Mine Action Strategic Plan 2005 – 2009 finalized and published.

Eritrean Demining Authority (EDA) and the Eritrean Demining Operations

- Formal undertaking by EDA stating that Mine Action in Eritrea will be carried out in compliance with the International Mine Action Standards (IMAS).
- National structures for both the EDA and EDO developed.
- Term of reference for EDA and EDO positions prepared.
- Staff recruited to support their respective field operations. (In this respect it is worth noting that the process of recruiting national staff for both EDA and EDO was not smooth and that as at the date of the suspension of the MACBP in October 2005 the following key positions within EDA had not been filled:)
    - Regional Office Managers;
    - Post Clearance Impact Assessment Team Leaders;
    - Information Management Systems for Mine Action (IMSMA) Officer;
    - Personnel Officer;
    - Logistics Officer;
    - Procurement Officer;
    - Vehicle /Generator Mechanic;
    - National Training Centre (NTC) Instructors;
    - NTC Logistics manager.
- Interim National Mine Action Eritrean Framework (2003 to 2007) prepared– the document describes the steps to be taken to set up a fully functioning EDA and EDO.
- EDA enters into Memorandum of Understanding with UNMEE-MACC for the in-kind services of the Information and Mapping Systems Technical Advisor – Development to EDA's Information and Mapping Department started.

EDA Information department:

- Plan to set up EDA's Information Mapping Department developed and implemented – Technical Assistance in kind donation from the Swedish Government.
- Local network for both EDA and EDO established and staff trained in the use of intranet and office automation systems.

47 Landmine Impact Survey – Eritrea -2004

48 E-mail MACBP Programme Officer to UNDP – New York - BCPR –Mine Action Office 02.12.2003)

- Standard Operation Procedures (SOP) developed for EDA and EDO Information Departments.
- Information Management Systems for Mine Action (IMSMA) software installed in EDA.
- Agreement reached between UNMEE-MACC and EDA for the overall policy, structures, operations and maintenance of the mine action database.
- Starts to produce maps.

EDA Operations department:

The following EDA field teams trained and deployed to the field:

- One Quality Assurance Team operational
- Two Explosive Ordinance Disposal (EOD) teams. The EOD teams responded to Mine Risk Education teams report on unexploded ordinance (UXO). Disposal operations were carried out in collaboration with UNMEE-MACC. The availability of the EOD teams meant that there could be quick response to UXO reports. This quick response built community confidence in mine action.
- A section of the EOD teams successfully collaborated with MECHEM (Mine Clearance contractor to UNMEE)49
- Accreditation, tasking and quality assurance procedures in place; and started to receive completion reports from implementing agencies.
- From 02 to 03 December 2004, EDA prepared and conducted an Operations Workshop- the workshop included the preparation of training/internal assessment programmes. Command, Leadership training carried out on a regular basis.
- Introduction to both EDA and EDO of loss/damage/ replacement procedures

EDO Operations department:

- Six EDO Mine Risk Education Teams, trained, accredited and deployed with the assistance of UNICEF
- Five Manual clearance teams operational (3x60 person manual clearance teams; 2x20person manual clearance teams), with ongoing capacity building and training. In part this involved the recuperation of national Manual Mine Clearance 50Teams that had been developed with the assistance of the Danish Demining Group (DDG).
- 3x60 person manual clearance teams fully integrated with Bronco's 51 Mine Detection Dog teams HIV/AIDS training for all mine clearance personnel in EDO and EDA.
- Yearly work plans produced by both EDA and EDO.

Land Mine Victim Support

- At the start of the implementation of the Victim Assistance component of the Mine Action Capacity Building Programme, 850 people at regional and sub-region level were trained in a method to identify and prioritize within their communities. The focus was people with disability including landmine victims. The training was done in close collaboration with the Norwegian Association for the Disabled (NAD).
- This activity became the foundation of the National Policy/ Plan on Disability and the setting up of co-ordination groups.
- Victim support component of the MACBP brought together the UN Policy on Victim Support and the Community Based Rehabilitation model existing in Eritrea.
- In compliance with the provisions of Proclamation 123/2002, a Proclamation to Establish the Eritrean Demining Authority (EDA), meetings were held between EDA, the Eritrean Demining Operations (EDO) and the Ministry of Labour and Human Welfare (MLHW) regarding Victim Support
- Ministry of Labour and Human Welfare (MLHW) developed a 4-year plan for Victim Support – ***"Direction to Establish a Model of Victim Support Utilizing Community Based Rehabilitation in Eritrea"***
- Assistance to the MLHW on matters of co-ordination – in this regard dialogues were opened with key ministries such as the Ministry of Education, and the Ministry of Health with a view to establishing Thematic Working Groups.

National Survey for People with Disability

- The proposal for the Enhancement of the National Survey for People with Disability was funded. Technology needs identified, tenders issued, equipment purchased The National Survey of People with Disabilities was to be the first countrywide information on landmine and UXO survivors. The plan was to directly link the survey to the Landmine Impact Survey (LIS).
- National Survey data analysis started.
- Meetings with UNMEE-MACC Information Management Systems for Mine Action (IMSMA) and Landmine Impact Survey (LIS) personnel and LIS to discuss the linkage of the National Survey to the LIS and IMSMA database.[52].
- Discussion of IMSMA and victim support data initiated at national, regional and international levels.
- Identified how to monitor key Millennium Development Goals for people with disability including landmine survivors - Indicators developed. The purpose of the indicators was to facilitate the process of evaluation and monitoring of the Community Based Rehabilitation and Reintegration model.
- Coding manuals completed.
- Literature review completed.
- Data Entry personnel hired. Pilot data input started – as at the date of suspension 8,000 questionnaires had been coded and edited.

49 Mine Action Capacity Building (MACBP) 2002-2006 Annual Report 2005

50 DDG – Danish Demining Group was one of the International Mine Action NGO's that had been asked to cease operations in 2002.

51 RONCO – International Mine Action NGO operating in Eritrea with Mine Detection Dogs

52 In accordance with capacity building principles the plan was that both the LIS and IMSMA database would in due course be a national database

- Quality Assurance and Quality Control of the National Survey initiated.

Psychosocial care and support

- Assist and facilitate the provision of psychosocial care and support by the MLHW and the Ministry of Health to: Assab Southern Red Sea region, including training, and screening of 255 children and adults.

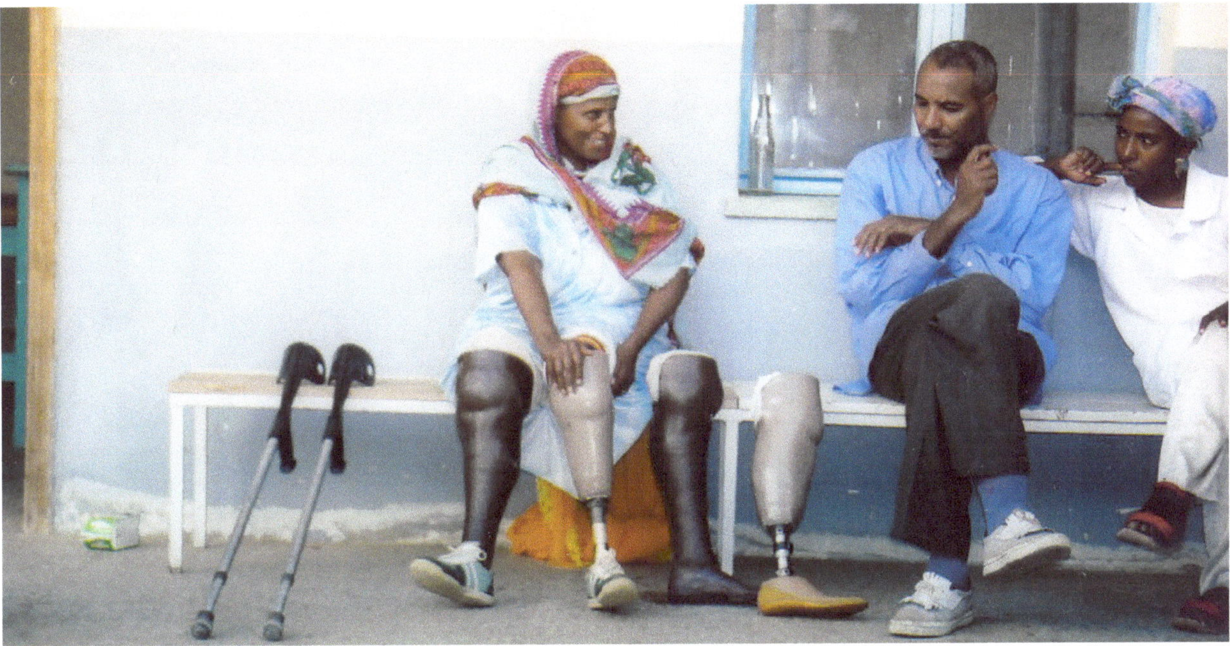

Orthopaedic workshop

Orthopedic Workshop

- Emergency Access to the Orthopedic Workshop - a project initiated in November 2004
- Logistics and finance training of personnel at the Orthopedic Workshop.
- Development of referral structures and relevant training started.
- Accommodation becomes available at the Maekel Orthopedic workshop through the support of the Mine Action Capacity Building Programme (MACBP) 2002-2006.
- Mobile Orthopedic Units prepare to visit Tesseney and the Eritrea/Sudan border to follow up on patients.
- Linkage between Maekel Orthopedic Workshop (also known as the Adi Guadad Rehabilitation Centre) and the physiotherapy department of the Ministry of Health started.

The work was done to:

- enhance the National Survey for People with Disabilities,
- Improve access to both the Maekel Orthopedic Workshop and the Mobile Orthopedic Units
- Demonstrate how the Mine Action Capacity Building Programme (MABCP) 2002 -2006 was at all times seeking to build on existing structures and partnerships.

Landmine Socio-economic Survey (LIS)

The Landmine Impact Survey – Eritrea was completed in April 2004 and received International Accreditation in October 2004. Total funds received from all sources during the period 2002 -2005, was USD **8,890,790.58**

Of the total funds received **USD 6,025,354.79** was expended during the period.

Further information on unexpended funds: Norway's USD 708,902.00 unspent funds was transferred to be used as part of the Norwegian contribution towards the implementation of the Joint Programme on IDPs return and resettlement in Debub and Gash Barka regions.

5.7.1 Mine Action Programme: Lessons learned

- UNDP in consultation with the Government and relevant stakeholders, through the mechanism of the Preparatory Assistance for Mine Action, initiated the Mine Action Capacity Building Programme (MACBP) in 2002. This two-year programme was subsequently revised and was extended to 2006 (i.e. Mine Action Capacity Building Programme 2002 – 2006). Because of the specific circumstances of Eritrea at the time, in particular in the mine action sector, the programme was directly executed by UNDP (DEX) with the Eritrean De-mining Authority (EDA), Eritrean De-mining Operations (EDO) and the Ministry of Labor and Human Welfare (MLHW) acting as implementing agencies.

- The MACBP was not as focused and time bound as it could have been; in the particular context of Eritrea this led to concerns by EDA about the motivations of the experts concerned and a desire to cut short, in some instances, international involvement. A more developed scoping could have helped to define a more focused program and thus establish an appropriate exit strategy for international involvement.[53]
- The initial Mine Action Strategic Plan (MASP) was over-ambitious and raised expectations that could not be met in terms of resource requirements. This was exacerbated by the Ottawa paradigm, which requires the clearance of all anti-personnel mines by a certain date.
- Mine action, and especially mine clearance, is an expensive activity with variable outputs. Therefore, it is important to prioritize the tasks in advance and to use the right analysis tools, including socio-economic analyses and technical analyses. Therefore, the size of the requirement should have been developed in a transparent and objective manner using a scoping exercise to identify which categories of land should be cleared to make Eritrea 'impact free'. It would then have made sense; to appeal for donor funding focused on support for these more important areas. An exit strategy for donor funding could have also been worked out based on the findings of this scoping study. Furthermore, an 'impact free' target provides a paradigm by which a risk-management approach might allow the de-mining teams to concentrate on the areas where they will do the most good without necessarily compromising safety, as set by international standards.
- In the view of the Eritrean Demining Authority EDA), the application of the International Mine Action Standards (IMAS) seemed to be slowing down progress. That is, criticism has been made by Government authorities of the 'scientific approach' of IMAS which resulted in an opportunity cost, i.e. more distress caused to an internal displaced persons (IDPs) population waiting to return to their homes than would have been caused by an 'acceptable' casualty level from faster clearance.
- Donor agencies did ask for specific assurances about Eritrean national technical standards for landmine clearance and explosive ordinance disposal (EOD) and that these national standards are no less safe than IMAS. This was raised as a 'due diligence' requirement in order to ensure the mitigation of liability that might be accrued to the donor. Therefore, for future mine action intervention the lesson learned is to compare the current national technical standards with IMAS to satisfy donor sensibilities about risk and liability. A common-sense, collaborative approach including suitable risk-management approaches should be able to accomplish this without a return to the past confrontations on this issue. .
- There were also communications problems between the MACBP staff and the implementing agencies, where the MACBP staff were not as good as they could have been at conveying what could realistically be expected from donor commitments, while on the part of the implementing agencies, several significant issues were not explained rather than being presented as a fait accompli, generating in turn dissatisfaction amongst the donor community. Even though, there were progress reports, these reports tended to 'accentuate the positive' and thus, when things started to break down in 2005, the developments came as a bit of a surprise to the stakeholders. There were some indications that problems had been made known to the UNDP via MACBP staff but there was little or nothing to reflect them in the routine reports made by MACBP, and indeed the EDA staff admit problems were discussed verbally rather than being set down in a formal report.
- Furthermore, the final report process was also not able to capture reports from the MACBP technical advisors in terms of what they had been able to complete in terms of their capacity development objectives before the technical advisors left.
- It is evident that the mine action programme requires technical expertise in several varied areas of specialization. However, the provision of technical assistance should have been focused to meet specific objectives and be time bound. Furthermore, the provision of technical assistance for specific capability gaps should have been carefully designed using a Training Needs Analysis process to ensure the assistance is demand driven and provides value for money.
- Training Needs Analysis (TNA) is helpful to design the requirement for technical assistance. The Training Needs Analysis should include a local specialist to provide advice about what is available locally. Moreover, local resources should provide the technical assistance wherever possible. For example, if there is a general need for training in methods of training, this should be provided through local training schools if available rather than paying for foreign training resources. Apart from increased cost it can also dilute the amount of time available for focused advice on subjects ***not*** available in Eritrea, such as the latest international landmine clearance techniques, which should be the core business of expatriate advisors.
- The mine action programme should aim to reduce the direct and indirect impact of landmines while simultaneously contributing to the economic and social development of communities. The integration of mine action into development emphasizes the importance of mine action as a priority in reducing poverty, as well as the importance of national ownership and community consultation. Hence it requires the involvement of actors across the development sectors and strong co-operation with a range of related stakeholders and bodies.
- The evolution of the mine action sector in Eritrea put conceptual strain on the original proposal, which was purely for technical assistance and therefore suitable to a direct execution (DEX) modality. The second version of the project document retained this DEX modality even though there was a substantial change in the scope of the project. It is believed that the DEX modality, which whilst initially appropriate for a technical assistance project, was less compatible with the later expanded operational support role of MACBP, exacerbated this problem as it led to concerns about ownership of the program amongst Eritrean authorities. Whilst it is reasonable for a technical assistance project to be provided under a DEX modality, if the international community is to encourage national

53 Evaluation of the Mine Action Capacity Building Programme

ownership of a mine action programme a NEX-DEX hybrid modality would probably have been more suitable, especially for operational support elements. This does not prevent expatriate technical specialists from having a monitoring role. .

- Hence, it is imperative, that any future programme would need to be compliant with government policy, provided it is in line with international norms, and needs to be under national ownership. Whilst it might conceivably be possible to provide Technical Assistance (TA) under a DEX modality, operational support would be more appropriately supplied in a NEX structure. Nevertheless, donors need to have access to an effective monitoring and evaluation process in order to provide them with a reasonable level of oversight on how their funds are being expended. This monitoring and evaluation process can be done on a periodic basis, but the monitors need the support of the government to allow them to access the work sites. .
- There needs to be coordination between mine action, and host government priorities and actions. It would have been prudent to establish an Eritrea Mine Action Coordinating Center (EMACC). Relevant UN agencies, NGOs and corporations could still provide deployable machinery, work force and commodities. This setup could allow each organization to focus on its specialty areas while the EMACC could work on integrating all activities. The EDA is at the moment the coordinating authority.
- There is also a need to improve the involvement of the programme with other government agencies, such as the Ministry of Defense and the National Police. That is, there is a need to find a home for a sustainable capacity able to deal with a residual landmine/UXO problem after donor funds have dried up. The Police are a potential home for such a capacity. As mutual confidence increases there may be increased options for military-military relations in terms of technical assistance for de-mining training; there is also an important coordination role for the Land Based Defense Forces. Hence, it is appropriate to develop a more sustainable capacity with a size commensurate to the likely size of the residual contamination problem and the ability of the Government of Eritrea to fund it.
- The Landmine Impact Survey (LIS) was a useful source of data to support a transparent and objective prioritization mechanism for resource allocation in the mine action sector. The successful completion of the LIS was considered a positive outcome of MACBP.
- The collection, management and analysis of landmine/ERW casualty data have proven to be a significant challenge for most mine-affected countries. With UNDP support of the development of IMSMA and the LIS process, the MoLHW is in the process of creating casualty databases but is often challenged to use that data productively in planning for mine action related activities. Landmine/ERW casualty data could be used for a number of different purposes within a national mine action strategic programme, depending on who will be using it and which questions they want to have answered. Lots of different types of casualty data can be collected, but only data that is of specific use to some component of the mine action program (mine clearance, mine risk education, mine victim assistance, and advocacy) should be collected and stored.
- Initial data collection should be part of a comprehensive and integrated start-up plan agreed to by the government and other stakeholders. Ideally, mine action data should be standardized (as much as is possible) and agreed before deployment to ensure compatibility. Subsequent mine/UXO data collection exercises should be done as part of an integrated information collection process – preferably orchestrated by the EMACC. The end-users of data collection exercises (especially the MoLHW and MoH) should play an active and major role in defining data to be collected. In situations where extensive mine/UXO data are likely to be provided, a rapid verification exercise after the data has been received would add value – especially if basic socio-economic impact data were also collected during this process.
- Mine action is not so much about landmine/UXO as it is about people. All the activities should be geared towards addressing the problems faced by populations because of landmine/UXO contamination. Therefore, its aim is not technical that is to survey, mark and eradicate landmines, but humanitarian and developmental. Considering this, when looking at mine action activities, it is necessary to examine not only landmine/UXO clearance, but also mine, awareness and victim assistance. Therefore, in addition to the LIS conducting a mine victims needs assessment can provide valuable information for defining the extent of the need for services and the particular types of medical and rehabilitation services required. These detailed surveys generally focus on landmine/UXO survivors but can also gather information on other victims such as family members of those injured or killed in accidents. The data collected could augment the accident data collected by EDA/MoLHW and could be of use to those working in landmine/UXO action plans and be of use to those working in landmine/UXO clearance and MRE activities.
- Some experience has revealed that where prosthetic and orthopedic programmes are handed over to government departments, they tend to fail. The Mobile Orthopedic car provided by the PoWER programme is now permanently parked in Keren town, Anseba region. The simple reasons for this are two-fold. First, the MoH has very limited resources and huge demands on those resources. The second reason is that staff salaries within government services are frequently very low: consequently, morale is low within the service and staff eventually leave. One of the solutions to these problems is to create a body that can continue the service outside the government. This body may be an autonomous Agency that operates in partnership between public and private organizations and should preferably be a non-profit establishment.
- In the implementation of the Mine Risk Education projects in Eritrea under the auspices of the EDA with support from UNDP and UNICEF, it has been noted that children not attending school in the areas targeted by mine risk education had limited information on mine risk behavior and were the most vulnerable economic groups with greater daily risks to mine accidents. Hence, every mine risk education (MRE) programme based on schools the Eritrean Demining Authority needs to develop a complementary, parallel approach to ensure that out-of-school children also receive mine awareness education.

- Landmines are major threats to food security which can be illustrated by the fact that the typical mine victims in Eritrea are farmers. The impact is even greater on farmers who have only a small farm with a large portion possibly infested by landmines, leaving them unable to support their family. Consequently, recent studies indicate that the procedure for identifying "the vision of a mixed and environmentally sustainable rural economy is seriously jeopardized by landmine and UXO pollution."
- The recently approved National Strategic Plan for Eritrea envisions that the implementing agencies ensure that casualties are cared for and that additional victims are kept to an absolute minimum. It is also necessary to determine which land areas should be re-opened in relation to pressing socio-economic needs, such as schools, farms, businesses, transport routes, water access, and even restoration of access to areas which could potentially provide sources of revenue such as tourism. Mine action is more than taking landmines/UXOs out of the ground.
- Eritrea had successful reconstruction/rehabilitation programmes since it has adopted the application of a rights-based approach. Mine action must provide the freedom of movement and the rights to housing, health services, schools and the cultivation of fields. Mine action also impacts on the right to ownership or user-right of land, which places focus on poverty reduction and development. Besides, mine action activities should include gender mainstreaming in all its aspects.
- Mine action programs are funded by diverse means and donors all have unique approaches. Mainstreaming of resources for mine action into overall development spending is a growing trend and one that can be used to harness funding for an integrated mine action. Mainstreaming mine action into the development agenda requires close partnership and joint action by all mine-action actors and the development community. Among the key stakeholders that must be involved in this process are the landmine/UXO affected regional administrations, traditional donors, international financial institutions, UN agencies, and national and international NGOs that have expertise in Mine Action.

5.8 Joint Programme on IDPs/Expellees–Return/ Resettlement: First Phase and Expanded

First Phase

The first phase of the Joint Programme (UNDP-UNICEF-WFP), with a duration of 15 months starting from its signing on 24 November 2004, was launched to support the ongoing programmes of the Government, which had already made substantial commitment to the return of IDPs. The programme aimed to address the return/resettlement of 30,000 persons (8,300 households) IDPs and Expellees from Adi-keshi, Kotobia and Mai-Wurai camps in Gash-Barka and Debub regions. The Programme was within the United Nations Development Assistance framework (UNDAF) for Eritrea for the period 2002-2006. The management and coordination of the programme was designed to comprise UNDP as the managing agent (MA) of the pooled funds and a Joint Programme Steering Committee (JSC) made up of UNDP, UNICEF, WFP, the Ministry of National Development (MND) and ERREC, chaired by the Government and UNDP.

The Joint Programme was implemented on two alternative modalities; namely pooled funding and parallel funding. The pulled funding was primarily resources provided by the UNDP and what it was able to mobilize. There was at one time a contribution of 240,000 USD which was incorporated in expenses related to makeshift school construction. Hence, all the achievements written below is that of the UNDP. All other UN agencies have been reporting their successes directly by themselves and are not reflected in this report.

The activities carried out by UNDP during the first phase joint programme are as follows.

Transportation of IDPs to villages of origin in Gash Barka

UNDP, in collaboration with the Eritrean Relief and Refugee Commission (ERREC), as well as UNHCR, which was not a signatory to the joint programme, accomplished the transportation of 19,000 IDPs and their belongings from Adi-Keshi camp to their villages of origin in Laelay Gash sub-zone in February 2005. Whereas UNDP mainly funded the procurement of commercial truck services and fuel, UNHCR made available some trucks for the operation.

Shelter

Emergency shelter materials (family tents, tarpaulins and '***Agudo***' frames with mats) were distributed to the IDPs upon return to their villages of origin. The temporary shelter component was provided by agencies outside the Joint Programme. ICRC distributed 2000 pieces of tarpaulins, UNHCR supplied 600 tents and 1500 dome shaped metallic frames ('***Agudo***' structures) to replace the worn out temporary shelter, which the IDPs used during their stay in Adi-Keshi camp. The rugs of the worn out tents and tarpaulins were also transported to the new sites as part of the transportation package of personal effects of the individual IDP households. The newly supplied temporary shelter materials fell short of the total number of the IDPs that returned.

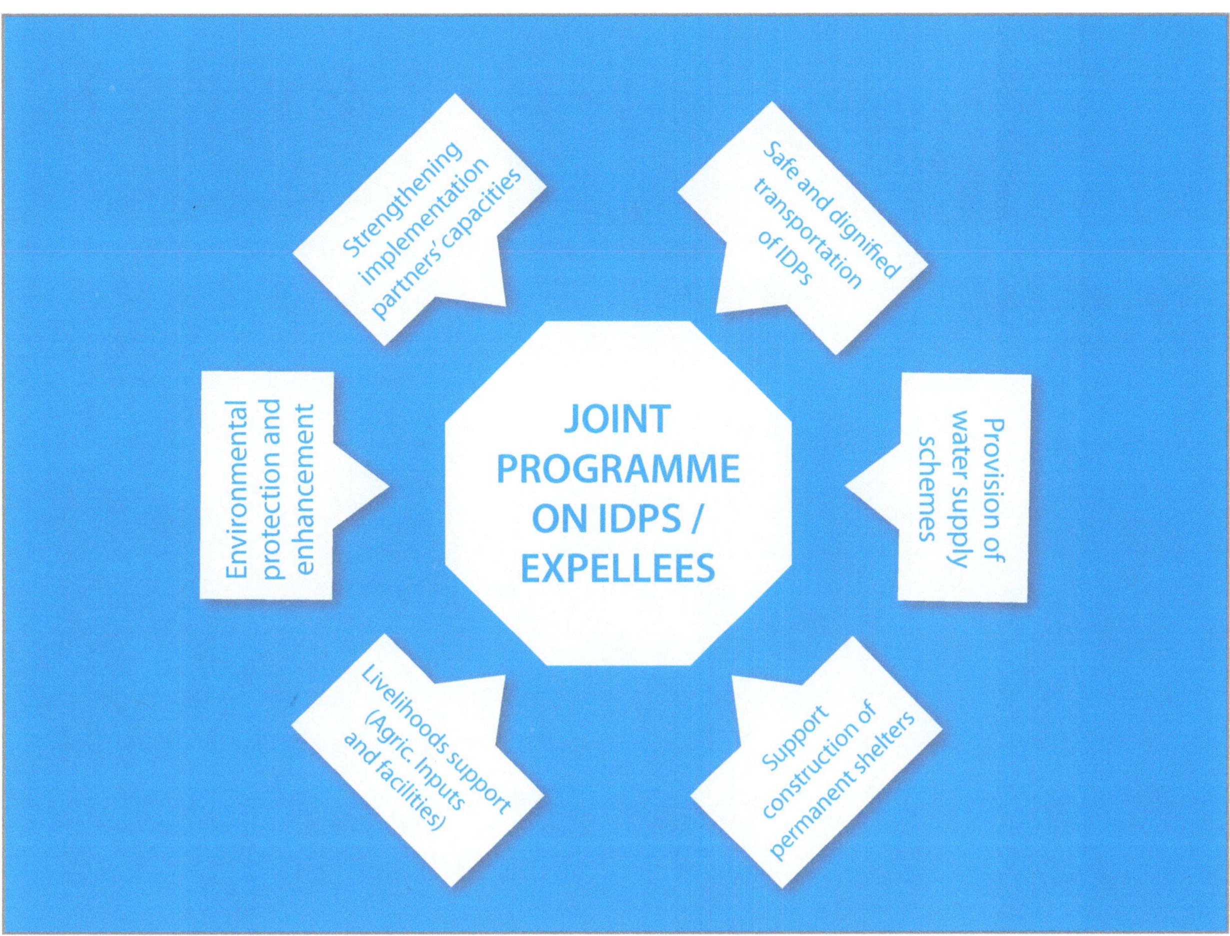

Permanent Shelter

UNDP provided 2200 shelter kits (comprising corrugated iron sheets, purling, rafters, nails and hinges) and cash for labor costs. Additionally the Norwegian Church Aid (NCA) provided 500 of the same shelter kits. The construction of permanent shelter was complex and controversial. During the implementation stages, there was disagreement between UNDP and the Gash Barka administration on the type of houses to be constructed.

Eventually, UNDP had to adopt a flexible approach, that is, provision of the shelter kits, and an additional cash equivalent contribution to the cost of constructing 5m x 5m stabilized soil block walls for each household. The households were given the option of deciding the type of walls they wanted. The extra cost beyond the UNDP's contribution was to be covered from the individual household's own resources or other sources to be identified by Gash Barka administration.

Food Aid

As a continuation of previous emergency relief, WFP continued the distribution of food assistance to the IDPs who returned from Adi-Keshi to their villages of origin.

Non-food Items

Items such as mosquito nets, metal ovens, blankets, soap, sickles, plough, axes, spades, hoe and kitchen sets were distributed to the returned IDPs and Expellees by UNHCR, ICRC, the Eritrean Red Cross Society and the government beginning February 2005.

Water and Sanitation

The Gash-Barka administration ensured the availability of water supply systems prior to the movement of the IDPs. The places where water supply was established were Shilalo, Habela, Sheshebit, Adi-Tsetser, Dembe-Dima, Tselale, Adi- Hakin, Mai-Kokah and Mukuti. Depending on the productivity of the wells, various types of pumping devices were fitted into the sources.

To ease travelling long distances, there was a need to bring to distribution stands close to the community, residences had been identified for some of the villages. Accordingly, 5 villages (Shilalo, Sheshebit, Dembe- Dima, Mai-kokah and Mukuti) were prioritized with a budget of USD 1,471,049.00.

Mukuti Water Supply Scheme

Health and Nutrition

The Health station in Shilalo was rehabilitated by the Gash-Barka administration prior to the return of the IDPs. The health facility serves 20 villages, including the 9 villages of return. However, since some of the villages are remote from Shilalo, many people are finding it difficult to get access to the health services.

Education

The plan was to dismantle the makeshift classrooms in Adi-Keshi and erect them in 5 locations of the IDPs' return villages. Overall, 49 classrooms and 16 teacher residences were to be constructed. Actually, 30 classrooms brought from Adi-Keshi and 18 new ones, and 18 new teacher residences were constructed. Thus, the plan was fully implemented, enabling the students to pursue their education back at home.

Sustainable Livelihoods

The returnee IDPs were assisted to build sustainable livelihoods through the provision of agricultural inputs and services to revitalize agricultural activities in their villages of return. Each household has access to at least one hectare of farm plot. About 70% of the land (3556 hectares) was cleared through cash-for-work schemes and ploughed by tractors and oxen. The total number of returnee IDP households from Adi- Keshi to their villages of origin was 5,054.

Second Phase

The revised Joint Programme, between UNDP, UNICEF, UNHCR and UNFPA, was launched following the decision of the Government to return all the remaining IDPs sheltered in camps in Gash-Barka and Debub to their villages of origin or to new resettlements. Like the first joint programme, this was designed within the overall framework of UNDAF.

It was signed in April/May 2006 for a duration of 20 months for recovery-related activities of some 40,398 IDPs/Expellees to their villages of origin or new re-settlement areas. The Programme covered 5 sub-regions, namely, Shambuko, Molki, and Laelay-Gash in Gash-Barka, and Tsorona and Senafe in Debub; with 14 Administrative Areas. The principal partners of the Programme are the Ministry of National Development, Ministry of Labor and Social Welfare (assuming the responsibilities previously conferred on ERREC), Gash Barka and Debub Regional Administrations, and Water Resource Department of the Ministry of Land, Water and Environment. The major donors are Norway, the Netherlands, Italy, USAID and UNDP. The adopted programme management options were pooled through UNDP and parallel through UNICEF, UNFPA, and selected NGOs.

The activities envisaged under the Programme include the safe and dignified transportation of the IDPs, provision of water and sanitation facilities, provision of temporary and permanent shelter, provision of agricultural inputs, credit, income generating activities for some of the most vulnerable households headed by women, food aid rations, school feeding and supplementary feeding, school rehabilitation and temporary school construction, provision of education equipment/materials and health facilities rehabilitation including health post construction. The expected outcomes of the programme were to bridge the gap between emergency, recovery, reintegration and development programmes; provide special attention to women-headed households in the emergency and recovery programmes; and assist in the provision of appropriate and environmentally friendly housing (and settlement) schemes for IDPs and expellees.
The activities carried out under the programme are the following:

Transport of IDPs to their places of origin or resettlement

The IDPs in emergency camps in Debub and Gash-Barka have been returned to their villages of origin or re-settlement. Hence, all camps are closed and no IDP HHs remain unsettled. The regional administrations of both regions have established an elaborate and efficient ad-hoc structure to undertake the safe movement of people and goods. A large number of buses and trucks were mobilized; ambulances were dispatched for emergency first aid services and emergency food and water supply were made available; and means of transport for the IDPs and their belongings were provided.

Transportation service from Kotobia camp to Tebeldia - Gash Barka

Transportation service from Kotobia camp to Tebeldia - Gash Barka

Access road to water development schemes

Tserona - Hadish Adi - Kinito

Transportation service from Kotobia camp to Tebeldia - Gash Barka

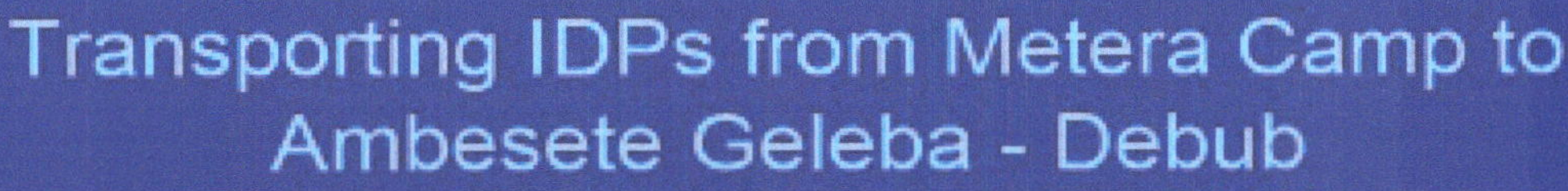

Water Supply Systems

In Gash-Barka, 47 hydro geological and 14 geophysical surveys were carried out in the villages of return, by the regional administration, starting February 2006. On the basis of these rudimentary surveys, water wells were drilled by ECDC in Girme, Ellala, She'hate, Tselim-Kelay, Adi- Maelel and Folina. Out of trials in 43 sites, it was only possible to get water in 12 villages. The yield of the wells varied from 1.2-15 lts/sec. The results were largely disappointing. Alternative water supply sources for Adi-Maelel and Tselim-Kelay were studied by UNDP contracted professional consultants and the construction a of micro-dams was implemented in accordance to the scientific study. Whereas, in Debub, the situation was more complex. The return villages were located in most cases on the top of mountains. The water sources were in nearby riverbeds. The water was brackish in sharp contrast to the clean water in the camps. The sources were not protected, thus exposing the returnees to waterborne diseases.

In June 2006, UNDP sponsored a preliminary study for water supply and sanitation programme for the returning IDPs in Debub administrative region. Based on the study, 2 workshops were carried out with participation of all stakeholders which led to the preparation of the design works of the desired water supply schemes. As a result, 7 bore hole based water schemes (Adi Mereta, Ahiz, Tahtay-Fihe, Unanazo-Kudoweiba, Unawelesti and Enta villages), three micro-dams in Hadish-Adi, Kinito and Ham villages and components of the water supply schemes, such as the building of water reservoirs and public fountains have been constructed in the return villages.

Kinito – Tsorona Sub region

Adi Shuhu, Tserona Sub region

On the other hand, in Gash-Barka region the water supply system construction of Folina, Ellala, Tselim Kelai and Adi-Maelel; rehabilitation works of Omhajer water supply project

Tselim Kelai Micro dam in Gash Barka

WATER DEVELOPMENT SCHEME

Solar Panels – Unanazo Kudewieba, Tserona Sub region

Reinforcement wire mesh for the construction of water reservoir in Ham village in Southern region

Carrying of sand and cement from the low areas by hired donkeys for the construction of micro dams

and 3 borehole-based water systems in the returnee villages of Mukuti, Sheshebit and Dembe-Dima have been completed.

Adi Maelel Mico Dam, Gash Barka

Shelter: Master plans have been prepared for Grime, Ellala, She'hate, Folina and Adi-Maelel return/resettlement areas with plots zoned for residence, social service infrastructures, recreational areas and market places and roads of 20, 15 and 10 meter width. In Gash-Barka, 1,643 HHs received three installments and 4,330 HHs received first and second installments of cash for the construction of permanent houses. The budget allocated was Nakfa 23,000 per HH to construct a 4m x 5m house. Out of the 1643 HHs who received the full housing grant,1061 (64.6%) were female headed.

Adimaelel shelter

Elala Shelter

Similarly, in Zoba Debub 1,352 HHs received the three installments and the first and second installments were disbursed to 2148 HHs for the erection of one multi-purpose room at the rate of 12,000 Nakfa per HH (4,000 and 8,000 Nakfa being the first and second installments respectively). 61.2% of the beneficiaries were women headed households. The settlement of the first and second installments was undertaken in 2006 and the remaining third installment was accomplished successfully in 2007.

Sustainable Livelihoods

Men and women former expellees in their farms in Gerenfit village

Agriculture: In **Debub** the support to agriculture for enhancing sustainable livelihoods of returnee IDPs and expellees consisted mainly of land development and clearing, terracing and tree planting through cash-for-work programmes, procurement and distribution of agricultural hand tools and provision of funds for the purchase of oxen for distribution to vulnerable IDPs.

In 2006, 4,659 sets of agricultural tools were distributed to returnee IDPs. 1,553 households received cash assistance to purchase one ox each in Tsorona, Senafe and Endeli. 74.38% of the agricultural hand tools and 65% of the oxen restocking beneficiaries were female-headed households. In Tsorona, tractor service was provided for about 700 hectares of land, in Itaro, Hazomo plains; 240 quintals of '***Taff***' seed was supplied to the 566 households who resettled in Una-Argena.

This support has continued during the year 2007, with different land development activities such as the construction of terraces, check dams, soil embankment and diversion; land levelling; stone collection and road construction and road maintenance. 676 qt. of improved seeds of different types of crops distributed to 3,281 HHs in Tsorona. 1,003 resource poor and women headed HHs has received cash assistance for restocking (one ox per each HH).

Tsorona - Debub Region

Tsorona Covered Market - Debub Region

Likewise, the returnee IDPs and expellees of the **Gash-Barka region** were assisted to build sustainable livelihoods through agricultural support. In 2006, in order to allocate one-hectare cropland for each of the new IDP/Expellee Households, 1,376 Hectares of new cropland surveys were undertaken in the villages of Girme, Ellala and She'hate. Whereas, for those who have returned to their villages of origin who have their own plots of land, assistance was made in land clearing and plowing. Plowing and planting activities have been carried out in all return areas in sub-zobas of Shambuko, Molki, and Laelay-Gash. These activities mostly have been conducted with Tractors in Laelay-Gash and Molki and in some areas with oxen in Shambuko and Molki sub-regions. The planting activity has been done following first phase plowing on 1,363 hectares while the remaining of the farmlands 3,467.75 hectares was planted without the first preparatory plowing. Moreover, 2,263 oxen to 12 beneficiary villages in sub regions of Laelay-Gash, Shambuko, and Molki were distributed and the beneficiaries (2263 HHs) were vulnerable households and mostly female-headed households. 1,650.55 Quintals of cereal seeds have also been distributed to returnee farming households and crops have been sown successfully. In addition, a total of 9,638 hectares of land was ploughed and planted in the 2007 crop production season. The returnee farmers in Gash-Barka have conducted most of the land clearing activity manually on a cash-for-work basis. 2,144 shovels, 3,663 iron plough tips, 2,500 Hoes and 7,472 sickles were distributed to returnee families. A total of 2,076 qt. of cereal crop seeds and 300 qt. of chickpea were distributed to about 140 HHs.

Agriculture (Contd)

Various Agricultural interventions in Gash Barka

Harvest time for former expellees in Gerenfit village

Harvest time for former expellees in Gerenfit village

Environmental Interventions

In 2006, the component on environmental interventions started procurring the necessary materials for energy saving devices; beneficiaries have been identified and training programmes given in consultation with the Ministry of Mines and Energy. The Implementing Partner in Gash Barka was the National Union of Eritrean Women Branch office in Barentu. This component envisaged the introduction of improved *'Mogogo'* (traditional stove) and related training; the provision of community solar PV. The improved stove (mogogo) was designed by the Energy Research and Training Centre (ERTC), part of the Eritrean Government's Department of Energy. It is a new stove for the cooking of 'injera', a pancake-like bread that is served with most traditional Eritrean dishes. Injera is made from the fermented batter of Taff flour (an ancient cereal grain) and cooked on a large, flat, black clay cooking plate below a hat-like metal cover. For centuries it has been cooked on simple clay stoves, built over an open fire. These stoves, known as mogogos, are smoky and dangerous and often difficult to start, requiring a lot of blowing, and large amounts of kerosene, to get them going.

They are very inefficient and require a lot of wood fuel to complete the cooking process. The new and improved stove is efficient in terms of firewood consumption (reduces up to 50%) and the time required to bake 'injera'. It is also safer to use. It has an enclosed fire-holder, with enhanced ventilation so that the fire burns more efficiently, and a chimney to take smoke out of the house or shelter where the cooking/baking is done. The stove also burns a wider range of fuels, working well with twigs and leaves and animal dung. Being raised above the floor and, having an enclosed fire-holder, the stove is no longer a danger to children.[55] Furthermore, related to terracing, and planting of trees and shrubs to enhance environmental conservation have also been carried. The Environment subcomponent, which is funded from the UNDP Trac II resources, has also recorded a remarkable accomplishment. Part of the core resource was allocated to install improved *'Mogogos'* within the IDPs areas of return and resettlement. NUEW, Gash Barka branch has carried out the procurement of improved Mogogo materials, conducted training sessions on how to install and use the system and provided 4,000 improved *'Mogogs'* to vulnerable female headed beneficiary households. Similarly, in 2007, improved stoves were distributed to 2,200 resource poor and women headed households among the returnee/resettled communities of Shambuko and Goluj. The beneficiaries also received training on the construction and use of the improved stove.

Soil and water conservation, Areza Sub region

55 The Energy Research and Training Center, Asmara – Ministry of Mines and Energy

Furthermore, soil and water conservation activities such as hillside terracing and construction of check dams were done by the returned/resettled IDPs in Laelay-Gash, Molki, Shambuko and Gogne. Different species of trees that are proved to be suitably grown in various areas of Gash-Barka region were distributed to families in returnee/resettlement sites of sub-regions Molki, Goluj, Laelay-Gash and Gogne for planting in the homestead areas.

5.8.1 Joint Programme on IDPs/Expellees (First Phase and Expanded); Lessons Learned

General

- In Eritrea, where more than 1.1 million people were displaced, the prime responsibility to avert human disaster rested on the national and local governments. The active leadership of the Government and involvement of the affected people played a central role in mitigating an imminent catastrophe that could have resulted from the aftermath of destruction and displacement.

LESSONS LEARNED FROM THE JP on IDPS/EXPELLEES BY COMPONENTS OF THE PROGRAMME

- Transportation of IDPs/Expellees to their original villages or to new resettlement areas
- Shelter (Emergency and Permanent)
- Sustainable Livelihoods (Input to Agriculture)
- Water (Potable water for humans and animals)
- Mine action (Survey, mark, demine, educate)
- Social and Economic Reintegration of Demobilized Soldiers
- Capacity Building (Implementing partners at regional level)

- The swift organization of the administrative and service giving government institutions was instrumental in avoiding chaos and a breakdown societal cohesiveness, as well as in maintaining the law and order that usually accompanies other similar situations of conflict or natural disasters. The government ensured that the administrative structures and functions were preserved in the course of prevailing situations of distress. Due to the recreation of an enabling environment, the provision of psychosocial protection, including security, food, shelter, water, health, education, etc. was possible in an orderly and equitable manner.
- The mobilization and active involvement of the affected population in all matters affecting their survival in the emergency situation, as well as in the subsequent restoration of their sustainable livelihoods upon their return or settlement is a rare experience that we can draw unique lessons from the coordination mechanisms put in place at various hierarchies of the administration and the stages of interventions, including studies, registrations, project identification and formulation, were in most cases participatory in nature. The cooperation between Government bodies, donors, the UN system, civil society and host communities was remarkable. The steering committees, sectorial work groups and joint field assessment missions were instrumental in the delivery of effective and efficient support.
- The joint programming in the implementation of the recovery/rehabilitation programmes was helpful in pooling together the meagre resources, minimizing transaction costs that would otherwise be incurred by various actors in harmonizing the diverse sectorial interventions and ensuring equitable distribution of resources.

- The registrations and rapid assessments/studies that were periodically carried out were useful in understanding problems, and obtaining up-dated correct information on the needs and gaps to be met.
- Special attention was given to the most vulnerable groups, such as women, children, handicapped and elderly headed households, and the community based targeting of beneficiaries enabled the Joint Programme to be transparent and fair.
- The no-war-no-peace situation extended the state of insecurity and uncertainty thus keeping in limbo actions that could have been taken for the long haul. This has also down played the level of commitment and support from the international community.
- The delay in the demarcation of the border slowed or postponed the release of the able human resources from the Defence Forces and this negatively influenced the pace of the emergency recovery programmes, since most of the returned/resettled IDPs and expellees were largely female and elderly headed with a big proportion of non-productive dependents.
- Non-flexible definition of displacement and eligibility criteria or approach for assistance has caused a number of seriously war affected people to be excluded from the packages of assistance. People in Senafe and Adi- Keyih areas that had stayed at home during the occupation (stayees), but had sustained heavy destruction and looting, were not registered as IDPs/Expellees and were thus left out ***initially*** from the recovery provisions.
- Lack of accurate updated population data of the returnee IDPs within the villages of return or resettlement hampered accurate planning of activities in the programme. Population surveys need to be carried out and periodically updated within the villages of return to have accurate population data so as to have a proper activities plan. This is of course easier said than done.
- There were budget shortages to implement and cover all the expenses of the programme. Allocations of sufficient budget to implement all components of the programme, in predicable and assured multi-year commitments were rare.

Senafe District Hospital – Lote 1

- Because of the emergency nature of the interventions, implementation of the Joint Programme started before the signing of the project cooperation agreement, and there were initial problems to effect payments on time. As a general rule, implementation of the programme activities needs to start after the signing of the cooperation agreement document. The construction of the District Hospital in Senafe is a case in point.

Senafe District Hospital Lots 1 and 2

- Construction work started on the premise that an agreement would be signed and a retroactive payment effected. Unfortunately, the EC funds earmarked for the construction of the Hospital expired and the agreement was not signed. After a lapse of several months it was possible to assign EC money contributed for Food Security related interventions to cover only the first phase of the constructions. The first phase envisaged the construction of OPD, Maternity Ward, and Administration Building etc. but did not include a block for surgical operations, Kitchen and Laundry because of lack of adequate funds. The MoH stated in no un-certain terms that the hospital could not be operational without the additional blocks. At a later stage and at the request of the Government, the UNDP provided the necessary funds to undertake construction of the additional blocks requested by the Ministry of Health.
- Implementation of the Joint Programme has been undertaken by the respective regional administrations. The establishment of a Project Coordination unit in both regions was vital to ensure the required coordination, timely implementation of activities and reporting of the performance of the overall programme components. However, to increase the implementation capacities of the regional administrations, a modest building capacity component for training and installation of medical equipment was also included and the need for training seems to be an important component of the recovery programme. Hence, the coordination, monitoring and supervision were instituted within the respective structures of the Regional Administrations of Gash Barka and Debub.
- Credit was among the activities envisaged under the expanded joint program however, there was no support provided by the programme through credit intervention.

Sustainable Livelihoods:

Agriculture

- It is to be noted that the agriculture component, as implemented, concentrated more on the immediate provision of inputs, and less on longer term sustainability and strengthening of extension and implementation capacity. Consequently, staff time was mostly spent on supplying packages, which left little spare time for training and extension of the beneficiaries.
- Obviously provision of assets needs to be considered as part of the envisaged subsequent phase of assistance which was planned to take place sometime after the return of the refugees, when returnees would have better ideas of the area, their capabilities and priorities, and their likely sources of livelihood; and the provision of assets should include a variety of possible forms of assistance to encourage investments in a range of income generating activities

Land provision and land development

It is apparent that clearing of land for agricultural use should be implemented by individual households, but a program to assist less able households such as women headed, elderly and disabled people, with initial clearing and land preparation would be necessary. It was realized early that the virgin lands assigned to the Expellees could not easily be ploughed using oxen and the shrubs could not also be cleared with manual labour. Hence, in such situations tractor ploughing was introduced and bulldozers for rooting out undesired shrubs. For instance, one bull-dozer and eight tractors were purchased to facilitate the settlement of the rural expellees from Ethiopia (UNDP: Focus on Gerenfit, August 2004).

Project Tractors in Gerenfit resettlement village

- During the land clearing process returning refugees were advised to leave some plants on their plots as windbreakers so as to protect the land from soil erosion. However, in some areas failure to follow the advice given by the MoA staff led to some land degradation. Furthermore, due to some cultural hindrances, in some areas women extension workers were required to address directly and maintain contacts with women returnees.

Provision of seeds and farm tools

- In war-affected communities, which were dependent on agriculture for their sustainable livelihoods, a key element in the reintegration of these communities is the provision of agricultural inputs. This can enable families to start to put together their lives after the chaos and distress of conflict.
- We have learned during the last programme that seed interventions, even if meant to address immediate and temporary problems, should also be considered as a long-term intervention. In adjoining projects of the TER we have observed that unnecessary distribution of seeds or distribution of poorly adapted seeds could disrupt and endanger farmer seed systems and actually undermine long-term food security. It is imperative that following seed distribution, capacity building and training may be necessary if the introduced varieties are to be used effectively. It should be remembered that traditional seeds were generally speaking drought and disease resilient. In times of food shortage farmers were obliged to eat their seeds which they normally put aside during harvesting time.

- Although farmers were keen to receive new and improved seeds, they are well aware of the adaptive characteristics of their own local varieties, especially in marginal areas and with low inputs. Farmers make every effort to hold onto their own seed stock, the varieties whose characteristics they know and trust.
- While emergency seed supplies were required in specific drastic situations there were disadvantages to the blanket distribution of imported seed. It is often not appropriate to local conditions, specifically to the marginal, low-input management conditions of displaced farmers. In highly variable areas with, for example, with differing growing season lengths, no single variety will be appropriate for all areas.
- The implementation of the provision of seeds in the PoWER program was mainly from local markets. However, there was an instance when the implementers were hard-pressed to obtain and distribute seeds in time before the cropping season and were forced to import Sorghum from Sudan which happened to be full of striga weeds. Such types of weeds were difficult to eradicate.
- Interventions and inputs must be kept to the most essential and to a level of technology well within the knowledge, experience and skills of the rural population. Introduction of hybrids and varieties excessively dependent on high doses of fertilizer, pesticides and insecticides should be avoided. 
- Emergency seed supplies were made in response to a food crisis. In such a situation the speed of response is critical, and blanket distribution of commercial/certified seed may be the only practical solution. However, any provision of such seed must not only be well selected and appropriate to the environment into which it is being sent, it must also be of the highest possible quality. This is essential if agriculture is to get off to a flying start, to delay the process of degeneration as long as possible and protect against exotic pests and diseases.
- Decisions on seed procurement were often made on the basis of availability and cost rather than quality. As a result there were several bad experiences. Humanitarian agencies have started to insist that seed is tested for germination percentage, but it was not possible to determine varietal's integrity from a physical seed inspection without actually growing out the crop. Where seed is concerned, a variety can be considered local when many farmers have adopted it within a specific agro-ecology and when it is locally appropriate to the particular farming system in which it is to be used. (In this case, the IDPs/Expellees in four regions have benefitted from the programme, namely: Debub, Gash Barka, Northern Red Sea (Near Ghinda who came from Adi Keyih area) and Southern Red, (Near Debai Sima and Musa Ali).
- Procurement of farm tools should be based on selection by farmers that is, they need to sample the tools, and this helps to ensure their ultimate suitability. Not the same type of farm tools should be provided for different regions where there is variability on type of soil. Furthermore, the farm tools were preferred to be locally made or modified so as to secure their repair and maintenance in the local market.
- Farmers need access to a wide spectrum of inputs and services in order to produce effectively. It is increasingly recognized that the potential gains that can be achieved through one service, such as provision of quality seed, may be dependent on access to other complementary inputs, such as fertilizer, water for irrigation and pest control, in addition to extension advice, credit and market information services. In Gerenfit the expellees farmers were given funds to buy their seed from nearby markets through the help of a local committee. That year a bumper harvest was registered, since they selected the seed that suits to the land and the special ecology.
- After farmers receive improved seed (together with other associated inputs) as emergency assistance, their requirements quickly progress from emergency, to rehabilitation and into development mode. Often this occurs even before the end of the first production cycle. Farmers themselves do not differentiate between these various phases of emergency relief, rehabilitation and development. On this basis, the programme also treats them as a continuum under its integrated strategy.

Provision of Livestock

- Livestock interventions that were based on a strong understanding of the affected system, the economic and cultural roles of livestock in the community and the various gender roles played in the management of animals can contribute to household food security and income. The livestock intervention of the PoWER programme mainly targeted the most vulnerable households, particularly female headed households who lack the resource as well as the labor required for agricultural livelihoods.

- The restocking of livestock was accompanied with effective training programmes which enabled beneficiaries to receive quality information on the keeping of livestock. Furthermore, there were many examples of close contact with MoA veterinarians. However, livestock interventions should have animal health programmes to prevent the spread of diseases and reduce livestock deaths.

- Even though the restocking of livestock had no major disasters, as can so often happen when restocking with non-indigenous or unaclimatised stock, such interventions should have considered the maintenance of the local breeds. Failure to give due attention to the local breeds would lead to extinction of local breeds and can have ecological impacts. Moreover, economic indicators were also important to recognize, including changes in the price of livestock and feed on local markets.

- The restocking component of the Joint Programme is being implemented through the provision of cash to the beneficiary households so that they can purchase livestock of their choice. This enabled farmers to select the right types which were suitable for their respective areas. As regards to the health conditions the staff of the MoA supervise the livestock and provide the necessary advice. It has been noted that when the MoA buys them through a committee, the price sky rockets. The originl budget called for USD 267 per ox, suddenly it jumped to USD 534 per ox.. During draught years farmers in return areas, sold their oxen at high prices, before the prices tumbled. It seems they were more astute in their decision-making. It is an asset that they dispose of when conditions were bad and buy when the situation improves.

Cash for Work

- The cash for work (CFW) projects do benefit a large number of beneficiaries and do produce assets that have a direct and positive impact on the communities in particular and on the improvement of the environment in general. These activities fit the general philosophy and spirit of the PoWER programme as a safety net for war-affected communities, as they distribute cash to needy households without huge overheads. The projects enhance the environment, ultimately soil fertility and food production. However, due to the lack of able bodied male manpower (works have been carried out mostly by the elderly and women) the technical outcomes of the cash for work projects were in most cases satisfactory.

- The cash for work activities were mainly agriculture related and regarding construction and/or maintenance of feeder roads. The participating communities were the war affected, drought affected villages of return/resettlement and returned refugees and resettled expellees. The benefits from such cash injection at the household level provided a very helpful kick-start to families as they struggled to regain their former livelihoods.

- Experience show that the identification of the types of Soil and Water Conservation (SWC) activities were entirely decided on by the regional offices (mainly agriculture &

administration) of the region and sub region without full consultation (a problem that was fully addressed in the subsequent programme – Transition and Early Recovery Programme) and participation of the direct beneficiary communities. The type of activities of the CFW programmes that were the priority needs of the communities vary from one region to another region even among sub-regions depending on the topography, size of land and water availability. In Gash-Barka region, the communities' prior demand is the construction of check-dams, micro-dams and ponds on the wider aspects, where as in Debub region, farmland terracing is preferred due to the small and limited size of farmland per household.

- The CFW programme had been targeting the returned /resettled IDPs/Expellees, those who were still in camps as well as the communities that receive or 'host' displaced persons, which were also considered as war-affected. The experiences on CFW activities under the PoWER programme show that the work is open to all members of these communities and there were no restrictions on the number of participants per household. Hence, older children can help their parents to complete the given daily work norm. These would benefit the parents especially women headed households who were overburdened with the domestic workload, and the disabled and elderly groups of the community.

Women participating in Soil and Water Conservation structures in Debub Region

- The levels of awareness of CFW programmes among the communities was found to be high because the communities have already participated in at least one programme and witnessed the benefits of the CFW activities on the ground. The level of awareness of the benefits of the SWC is not the same in the two regions. Communities with land problems and water shortages do really understand the effectiveness of SWC activities. In some places of Gash-Barka, they refused to participate in SWC activities for they did not understand the benefits of such activities. Most of the time they were very concerned about the direct benefits to them rather than the long-term benefits or indirect benefits such as improving the environmentally degraded areas.

- Based on the discussions with the experts from the MoA and the community representatives, the most effective activity from the past CFW is the construction of check dams. The farmland terracing is also more effective than non-farmland terracing. Effectiveness is highly correlated to sustainability of the outcome of the CFW activities. In the past successive years,asignificant amount of SWC activities have been performed through mobilization of the communities. However, due to lack of a sense of ownership, improper management, mishandling and unsafe guarding by the communities and other concerned bodies, the outcomes were not as expected. In both regions, the level of technical expertise on Soil and Water Conservation (SWC) and forestry could be regarded as satisfactory. However, due to lack of transport facilities and insufficient fund, designated for daily Subsistence Allowance (DSA), the experts could not reach all the areas under their respective sub-regions as frequentLY as the work required.

- Payment to participants for the CFW activities was done based on the completion of daily work norm that has several advantages. Primarily, it reduces inefficiency in the implementation of CFW programme because payment is based on the number of hours worked rather than output produced, which enhances the tendency of extending the number of days to complete the job by working actively for less hours per day, to earn more income that resulting in delay and inefficiencies in the use of resources. Secondly, output based labor payments instead of hourly wages increases accountability. Thirdly, workers can have flexible times to complete the job so older children can help their parents after school; women can also make adjustments with their domestic workload.

- Past records of the CFW program shows the duration of CFW programmes on the average was less than a month where the remuneration ranges between Nakfa 520 to 1,200. The average cash distribution per beneficiary was not sufficient for most people to invest in buying new assets. Therefore, there is a need for larger cash transfers or to run the programme concurrently with other safety nets for greater impact for recovery.
- Cash-based employment generation schemes were best implemented when the main constraint to food security was access to food, not availability of food. In 2007, in both regions, there was reasonable access to grain in the ordinary market areas as well as in the government distribution centers; hence, there was no shortage of food grain in the market. Concerns that distributing cash could lead to higher food prices were not relevant because the influx of cash was not big enough to distort the market. However, the importance of frequent monitoring of market prices to check on inflation in CFW programmes cannot be denied.
- It became apparent that the importance of the CFW activities itself is in psychosocial recovery. Communities prefer cash to food relief and want to work. Most of the communities believe that food aid is not a sustainable means of livelihoods. Distributing money rather than food enabled households to choose how to spend the cash – whether on food or on longer-term food security strategies (e.g. investing in tools or livestock). While cash is easier and quicker to distribute than food, there were also concerns over handling of cash. It has been observed that women were the best inhandling the extra cash. However, the misuse of cash for unintended purposes even among men (e.g. drinking of alcoholic beverages) was not common among the beneficiary communities.

Non-farm livelihoods:

- Given the unreliable and erratic rainfall, arid and semi-arid climates and the pursuit of traditional rain-fed farming, diversification of the means of livelihood is indispensable. However, the non-farm component of PoWER did support a very limited number of households to establish small non-farm businesses so as to make real and sustainable improvements in their livelihoods. With a thorough study of the potential of non-farm enterprises there is a need to expand the opportunity to larger groups of the rural communities.
- Implementing NGOs of the non-farm component of the PoWER programme were assisting people, especially women in learning how to establish and manage businesses to achieve financial sustainability. Furthermore, these projects were encouraging the development of social capital. Hence, the owners of businesses were establishing networks and a range of market relations.

Earthen Water Pots – Import substitution and income generating project

- While it would be necessary to provide initial tractor services to assist the IDPs/Expellees in their return/resettlement areas, to resume agricultural activities; the restocking of animals will be a very essential element in the creation of sustainable livelihoods of the communities in the long run. Given the low technological levels and the diverse benefits and incomes that were derived from livestock, mechanisation does not appear to provide a guaranteed sustainable substitution at household levels.

Shelter

- The PROFERI did not have a shelter component supported by the UNDP. However, there were other parallel projects that supported returning refugees with their shelter needs. The construction of one room in Sabunait resettlement area was a total disaster (German NGO). The houses were presumably built from Adobe and roof from onsite manufactured corrugated Asbestos roofs. All the units without exception cracked and were uninhabitable and had to be abandoned. The idea was good but it was not based on well tested scientific analysis. There was another initiative to address the shelter needs of returning refugees but it also lucked sensitivity to local factors such as weather and tradition in the design of homes. For instance, in Mahmimet the houses were too small, the ceilings short and the room too hot. The roofing was made of corrugated iron sheets, which was not suitable for the climate of the region. Consequently, the beneficiaries had built their respective grass houses besides the new units and their animals were sheltering in that shelter with corrugated iron sheet roofing.

- In the planning stages the initial shelter component of the PoWER Programme was misdirected because a lot of resources were earmarked to cater to the needs of a small target group at the insistence of the local government representatives. 60 expensive houses were built in Goluj and Tessenei to cater to the needs of a higher echelon returning refugees (teachers, skilled technicians, administrators) that were supposed to help the implementation of the recovery programme in Gash Barka. The same amount of money could have covered the construction needs to build one multi-purpose room for at least 1,000 households. This was immediately corrected and no similar houses were built thereafter.

Training on the use of new building materials for low cost housing (stabilized soil block and corrugated cement roofing in Goluj-Gash Barka

- By the same token, the rest of the refugees were also housed in equally expensive imported family-tents, which were in tatters in few months time, due to rain, excessive heat and winds.
- Shelter projects in rural areas need to be carefully planned in order to ensure that as much as possible they empower beneficiaries by utilizing to the full their skills and abilities and pump capital to the local economy. (Women in Tsorona Sub region, projects carried water and sand from the river beds – on their backs and on donkeys - to high mountain areas where dams were built: infusion of capital to the local economy. carrying water, reinforcement bars and sand on their back and on their donkeys and were paid amply at market prices.

- The experience of the shelter projects of the PoWER programme showed that when the option of cash provision is selected as opposed to shelter materials, the availability of building materials in the areas needs to be assured. In one instance the price of one corrugated iron sheet (state the size) used to cost 125 Naka and suddenly due to shortage in the local market jumped to 800 Nakfa a piece if you could get it. Furthermore, if the building materials to be used for construction were from natural resources, their impact on the environment needs to be assessed.
- PoWER revealed that construction of shelter should be done based on participatory methodology that involves the direct participation of local populations in providing their labor. However, in some of the PoWER projects the implementing NGOs found it difficult to mobilize and manage the local labor. Furthermore, the beneficiary households were mainly women, children and elderly who lack the physical labor required for construction.
- The benefits gained by harnessing people's skills and abilities to refurbish their own houses was not learnt and applied across agencies. Some NGOs placed a undue reliance on contractors in the construction of new houses. This resulted in resources going to feed contractor's profit margins rather than being applied to materials and technical support to assist with self-reconstruction.
- The shelter component of the PoWER programme confirmed that the mere construction of shelter does not lead to the settlement of a targeted group in resettlement sites. That is, the construction of shelter needs to be accompanied with the provision of water, health and educational services that serve the community. Furthermore, the targeted group should be engaged in the planning stage of the project for a better community buy-in of the output of the project.
- There were instances in Tsorona town, where the shelter package offered by PoWER was initially to rehabilitate existing housing units destroyed by the war and vandalism regardless of which they belonged. The idea was to put a roof on the head of those who were returning. Hence, it was agreed by the local authorities that the money collected from renters would be put in a revolving fund until the rehabilitation cost of the owner-renter is fully covered. Moreover, the PoWER programme was also catering to the needs of IDP farmers who were the poorest among the poor and where ownership of houses in the community was one hundred percent.

Permanent Shelter - Ambeste Geleba - Dubub region

- Experience from shelter construction in all the recovery programmes revealed that it is a very complex undertaking. In the Joint programme different options have been tried. The first was provision of shelter kits and money to cover labor costs, especially women/elderly headed households, and the second was provision of a fixed amount of money. This was the least desirable option. There was no effective mechanism to push the beneficiaries to complete the building. In some villages, it even had undesirable results. The returnees started to sell the corrugated iron sheets and make money. However, the very high material cost for constructing permanent shelter and the labour it demands against the demographic composition of the beneficiaries has constrained the progress in this sector. The provision of cash to individual households does not appear to provide a quick fix to the housing problems. Furthermore, the absence of readily available construction materials and the delays in shelter construction is forcing people to cut whatever scarce vegetation existed in the return or settlement areas, thereby causing devastation of the fragile ecosystem prevailing in the semi-arid conditions.

Mihrad Chele, Southern region

- The shelter component of the Joint Programme revealed that cash assistance on installment basis triggers the beneficiaries to complete construction of their shelters on due time provided that the availability of construction materials in the market was secured. (Arrangements were made to procure such materials from international markets at considerably reduced prices).

Inauguration of the Shelter Programme in Mihrad Chele

Mihrad Chele Youth singing on the inauguration day

Shelter Assistance &Rehabilitation

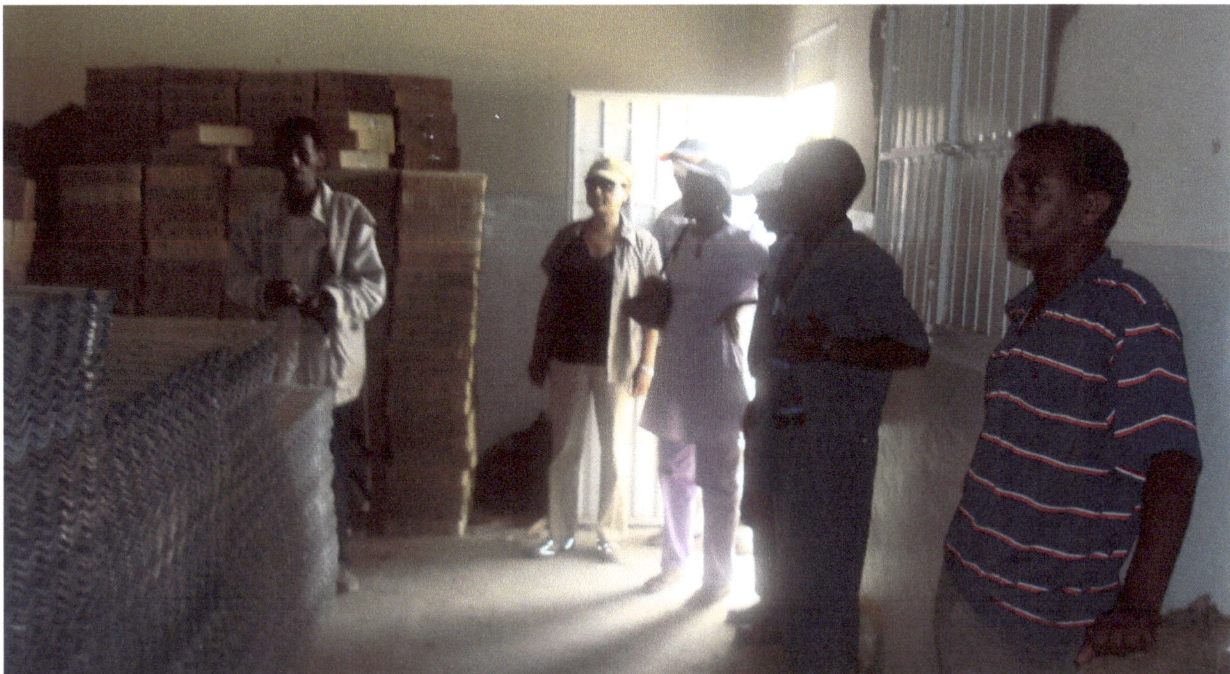

Mihrad Chelle – store for corrugated iron sheets for the shelter programme

Mihrad Chelle – Partial View of houses built

Water and Sanitation:

Water Supply

- The UNDP Recovery Unit that oversaw the implementers of the joint programme ensured the availability of water supply systems prior to the movement of the IDPs/Expellees from camps to their place of origin and resettlement sites. In some of the villages with acute water source shortages, micro dams and ponds have been constructed to upgrade the recharge capability of the water sources as well as bore holes and spring protection measures.
- There tended to be strong community buy-in to these projects. The expense and technical complexity involved in making improvements to water supplies made this sub-sector, one which communities were unable to execute alone without external assistance.
- The water components of PoWER revealed that coordination with local representatives of the project areas was imperative for speedy and effective implementation of the projects, in order to benefit from the professional experience of local technicians and from their knowledge of the whole water supply system in their respective localities. Moreover, their involvement in works and discussions on how to construct the works would enable them to maintain it better once the system is rehabilitated and/or constructed. The technicians were not brought in from nearby towns; they were local people living in the villages.

- Community involvement also added an element of sustainability to the projects. The heavy involvement of the communities at all phases is such that they felt a strong stake in the project and its product, a strong sense of ownership, and therefore were assets in the operation and maintenance of the water supply schemes.
- It was agreed at the planning stage that repair and maintenance of the water supply system should be borne by the benefiting community to ascertain the sustainability of the outputs of the water projects. In some other areas lack of a sense of ownership led to negligent use of the water facilities. Apparently, the need for training and capacity building of the local communities was crucial the a sustainable organization, operation and management of the water supply system. Furthermore, the salary of operators and fountain caretakers should be covered by the community so as to assure its after the external assistance ceases. Hence water committees were established in each water project site and they generally charge the beneficiaries for water they consume to cover the cost of maintenance and the salary of a guard, if the situation warrants it.
- Another important lesson learned from successful water supply systems was that the early establishment of a village water committee could foster greater beneficiary participation, resulting in a stronger sense of ownership and willingness to accept operations and maintenance responsibility among project beneficiaries. Furthermore, representation of women in the village water committee needs ensured better results. The water supply component of the PoWER programme had established village water committees and the committee received relevant training to support their participation, but much more is required such as incorporating this into national policies.
- The water supply system intervention was accompanied with establishing a water committee and provision of training to the committee on water management, the rules governing water usage, protection of the water schemes and the responsibility of the water committee. Again, adequate representation of women in the committee was ensuring at least two out of the five members of the committee were women.
- Even when a rural community is well trained and organized to operate and administer its water systems, it still needs some form of external support and guidance over the short term. This is especially the case for a smaller rural community, which may lack the economies of scale and resource base of a larger community. The long-term support to a rural community is based on a number of important functions, which includes active monitoring of system performance, coordination and facilitation of linkages between the community and key resource entities, and, where appropriate, direct interventions to resolve specific problems that the community itself cannot manage alone.

- The shortage of diesel oil to power generators that power pumps has also pushed the introduction of solar panels to pump the water. These solutions although expensive in the short term were cost effective in the medium and long term, since the alternative energy is in abundance in Eritrea and the maintenance for at least the first three years is minimal compared to diesel powered generators.
- Despite the widespread popularity of community water management committees among donors and implementing agencies, low water supply sustainability levels and a cursory look at existing systems indicate that it is not the panacea it is often presented to be. Hence, if community management systems were to be sustainable, they require ongoing support from an overseeing institution, such as the MoLWE Water Resources Department, to provide encouragement and motivation, monitoring, participatory planning, capacity building and specialist technical assistance.
- The choice of the water supply system in addition to technical criteria, needs to take into account the cost effectiveness not only for its construction but also its future maintenance. For hand dug wells, which were by and large not very deep, the returnees have expressed their preference for hand pumps rather than diesel generators, which were expensive to operate. Again hard duty hand pumps have to be selected that can easily weather rough treatment and accelerated wear and tear.

Kinito Microdam, Southern region

- Moreover, it has often been observed that the diesel run generators for water pumps have either been encountering intermittent mechanical failures or been running out of fuel supplies, thereby causing interruption in the water supply for people and livestock. The water supply systems have been revisited in light of their appropriateness to the remoteness of the places, the low technical levels, scarcity of spare parts and high fuel prices. Hence, for the period 2007 to 2012, only solar energy based water supply schemes have been constructed.
- In some water projects of the PoWER program the shortage of qualified local contractors hampered and narrowed the choices of selecting the best who could deliver quality projects. This also added to the overall cost of the projects resulting from uncompetitive prices.

- In some of the mountainous villages of Debub region, it is very difficult to undertake any construction of water supply schemes because the villages were inaccessible by vehicle. Hence, all the construction materials need to be transported by pack animals or on the backs of people. At times, the terrain is rugged and not suitable to lay the pipelines from the water source to the reservoirs and to the public fountains. However with full commitment and participation of the community, through cash for work, the construction of the water supply schemes have been highly successful.

Sanitation

- In most of the projects of the programme, return/resettlement latrines were non-existent. Once these limited number of latrines were constructed, it has been noted that orientation regarding their use, cleaning and sterilization and conservation should immediately follow.
- Sanitation technologies/typologies need to be in accordance with availability of local materials and building practices, local economic conditions, and local cultural practices and beliefs. In this way, many practical problems could be avoided, and 'ownership' of the technology is more likely to develop. Technical solutions to the problem of safe excreta disposal do not translate easily from one country to another. For instance, the toilets constructed by PoWER projects in some areas were inappropriate since they required water to flush solid waste and ample water supply may not be available.

Pit Latrine: Ham, Southern region

- Space and ground conditions affect the choice of technology, as do social and cultural preferences. The success or otherwise of sanitation programmes is often based on the appropriateness of technology being promoted and unfortunately is often either too prescriptive or based on little community consultation. Each variation of construction has advantages and disadvantages depending upon the local circumstances and therefore the choice of technology should, as far as reasonably possible be left to the household/village to determine.

Pit Latrine: Akran, Southern region

- It has been observed that the Ventilated Improved Pit (VIP) Toilet, when correctly designed, operated and maintained, has proved to be an acceptable, cost-effective, hygienic and environmentally friendly sanitation system. While there were always certain disadvantages associated with any sanitation technology, if the required attention is paid to all the diverse aspects involved, particularly the social and cultural aspects, then there is no reason why VIP toilets should not become acceptable to the vast majority of people who do not presently enjoy the benefits of a well designed and constructed toilet. (Cite the experimental five villages in Debub and Gash Barka. Emphasis to protect water sources and catchment areas. Difference between rural setting and semi-urban layout of villages require different solutions). (Attach some photographs)
- Sanitation facilities rarely improve health or hygiene on their own. However, hygiene promotion can change people's hygiene behavior and translate water and sanitation investments into health benefits. Therefore, an effective health education and hygiene promotion by Ministry of Health have been vital to improve hygiene behavior, to encourage the proper use and maintenance of sanitation facilities and to generate strong demand for improved sanitation facilities.

PHAST Training in Senafe, Southern region

- While maximum community participation is highly desirable, it is not the number one priority in the middle of a potential epidemic, saving lives is the top priority. This may mean also taking a more directive approach in terms of latrine construction and use. Under this scenario the community participation approach is not abandoned completely, it is only reduced or adapted in light of the life threatening circumstances. (Camp Hygiene and health issues)
- Learning from other experiences, it has also been noted that Water and sanitation support demands the participation of prospective beneficiary communities starting from problem identification all the way to implementation. In the identification of needs it was noted that community consultations led to a realization that there was also an urgent need not only to build water-points and public fountains but to construct laundry facilities as well, close to the boreholes to meet women's needs. Culturally, washing is done at the water source and this can lead to a polluted water site.

Social Facilities:

Health

- Sanitation must be provided and planned for all return and settlement sites to avoid the outbreak of epidemic diseases
- Health related activities supported by PoWER were an integrated package composed of building rehabilitation, the provision of medical supplies and equipment, supplemented by the provision of technical advice and support. It was evident that health practitioners owned their facilities and benefited from the transference of skill and best practices in their field.

Health Station in Gerenfit Resettlement village, Gash Barka region

- The assistance of the health component of the PoWER programme was being dove-tailed into long term preventative campaigns such as malaria control and HIV/aids. There was also a high degree of mutual respect and co-operation between international NGOs and their Eritrean counterparts.
- For some communities the preventive and curative health facilities being offered by the PoWER programme is much better than what they had before the conflict.
- The health sector intervention of the Joint Parallel financed projects focused on the objective of contributing to the improvement in the quality of life, with particular reference to the reproductive health of women, men and adolescents and to the achievement of broad-based sustainable development. The beneficiaries of the project were the most vulnerable, primarily pregnant and lactating women and adolescents and youth of reproductive age living in humanitarian crisis situations (IDPs, refugees and returnees) in selected regions.

Education

Make-Shift School in Gerenfit

- The school construction programme have given UNDP an opportunity to work outside traditional urban areas; to have direct contact with the beneficiaries particularly the rural poor and grassroots organizations; to take a leadership role in empowering the poor by assisting them build/construct, and manage/maintain their facilities.
- The possible change of the School Academic Calendar to suit the lifestyle of Pastoralists is an encouraging innovation that needs to be pursued vigorously. By the same token, it may also be helpful to examine, the Mobile School concept, as recommended by the Evaluation Team of the PROFERI programme that have has successfully tried in many parts of the Asian Sub-continent.
- The PoWER funded activities in the education sub-sector were mainly focused on the reconstruction and rehabilitation of schools and the provision of furniture and teaching aids. These inputs brought benefits to the war-affected students as well as other students that were provided with learning materials. That is, the intervention reached a wider community.
- The PoWER programme revealed that in situations of planning for emergency, education needs also should be given top priority like shelter, health and food. Hence the educational component of the programme had started immediately side by side with the other interventions. In the emergency situation the PoWER programme contributed to the continuity of education for the IDPs and Expellees when they were in camps as well as when they returned to their place of origin and resettlement places, through the provision of makeshift class rooms and learning materials.
- Interventions in the educational sector have enhanced the transition to more sustainable development in Eritrea.
- In some instances, the makeshift classrooms in the camps were dismantled and erected in the locations of return/resettlement villages and this enabled students to pursue their education without any interruption.
- The construction of schools through the Joint Programme enhanced continued access to education. However, this needs to be augmented with some facilities such as teachers' houses, library and demonstration rooms etc. to improve the quality of education.

To support the achievement of this UNDAF outcome, the CPAP was focused on three programme areas as follows: (i) supporting community based reintegration of IDPs, expellees and host communities (JP with UNICEF, WHO, UNFPA, UNHCR, UNAIDS); (ii) Support to Mine Action; and (iii) Social and economic integration of demobilized soldiers. UNDP placed substantial efforts on the first component dealing with reintegration of IDPs and Expellees, with far less emphasis on the last two components.[56] Thus the evaluation focused more on the first component - ***Support to community- based reintegration of IDPs, expellees and host communities***[57]

56 The Land Mine Action Programme was undertaken between 2002-2006, while the bulk of the work on demobilization also took place earlier.

57 This section draws extensively on the Final Evaluation of the Joint programme on IDPs and Expellees undertaken in 2010 and has been complimented by field visits during this CPAP Final Evaluation.

However, several thousand faced obstacles to return, for a variety of reasons, including their farmlands not being safe from landmines and UXOs, and remained in camps, receiving assistance from government and the international community.

External Independent Evaluation/Assessment

Ensuring that IDPs, expellees, returnees and other war-affected and drought-affected were reintegrated and had secure livelihoods and access to basic social services, was one of the national priorities of the Government of Eritrea. In accordance with this, the UN System and the GSE agreed that Emergency/Recovery to be one of the focus areas of the UNDAF (2007-2011). The goal of UNDAF was in this regard was "By 2009, assist the Government through an integrated multi-sector approach, to ensure that IDPs, expellees, returnees and other war and drought-affected are reintegrated and have secure livelihoods and access to basic services".

According to the External Evaluation of the Programme, "Contributions to support the JP came from a variety of sources: UNDP and GoSE, financial support by the Norwegian Government, Italian Government, USAID, UNOCHA and European Union. Out of a total program budget of USD 60 million, some USD 46 million has been mobilized of which over 90% has been delivered, making it a highly efficient operation".

The evaluation team of this programme led by Tijan Jallo and Gebremedhin 58 judged the JP was a highly successful programme, all the more remarkable given the complex socio-political context within which it was implemented. All IDPs and expellees that were still in camps at the start of the programme (17,690 households or 71,207 persons) have been successfully and safely transported with their belongings from camps to their villages of origin or new settlements in the designated areas from 2005 to 2008. Hence, all IDP/expellees camps were closed by March 2008.

The evaluation team concluded that "the JP has been an effective and successful programme and has undoubtedly helped and provided an opportunity for large segments of the war – affected population to begin to restore their lives and livelihoods. It has been effective in addressing the needs of the vulnerable such as, female-headed households, children and poor families, and contributed to closing the chapter on war and displacement in Eritrea, and by helping to rebuild critical socio-economic infrastructure, restore livelihoods is also contributing to laying the foundation to medium and long-term socio-economic development, to poverty reduction and attainment of the UN Millennium Development Goals for the country. The JP has succeeded inconsistently responding and providing support to very deserving communities in a very complex and politically sensitive context in a commendable way. Furthermore, there were several obvious indicators of positive impact on the ground and on the lives and livelihoods of individuals, households and communities."

The functional movement areas of villages of origin and resettlement areas were cleared of land mines and/or marked with signs, and Mine Risk Education given to communities. Additional surveys were conducted, and continuous road and farmland verification is being conducted. Mine action, as part of the overall recovery programme, has been very effective, and

58 Tijan Jallow

there were no reports of casualities in villages of origin or resettled areas so far. Massive rehabilitation, reconstruction and reintegration works have been going on between 2005 and 2011. IDPs/expellees and returnees were provided with shelter, basic social services, improved stoves, home solar systems, farm tools, oxen, land clearance and traction, seeds (12 kg/ha), and land (1-2 ha/household) to ensure livelihood security. Consequently, IDPs and expellees have started a dignified and purposeful life, free from the uncertainties of camp life. In the focus group discussion, beneficiaries reported: ***"In the camps, yes we had enough to eat, but now we have our own land, our own houses, and we are now in full control of our lives"***.

Provision of agricultural inputs (farmland, oxen, tractor service, seed, and pesticide the improved agricultural production, which in turn helped households become more food secure. Due to good rain in 2010, supported households were able to harvest enough food, which allowed them to meet their food requirements from their own production. They were able to store seed from their 2010 harvest for the 2011 planting season and also managed to pay for tractor services. This clearly shows that IDPs and drought-affected population in the target regions were in a much better position in terms of food production and were on track to achieve household food security. The good harvest of 2010 has already impacted on the market as evidenced by the reduction in the price of cereals such as sorghum and taff (a stable food for the highland areas). Beneficiary communities also got a fairly good harvest in 2011. The favorable climatic conditions of 2010 and 2011 improved animal feed situation which in turn contributed to increased livestock production.

The joint programme succeeded in securing underground water in most IDP areas, but it also built micro dams in communities where studies have shown that only surface water harvesting was feasible. Overall, the construction of the micro-dams brought great relief to beneficiary communities in targeted areas as they no longer have to endure the pain of travelling long distances in search of water for themselves and livestock. In annual evaluation and assessment meetings in 2010 and 2011, the communities have always expressed their satisfaction with the projects as they have already started to enjoy the benefits resulting from improved availability of water for them and their livestock. In Adi Maelel and Adi Tsetser, the representatives of the communities have expressed their desire to see the construction of the water distribution system completed in 2012, so that they would derive the full benefits of the projects. With the exception of the micro dam in Megel Shilalo, the construction of water distribution systems for the remaining micro dams is completed and fully operational. To reduce livestock pressure in areas where micro-dams were constructed, the joint programme financed the construction of several ponds to serve as a source of livestock water during certain months of the year until the onset of the rainy season.

Adi Maelel Micro Dam, Gash Barka

The distribution of improved, fuel efficient stove (Adhanet) to IDPs/expellees return/resettlement areas contributed to reduced deforestation and time and energy wasted to collect firewood, as well as improved health for women and other members of the household due to less emission of smoke. The provision of solar home systems, although limited in number, resulted in households having healthier and better living conditions and being allowed to carry out evening activities including the school children being able to study at night with adequate/proper lighting.

Household Solar Panel for lighting, mobile charging and powering radio

Traditional Stove - Mogogo

Improved Fuel Efficient Stove

The programme was characterized by sound and effective partnerships (donors, UN agencies, government, regional administrations, and affected populations). By developing strong links with regional administrations, the program has not only ensured rapid and effective implementation, but has strengthened programme ownership by the regional administrations and contributed critical capacity building support. The lean and efficient programme management structures and integration within existing regional structures have ensured that most of the programme resources were directed at the beneficiaries rather than the traditional heavy and costly programme implementation structures. However, while maintaining the strong decentralized operational links with regional administrations, there were benefits to establishing stronger links with central government/line ministries in order to better anchor the future programme to evolving national policy but importantly also to feed the very significant lessons learned from the JP into national policy making process as Eritrea shifts to longer-term development.

According to the international and national evaluators, the JP was highly effective as it was a government-driven initiative and the structures established were appropriate and accountable to authorities/stakeholders at different levels (Central government, donors, UNDP, regional/local Administrations, communities).

The main lesson to be derived from this experience was that it is possible to handle emergency/humanitarian operations within existing structures in an effective and efficient manner without recourse to costly and unsustainable parallel structures. In the case of the UNDP Recovery programmes, Eritrea appears to set a good example in this regard. The planned outputs were delivered well and the outcomes largely achieved, except when budget constraints stood in the way (e.g. shelter for Gash Barka where 8,000 housing units were constructed but an equal number of households were left to fend for themselves). Factors that contributed to such effectiveness were the relevance and appropriateness of the support provided, as well as the fact that the regions were in the driving seat and the planning process was flexible and adaptive.

The joint programme also enhanced the planning, implementation, monitoring and reporting capacities of the regional and sub-regional administrations in Gash Barka, Debub and Southern Red Sea regions. This was achieved through the provision of training and office equipment. The capacity building support has also benefited sub-regional administration responsible for the provision of technical support to communities and monitoring implementation of joint programme activities. Consequently, regions have become more efficient in coordinating programme activities and delivering projects, though their monitoring activities were affected by occasional shortage of transportation facilities. UNDP Recovery Unit made efforts to improve the quality of progress reports prepared by the regional and sub-regional administrations by developing and disseminating reporting templates or formats which were also translated into local languages e.g. Tigrigna to serve as a basis for the preparation of quarterly progress reports.

Beneficiary communities actively participated in project implementation by contributing labour and materials (e.g. shelter, micro dams, ponds, soil and water construction). In addition to saving cost for the project, community participation resulted in quick project delivery, improved sense of ownership, improved implementation capacity, and enhanced sustainability. To enhance project implementation, communities were empowered through training, coaching and mentoring in a number of areas including project planning and management, rangeland management, animal husbandry, soil and water conservation, etc. Capacity building interventions also strengthened community-based organizations by establishing rangeland and water committees and facilitated the development of water and rangeland bylaws.

Impact of the Results Achieved

In terms of impact, the evaluation team noted that there were significant indications of positive impact – the statement recorded by a Research Assistant of one beneficiary: "***In the camps, yes we had enough to eat, but now we have our own land, our own houses, and we are now in full control of our lives***", perhaps best sums up the measure of overall impact. Moreover, the Chief Priest of Ham Village located on the top of a mountain range informed the Recovery Senior Technical Advisor that they would soon be equal to Asmara and receive door to door connection to the main water system. Much socio-economic infrastructure has been built where previously there was none, and this has definitely improved access to social services. Previously women in Ham and other villages' trekked long distances on treacherous foot pass, on a daily basis to fetch water but this is now much reduced in many communities. Conservation works were rebuilding the natural resource base that will contribute in the long-term not only to enhancing productivity but also conserving biodiversity and reducing soil/land degradation and ensuring long-term sustainability. Moreover, SWC structures were often built on farmers' own land which means that their maintenance over the long run is taken care of.

Compared to their pre-displacement situation, IDPs have now better access to basic social services such as water (for human and animal consumption), shelter and school facilities. However, they were still on the road for some mountain communities to reach their pre-displacement position in terms of their livelihoods.

This is in sharp contrast to communities in Lalai Gash (Adi Maelel, Tselim Kelai, Adi Tsetser, She'hate, Girme and others who were already on their feet and achieved sustainable livelihoods far beyond what they had before the displacement.

Field visit to a Micro Dam with Donors

Field Visit to Shelter project for IDPs with a Donor in Girme, Gash Barka

Sustainability of the various components

Since shelter and school facilities were locally made, beneficiary communities in sustaining it have so far experienced no major technical problems. Beneficiaries have augmented UNDP cash and material support through their labour and material contribution, which, in addition to saving cost, resulted in improved sense of ownership, which is an important prerequisite for project sustainability. During the field monitoring visits, it was observed that some beneficiaries made efforts to improve the interior or exterior parts of the houses, build additional rooms and constructed latrines.

Micro dam construction was carried out with the active involvement of beneficiary communities who contributed labour to treat catchment areas and collect stones needed to strengthen the embankment and spill ways. They have willingly participated because the micro dams have addressed their most crucial problem, which is shortage of water for human and animal consumption. The participation of the communities during project implementation was expected to improve project sustainability. They have also established water point committees who were trained by the technical staff of the Ministry of Agriculture. As part of ensuring project sustainability, most communities hired guards to protect the micro dams (e.g. Shilalo community was paying a monthly salary of 1,500 Nakfa for the guard). They have also developed water bylaws to govern communities' water use and management activities.

In addition, the regional Infrastructure Departments in the respective regions have, through their water supply units established and trained village water committees on how to operate and maintain water supply systems. Communities pay for fetching water from the public fountain, and the cash collected is used to cover the salary of a guard and the cost of operation and maintenance. Although there has so far been no damage to the solar system, communities may in future face problems getting maintenance services for this technology. Solar power maintenance expertise appears to be limited at the regional level, and as a result they will continue to need support from the Water Resources Department of the Ministry of Land, Water and Environment or the private sector. It is therefore important to put in place maintenance arrangement, as the skills may not be available close to the project areas.

Ensuring that IDPs, expellees, returning refugees and other war-affected and drought-affected communities were reintegrated and have secure livelihoods and access to basic social services, as one of the key national priorities of the Government of Eritrea in its quest to ensure post-war rehabilitation and reconstruction of the country after years of war and displacement. The evaluation team concluded that the JP has undoubtedly helped and provided an opportunity for large segments of the war – affected population to begin to restore their lives and livelihoods. It has been effective in addressing the needs of the vulnerable such as, female-headed households, children and poor families, and contributed to closing the chapter on war and displacement in Eritrea, and by helping to rebuild critical socio-economic infrastructure and restored livelihoods is also contributing to laying the foundation to medium and long-term socio-economic development, to poverty reduction and attainment of the MDGs for the country.

The JP has succeeded in consistently responding and providing support to very deserving communities. IDPs/expellees and returnees were provided with shelter, basic social services, improved stoves, home solar systems, farm tools, oxen, land clearance and traction, seeds (12 kg/ha), and land (1-2 ha/household) to ensure livelihood security. Consequently, IDPs and expellees have started a dignified and purposeful life, free from the uncertainties of camp life. In the focus group discussion, beneficiaries reported: "In the camps, yes we had enough to eat, but now we have our own land, our own houses, and we are now in full control of our lives".

Household level solar system for lighting, mobile charging and radio listening

Provision of agricultural inputs (farmland, oxen, tractor service, seed, and pesticide) improved agricultural production which in turn helped households become more food secure. Due to good rain in 2010, supported households were able to harvest enough food which allowed them to meet their food requirements from their own production. They were also able to store seed from their 2010 harvest for the 2011 planting season and also managed to pay for tractor services. This clearly shows that IDPs and drought-affected population in the target regions were in a much better position in terms of food production and were on track to achieving household food security. The good harvest of 2010 has already impacted on the market as evidenced by the reduction in the price of cereals such as sorghum and taff. Beneficiary communities also got fairly good harvest in 2011. The favorable climatic conditions of 2010 and 2011 improved the animal feed situation that in turn contributed to increased livestock production.

The construction of the micro-dams brought great relief to beneficiary communities in IDP areas as they have no longer have to endure the pain of travelling long distances in search of water for their livestock. The communities visited during the regular monitoring trips expressed their satisfaction with the projects as they have already started to enjoy the benefits resulting from improved availability of water for them and their livestock. The distribution of improved, fuel efficient stove (Adhanet) contributed to reduced deforestation and time and energy wasted to collect firewood, as well as improved health for women and other members of the household due to less emission of smoke. The provision of solar home systems resulted in households having healthier and better living conditions and being allowed to carry out evening activities under superior lighting. The problem of maintenance of the solar home system is already felt in certain areas as some of bulbs were out of use and beneficiaries do not know what to do with them.

Field visit to Gash Barka region with two Donors

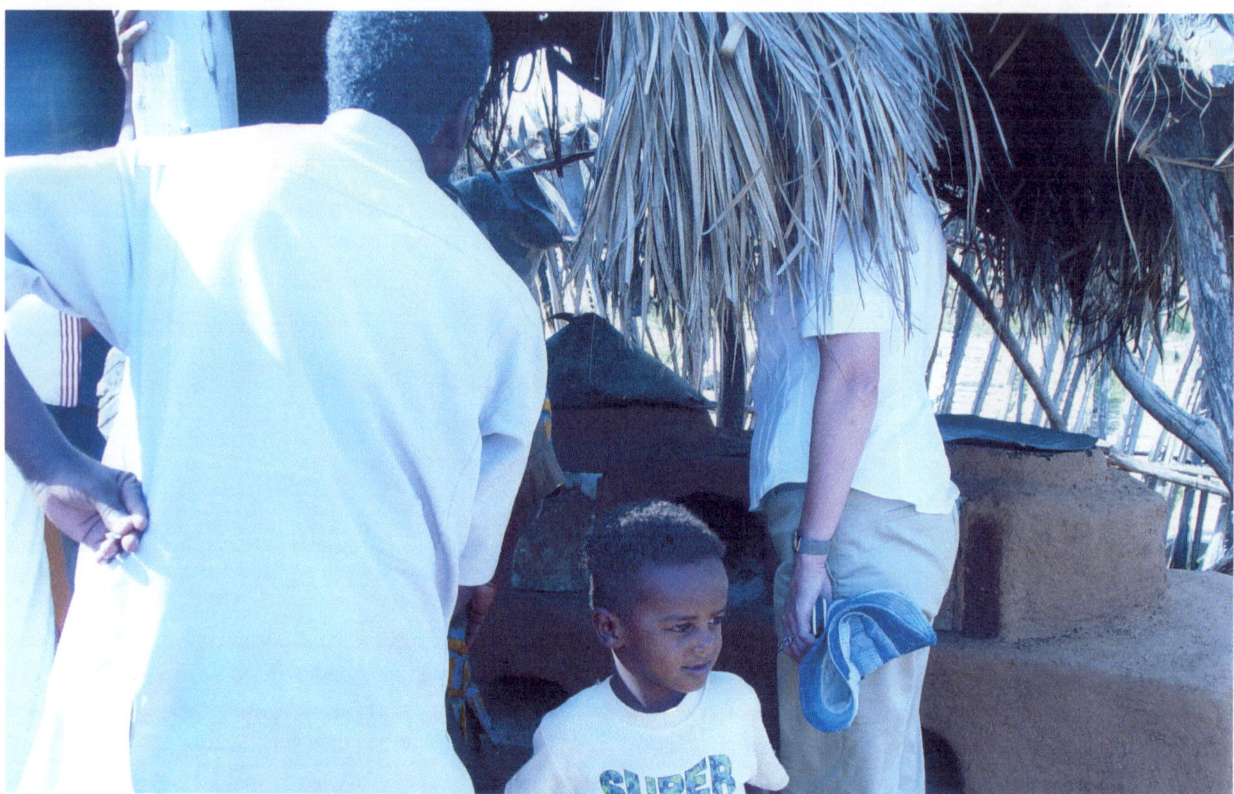

Visit to Fuel efficient traditional stove – Adhanet (Mogogo) with a Donor

Fuel efficient traditional stove – Adhanet (Mogogo)

5.9 Transition and Early Recovery Programme (TER)

The Transition and Early Recovery programme (2010 – 2012) is a continuation and an expansion of the previous program "Supporting the Return/Resettlement of IDPs/Expellees to the Communities of Origin/new resettlement areas in Eritrea (2004-2009)". It came into being following the recommendations made during mid-term review and by the final independent evaluation of the previous programme, and has mainly addressed livelihood security of drought affected vulnerable populations in three target regions of Gash Barka, Debub and Southern Red Sea.

OBJECTIVES

The main goal of the programme is to increase and diversify livelihood security and opportunities for 30,000 Resource Poor HHs (64% F). In order to attain the goal, the programme set the following objectives:

- Increase crop productivity and resilience to recurrent drought and effect of war
- Restocking and improvement of animal production
- Improve water supply in the communities
- Diversify the source of income
- Promote environmental protection
- Enhance access to basic social services and shelter
- Increase the capacity of partners and communities in participatory methods and project management

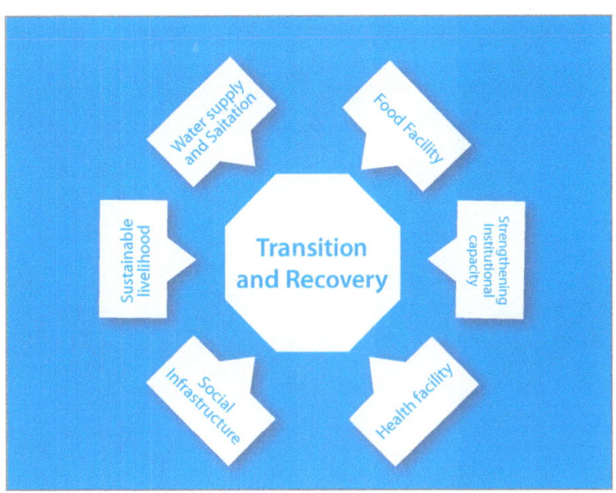

The programme addressed the main emergency needs including food insecurity, emergency shelter, potable water supply, emergency educational and health services. All planned activities were performed and their results were attained within the implementation period of the transition and early recovery program. Despite challenges related to lack/shortage of fuel for tractor ploughing and for field monitoring as well as other operational difficulties including the Government's change in its cooperation policy with the UN system, remarkable results were achieved. For all the indicators, the performance has reached the planned targets. In this case, substantial early recovery interventions, which were pre-requisites to the long term stabilization and development, have been successfully undertaken in the drought affected vulnerable communities of the country.

Special mention has to be made regarding the Water Supply component– especially the use of Underground Cisterns.[59] Provision of water is an important component of the recovery activities in the return/resettlement villages of former IDPs/Expellees in Eritrea. The most difficult challenges were in two categories: a) those who returned to Highland areas on top of mountain ranges, and those who live in arid zones of the country like the Southern Red Sea region.

In Highland Villages, it is futile to dig a borehole for underground water on top of the mountains which range from 2,000-2500 meters above sea level. The villagers used to go to the nearest riverbed, a journey that takes on the average 1-1.5 hours one way which was a great burden on women and girls. The only solution was to impound every drop of water in the rainy season in the form of micro-dams, and ponds (28 dams were built in 2007-2012).

Villages in arid areas where the annual rainfall is less than 100 mm per year; the only source is the runoff from the highlands. We could not build micro-dams, since the climate is harsh and any impounded surface water will evaporate completely in a week or two.

Traditionally the villagers have been using underground cisterns for centuries. It was therefore, prudent to build creatively on this age old wisdom of construction.

59 Final Report on Transition and Early Recovery – 2010-2012

Tractor Ploughing in Tsorona

Eritrea is highly vulnerable to climate change and variability which in many cases leads to droughts, floods, and rainfall unpredictability, drastically affecting pastoralists and internally displaced persons or returnees affected by the 1998-2000 Eritrea/Ethiopia border war. The affected communities in this programme were mainly in Southern Red Sea region, with vast and arid coastal plains stretching parallel to the Red Sea for almost 400 kilometers. The climate is hot and dry for most of the year. Temperatures reach up to 46 Celsius in the hot summer months (April to September) and 36 during the day/20 Celsius at night from October up to March. As much as 85% of the population are pastoralists seasonally moving with their goats, sheep and camels, 10% are involved in salt farming, trading and workers, while 5% are involved in the fishing industry.

In the villages selected, the area is inhabited by pastoralists who move with their animals mainly goats, sheep and camel from oasis to another oasis, in search of pasture and water. Traditionally they have depended on seasonal rivers and their customary knowledge to access water. These rivers dry up quickly and when they flow, it is for a very short time and in an unpredictable manner. The pastoralists' traditional means of survival is continually being challenged, their indigenous knowledge of collecting and harvesting water is put to test as a result of climate variability. Wells become saline due to intrusion of sea water. Communities and animals travel long distances to find fresh water. This search can sometimes take close to nine hours. In general, households are less able to recuperate from the increase in recurrent droughts, putting pastoralists' livelihood at risk

Traditional water harvesting structure

The pastoral households dig wells and harvest runoff. At least for the last 50 years they have dug water basins (***Birikuts)*** and lined them with cement. Traditional water management practices are stressed due to recurrent droughts. Additional or improved types of water sources are required to cope with the increasing water shortages by collecting run-off and flood water, which increases access to water and recharges underground water tables.

Supported by the UNDP and the regional administration of the Southern Red Sea, the pastoral communities were organized to construct innovated structures of underground cisterns around their grazing lands; where the sizes of cisterns fed by river flow were expanded three times larger than the traditional size; where ladders were provided to gain entry into the cisterns to clean and avoid siltation; livestock troughs were provided separately.

Restocking of goats and construction of Cisterns for both human and livestock

3 underground cisterns, each of them containing $217M^3$, $217M^3$ and $1{,}190M^3$ of water were constructed in Debai Sima village according to the new innovations. An additional 4 innovative cisterns were built in 2012 in Ferere, Areta, Allale, and Shekaito villages in the SRS region. These reservoirs are capable of providing water for some 4,000 animals and can keep water during the critical water shortage periods for up.

Parallel to the provision of access to water: initial restocking was conducted in four villages in Southern Red Sea Region including Debai Sima. 334 returned/resettled former IDP households received 4,008 goats, 12 goats were given to each of the households. Due to the short breeding cycle of small ruminants, the target households have been able to regain normal herd size of 20 goats per household.

The programme was implemented over a period of three years starting 1st April 2010 to 31st December 2012, and a total amount of 21,450,370 USD was disbursed towards its implementation. The following were major results attained by the programme.

TRANSITION AND EARLY RECOVERY – ACHIEVEMENTS (APRIL 2010 –DECEMBER 2012)

- Shelter: Some 2,213 household in Debub and Gash Barka regions were able to construct their own houses and started to live in dignified shelters.
- Water Supply: a total of 17 water supply structures have been constructed and some 10,289 households and their livestock (72,845 heads of animals) have secured year round access to safe water supply in Debub, Gash Barka and Southern Red sea regions
- Sanitation: A total of 2000 household have constructed improved pit latrines in their homesteads and attended health and sanitation training, as a result of which health conditions of the target households have greatly improved.

Household Pit Latrine in Ham village, Senafe sub –region

Senafe District Hospital

Meshal Akhran Community school, Southern regiom

Adi Gulti – Southern region

Livelihoods security: the programme restored human capital, physical assets/social services, natural capital, financial assets and social capital of vulnerable pastoral and agro-pastoral families in the three regions through initial restocking, distribution of agricultural inputs and provision of ploughing services, emergency employment through cash for work as well as rehabilitation of grazing lands through soil and water conservation works and reseeding with improved grass seeds.

Basic social services: A district hospital, a health centre and 2 schools have been built in localities that were most deprived from basic social services and greatly contributed to achieving minimum conditions for living with dignity for some 21,547 and 751 households respectively.

Resource Mobilization & Partnerships: The UNDP Recovery programme was once again highly successful and effective in mobilizing, managing and delivering substantial amount of resources to meet its programme objectives. For the period 2010-2012, UNDP ear-marked USD 6,283,837.00 of its core resources. Figures show that UNDP Recovery Unit, over the 3 years of the TER, mobilized USD 15,711,419 for its TER programme, exceeding its resource mobilization target by three times. The UNDP Recovery Unit raised USD 2.50 for every 1 USD spent from core resources, demonstrating a high leveraging capacity. The Transition & Early Recovery programme was the most successful and delivery of the recovery programme resources was also excellent.

UNDP Recovery Unit forged highly effective partnerships with relevant central government ministries (MND, MoH, and MoLWE), regional administrations, project communities and donors. At all these levels, the Recovery Unit has earned respect and trust. At all these levels, UNDP was regarded as a credible and trusted partner, recognized for its flexibility and adaptability.

Programme Management: The Transition and Early Recovery (TER) programme was implemented through a high breed of national execution modality and was efficiently managed at all levels. Moreover, TER adopted a highly successful project implementation modality (learning from the earlier recovery programmes) by working directly through regional administrations, and in the process strengthened their capacities to plan, execute and monitor and report on projects. This modality in the view of the Evaluation team represents best practice in the field of post-conflict recovery internationally.

Despite the restrictions imposed by the central government on the movement of Recovery Unit Staff, monitoring and evaluation was performed in a creative and effective manner. On site monitoring was done by the Recovery Unit technical staff when allowed, the respective Governors of the three regions had meetings with the Recovery Unit whenever they were in Asmara for other meetings, consultations by telephone were made on major policy issues that needed immediate attention between the Senior Technical Advisor and the respective Governors as needed. Special efforts were also made to develop the appropriate instruments and templates to enhance follow up and reporting.

Adi Beza, Southern region

Adi Beza, Stone Bunding, Southern region

Adi Kemcho – Soil Bunding

Areza, Stone Bunding, Southern region

Areza, Stone Bunding, Southern region

6.9.1 Transition and Early Recovery: Lessons Learned

- IDPs are now living in dignified shelter which protects them from the vagaries of nature such as rain, heat, cold, and dust. Compared to tents or even huts in which they lived, either in IDP camps or in their home villages before being displaced, the shelter support provided them cleaner, comfortable, safer and more hygienic houses. The shelter support enabled households to live in more secure dwellings, being less exposed to malaria and wildlife attacks.
- According to the participants of the Annual Assessment meetings in the 2 large Regional Administrations, the good rains of 2010 and 2011 contributed to improved food security for assisted households. Moreover, the Heads of the Agricultural Departments in Debub and Gash Barka have indicated that as a result of the good harvest in 2010, the prices of cereals have gone down in the local market. Beneficiaries were also able to meet their own seed requirement for the 2011 planting season. In most cases, they have also generated enough financial resources to pay for tractor services. Livestock population in targeted areas also increased due to improved water and feed situation, though they would still need time to reach their pre-displacement position in terms of livestock possession.

Fathma Mohammed and other beneficiaries on the Honey Development Project

- Restocking support such as the provision of oxen, dairy goats and bees contributed to food security and poverty reduction. For example, supported farmers on average produced 10 to 15 kilograms' of honey per harvest season which represents an important increase in household income. Others have also sold goats to meet their immediate household needs. Moreover, households' nutritional status for some of the supported households improved due to their ability to produce meat and milk.

Soira, Gollo kebabi, Debub

Soira, Gollo kebabi, Debub

- Construction of micro dams, ponds and water supply systems relieved beneficiary communities from traveling long distances in search of water. For example, beneficiaries from Teslim Kelay and Adi Maelel used to trek with their livestock for hours towards the Ethiopian border.
- In some areas, a small number of beneficiary communities have already started to engage in downstream horticultural production around the newly constructed micro dams. The regional and sub-regional offices of the MoA were making necessary preparations to encourage targeted beneficiaries to engage in small scale horticultural production both for household consumption and for supply the local market.
- After starting to live under a cleaner environment due to the shelter support, IDPs have now become more conscious about hygiene and sanitation as evidenced by the construction of latrines (in 4 villages in Oubel, Ham, Hadish Adi etc.) within their premises. Once widely adopted, it will generate greater impact on the public health situation of the supported areas.
- By participating in soil and water conservation activities, community members mainly women (in some villages more than 90% of the HHs) have earned new incomes that enabled them to meet their immediate household needs. In addition, they have become more aware of environmental protection and rehabilitation and have acquired skills that they would in future use to sustain physical structures left behind by the project.

- Planning, implementation and monitoring capacities of the regional, sub-regional and kebabi administration have been enhanced. As a result of training and due to the establishment of water and rangeland committees, local communities were capacitated to operate, maintain and sustain their resources.
- The PV solar provided to beneficiary households allowed women to do their household activities at their own convenient time as they do not have to rush to do it before dusk. It allowed children to spend more time on studies which is expected to improve their educational performance.

Restocking of goats and construction of cisterns for both human and livestock

- The programme also enhanced the planning, implementation, monitoring and reporting capacities of the regional and sub-regional administrations in Gash Barka, Debub and Southern Red Sea regions. This was achieved through the provision of training and office equipment. The capacity building support has also benefited sub-regional administrations responsible for the provision of technical support to communities and monitoring implementation of joint programme activities. Consequently, regions have become more efficient in coordinating programme activities and delivering projects, though their monitoring activities were affected by the shortage of transportation facilities.
- Beneficiary communities actively participated in project implementation by contributing labour and materials (e.g. shelter, micro dams, ponds, soil and water construction). In addition to saving costs for the project, community participation resulted in quick project delivery, improved sense of ownership, improved implementation capacity, and enhanced sustainability. To enhance project implementation, communities were empowered through training, coaching and mentoring in a number of areas including project planning and management, rangeland management, animal husbandry, soil and water conservation, etc. Capacity building interventions also strengthened community-based organizations by establishing rangeland and water committees and facilitated the development of water and rangeland bylaws.
- In order to assess the effectiveness of this knowledge/innovation sharing mechanisms, however, a well-defined feedback mechanism that assesses adaptability or adoption of the innovation elsewhere, needs to be established
- It is important to scale up the innovated cistern in other suitable areas and continue the research in new water lifting technology rather than the use of buckets.

- Compared to their pre-displacement situation, IDPs now have better access to basic social services such as water (for human and animal consumption), shelter, and schools. However, they were far below their pre-displacement position in terms of their livelihoods.
- The programme was implemented through national execution modality and was efficiently managed at all levels. The TER continued to use a highly successful project implementation modality by working directly through regional administrations, and in the process strengthened their capacities to plan, execute and monitor and report on projects. This modality in the view of the team represents best practice in the field of post-conflict recovery internationally.
- Monitoring and evaluation was largely satisfactory, and efforts were made to develop the appropriate instruments and templates to enhance follow up and reporting. A key problem area was associated with getting permits for field visits by UNDP staff and management, as well donors.

5.10 Gender as a Cross Cutting Issue in all Recovery Programmes

Gender considerations have been an essential component of all the UNDP Recovery Programmes from 1992-2012.

Under the PoWER programme, more than 60% of the total target populations were women-headed households. In all livelihood security interventions, women-headed and resource-poor households were priority targets. This is true in all subsequent programmes where women-headed households constituted about 74% in the provision of shelters, 53% in provision of seeds and 65% in provision ploughing services, 100% small ruminants for income generation and child nutrition and 67% participants in cash for work were women.

Interventions under the JP on IDPs and Expellees return/ resettlement have promoted gender equality and women's empowerment in many ways. Overall, more than 60% of the total target populations of the programme were female-headed households. Environmental interventions which addressed reduction of fuel wood consumption through the provision of fuel-saving stoves in households and provision of community solar-based household energy exclusively targeted women and female-headed households. In all livelihood security interventions, female-headed and resource-poor households were priority targets. In this case, female-headed households constitute 60% in provision of shelter, 64% in provision of seeds and tractor ploughing, 100% in small ruminants for income generation and child nutrition and 67% participants in cash for work were women. In the target communities, women and girls are responsible for fetching water and fire wood. Provision of access to potable water implies a reduction in women's workload and having more time for income-generating activities as well as time for schooling for girls. Hence, the intervention enhanced women empowerment and gender equity. Women were well-represented (40%) in local development committees. Women's increased representation and participation in the programme has influenced resource allocations and policies by making them to address women needs and prioritized concerns.

The Transition and Early Recovery and/or Food Security and Sustainable Livelihoods project purposefully targets the extreme poor whose livelihood assets and capabilities have been depleted due to war, drought and volcanic eruption. These were people whose livelihoods have been entirely supported with relief aid during their stay in camps; they reside in the remote area bordering Ethiopia, mostly deprived from basic services, and were seriously affected by the stalemate of the unresolved border conflict. Many of them were pastoralists with nomadic/ semi-nomadic lifestyle whose mobility across the border in search of feed and water is curtailed since 1998.

Across all the Recovery Programmes women constituted the highest proportion amongst the extreme poor. Gender issues have been addressed at two levels: as a cross cutting issue gender is mainstreamed in all programmatic areas and it has also been represented as a stand-alone strategic area as well. Women benefited directly through cash payments for work, access to services and natural resources and income generating activities such; honey and poultry developments.

Training sessions in Lahiyo, Senafe sub region

Training session in Lahiyo, Senafe sub region

Training on Beekeeping in Debub region

Training on bee keeping in Soira mountain range

ACRONYMS

APS	Associazione per la partecipazione allo Sviluppo
AWP	Annual Work Plan
CCA	Common Country Assessment
CESVI	Cooperazione e Sviluppo Onlus
CFW	Cash for Work
CI	Cooperazione Italiana
CP	Country Programme
CPAP	Country Programme Action Plan
CPD	Country Programme Document
CRIC	Centro Redgionale d'Intervento per la co-operazione
DEX	Direct Execution
EDA	Eritrean De-mining Authority
EDHS	Eritrea Demography and Health Survey
EDO	Eritrean De-mining Operations
EFE	Employers Federation Eritrea
ERREC	Eritrean Relief and Refugee Commission
ERW	Explosive Remnants of War
ESCA	Eritrean Solidarity and Cooperation Association (Special contract)
EU	European Union
EWDFA	Eritrean War Disabled Fighters' Association
FACE	Funding Authorization and Certificate of Expenditure
GoE	Government of Eritrea
GoSE	Government of the State of Eritrea
HHs	Households

HIV/AIDS	Human Immuno deficiency Virus/Acquired Immune Deficiency Syndrome
IDP	Internally Displaced People
IDPs	Internally Displaced persons
ILO	International Labour Organization
IMAS	International Mine Action Standards
IP	Implementing Partner
IRS	Information and Referral Service
JP	Joint Programme
JSC	Joint Steering Committee
LFM	Logical Framework Matrix
LIS	Landmine Impact Survey
MA	Managing Agent
MACBP	Mine Action Capacity Building Programme
MACC	Mine Action Coordination Centre
MCH	Maternal and Child Health
MD	Millennium Declaration
MDGs	Millennium Development Goals
MDGR	Millennium Development Goals Report
MLHW	Ministry of Labor and Human Welfare
MoA	Ministry of Agriculture
MoE	Ministry of Education
MoF	Ministry of Finance
MoH	Ministry of Health
MoLWE	Ministry of Land Water and Environment
MoMR	Ministry of Marine Resources
MND	Ministry of National Development
MRE	Mine Risk Education
MTR	Mid-Term Review
NAP	National Adaptation Plan
NCDRP	National Commission of Demobilization and Reintegration Programme

NCEW	National Confederation of Eritrean Workers
NEX	National Execution
NGOs	Non Governmental Organization
NGP	National Gender Policy
NSO	National Statistics Office
NRS	Northern Red Sea Region
NUEW	National Union of Eritrean Women
NUEYS	National Union of Eritrean Youth and Students (Parallel Market)
PHC	Preventive Health Care
PIR	Project Implementation Report
PMU	Project Management Unit (Not creating a parallel structures)
PROFERI	Programme of Reintegration and Rehabilitation of Resettlement Areas in Eritrea
PoWER	Post War Emergency Recovery
RR	Resident Representative
RRF	Results and Resources Framework
SRS	Southern Red Sea Region
SWC	Soil and Water Conservation
SHD	Sustainable Human Development
TER	Transition and Early Recovery
ToT	Training of Trainers
TNA	Training Needs Analysis
TWG	Technical Working Group
UK	United Kingdom
UN	United Nations
UNCT	UN Country Team
UNDAF	United Nations Development Assistance Framework
UNDP	United Nations Development Programme
UNEP	United Nations Environment Programme
UNFPA	United Nations Population Fund
UNHCR	United Nations High Commissioner for Refugees

UNICEF	United Nations Children's Fund
UNISP	UN Implementation Support Plan
UNMEE	United Nations Mission in Ethiopia and Eritrea
USAID	United States Agency for International Development
USD	United States Dollar
UXO	Unexploded Ordinance
WFP	World Food Programme
WHO	World Health Organization

(Footnotes)

1 Interview by Yodit Woldegabriel, Research Assistant to the Author of this manuscript

2 Interview by Yodit Woldegabriel, Research Assistant to the Author of this manuscript

3 Interview by Yodit Woldegabriel, Research Assistant to the Author of this manuscript

4 Techeste Ahderom, Tesfai Haile and Gebremechael Tesfaselassie, PROFERI Post Facto Evaluation, 1996

5 Interim Evaluation Report of the PoWER Programme.

6 World Bank, ***Aide-Memoire Implementation Support Mission,*** 20—30 September 2004, ***op.cit.,***p.7.

7 The National Mine Action Authority in the Preparatory Assistance was referred to as Eritrean Mine Action Agency (EMA) as events subsequently evolved the role of the Eritrean Mine Action Centre was executed by the Eritrean Mine Action Programme (EMAP), which subsequently became the Eritrean Demining Authority. Proclamation 123/2002

8 Sub-regions – administrative units directly above communities

9 Suspected Hazard Areas (SHA) are those areas that are either know or thought to be contaminated by landmines and/or unexploded ordnance (UXO)

ANNEXES

RECOVERY PROGRAMMES IN ERITREA
1992-2012

LIST OF PROJECTS UNDERTAKEN BY THE UNDP RECOVERY PROGRAMMES IN ERITREA 1992 – 2012

(Prof/Eng) Techeste AHDEROM

Final Draft, Asmara, 19 December 2013

Table of Contents of the Annexes

Annex 1 PROFERI

No.	Component	Packages	Region/ Sub-region Locality (ies)	Implementing Agency (ies)	Sector (s)	Beneficiaries	Total Budget USD	Project Description & Notes
1	Capacity building (Local, Regional and National	Capacity Building & Institution Strengthening					1,063,290	The design of the programme required that a Programme Management Unit (PMU) be set-up within ERREC to coordinate and implement the programme. It also required that all the various institutions whose services are essential and critical to the well-being of the refugees implement the aspects of the programme which fall within their domain.
		ERREC, Line Ministries and others				4,606 ex-combatants, returnees and disabled 47 staff of ERREC		In the areas of local-level capacity building/skills training for sustainable livelihoods, ERREC with UNDP support trained 4606 persons in book keeping, financial management/business planning; electricity, carpentry/masonary/plumbing; metal work and secretarial sciences. 47 staff of ERREC trained in management, finance, programme and project planning; monitoring and evaluation and logistics and procurement.
		UNV-SERV						In conformity with UN inter-agency consultation made with the GoE in 1993, the Government sought assistance of the UNV in designing a programme that would facilitate the return of professional Eritreans from the Diaspora. In July 1995 9 Eritreans specializing in such fields as water supply, statistics, legal services, health, construction, logistics, auditing, procuring and social work were recruited.
		Survey of Vulnerable Groups	Covered over 2000 villages all over Eritrea				63,290.00	The survey was designed to investigate the level of vulnerability among Eritrean communities, especially in terms of food security and needs for relief/welfare assistance with a view to determining their productive capacities and medium-to-longer term development opportunities.
2	School building	Construction of 14 schools; 9 Elementary, 4 Junior Secondary and 1 Senior Secondary schools; rehabilitation of 1 primary school	Gash-Barka (8), Northern Red Sea (4), Maekel (3) and Anseba (1)	Ministry of Education	Education	15,000 students every four years	3,213,773.49	The construction of these schools targets the refugee resettlement areas and the communities around these areas in a bid to promote reintegration and to increase access to education in remote parts of Eritrea. Regarding the literacy and numeracy component of PROFERI, 20,879 adults (Gash-Barka 9182, Anseba 7983 and Northern Red Sea 3714) have participated, 89.6% of which are women.

No.	Component	Packages	Region/Sub-region Locality (ies)	Implementing Agency (ies)	Sector (s)	Beneficiaries	Total Budget USD	Project Description & Notes
3	Provision of Agricultural inputs	Livestock	Gash-Barka region	Ministry of Agriculture		467 HHs	2,054,795	About 80% of the returnee households have benefited from the provision of livestock between January and June 1996.
		Crop Production (land clearing and ploughing, distribution of seeds and provision of farm tools)	Gash-Barka region					For the 1996 crop season, 12,045 ha of land had been distributed to 5,150 households. 11,150 ha of this had been cleared for ploughing. In the 1997 crop season 12,045 ha have been ploughed and cultivated. Purchase and distribution of seeds and farm tools have also been done for these planting seasons.
		Construction of water ponds, boreholes and hand dug wells	Gash-Barka region, sub-zobas Tesseney, Goluj, Hykota, Molki, Mensura, Gogne, Forto and Dige					In this activity 4 water ponds (Ruba Kamiap, Fanko, Gerset (A & B), Aklelet); 3 boreholes (Adi Shekgallo, Tebeldia, Alebu, Gonai Sagla); and 7 hand dug wells (Koret, Adi Kuky, Dase,Wakay, Molki, Deret, Tekrert) were constructed.
		Support to vulnerable households	Gash-Barka			1,800 HHs spontaneous returnees and disabled people		The assistance package included extension services, tractor services and seeds etc. for the 1996 and 1997 planting seasons. These beneficiaries were expected to engage in agricultural production either cooperatively (e.g. Sabunait) or individually.

Annex 2 Pre-PoWER Programme

No.	Implementing Partner	Type of Intervention	Region/Sub-region Locality (ies)	Sector (s) & Cost per beneficiary	Beneficiaries	Total Budget	Months	Project Description & Notes
1	CRIC I	Health, Nutrition & Sanitation	Northern Red Sea Region, Afabet Sub-region, Mekete Camp	Health 150,000 5USD/beneficiary	30,000	150,000	2	This project is part of the overall strategy for the provision of an immediate response to the urgent needs of the IDPs in Eritrea. It is planned to assist the health in the camp through the provision of medical staff and drugs and to supply additional quantities of supplementary food. (Starting date 24 July and completion date 30 September, 2000)
2	CRIC II	Health	Northern Red Sea Region, Afabet Sub-region, Afabet town	Health 284,280USD 21.86USD/beneficiary	13,000	284,280	6	This activity aims at improving Afabet hospital delivery services through rehabilitation of the hospital building and specialized technical assistance with particular emphasis on the obstetric and surgical emergency care. (Starting date 04 December 2000 completion date 15 May 2001)
3	APS	Water and Sanitation	Debub, Areza, Obel, Aleda and Adi-Bal	Water 150,000USD 18.75USD/beneficiary	8,000	150,000	3	Areza town has a population of about 6,000 and additional IDPs of 2000; the population get water from a dam through pipes and public fountains with the help of an engine. The water system needs to be restored and adapted to the increased population. In particular it is very important to maintain the filtration system and to construct additional fountains since the population is expected to increase. Therefore, this project will include the drilling of the wells in Obel, Aleda and Adi-Bal and restoring of the water system of Areza town. (Starting date 21 August 2000 and completion date 30 November 2000)
4	CESVI	Water and Supply of NFI	Debub, Awhne and Derra		20,000	172,182	3	The aim of the project was to supply NFI to the IDPs from Senafe area and to provide sufficient water to the IDPs and to the host communities by drilling wells and constructing reservoir. (Starting date 11 September and completion date 12 December 2000)
5	MANITESE	Provision of sanitation, school and kindergarten activities and other social services and training to women in Mekete camp	Northern Red Sea Region, Afabet Sub-region, Mekete Camp	Emergency intervention 150,000USD 6.25USD/beneficiary	24,000 IDPs	150,000	3	This project was aimed to support the IDPs in the Mekete camp in the following areas introduce educational and hygiene environmental activities related to proper use of water, fire and energy resources; improve the sanitation activities in the camp; organize workshops for women IDPs and supply them with materials for small handicraft activities for personal and family use and help children to follow their primary education and engage them in recreational activities. (Starting date 01 September and completion date 30 November, 2000)

No.	Implementing Partner	Type of Intervention	Region/Sub-region Locality (ies)	Sector (s) & Cost per beneficiary	Beneficiaries	Total Budget	Months	Project Description & Notes
6	ESCA	Distribution of kerosene (emergency assistance in distribution 900,000 liters of kerosene and 3,000 pcs of Jerryicans	Debub, Tsorona and Senafe Sub-zobas	NFI 262,032USD	30,000	262,032	3	The project aims to assist 30,000 families in sub-zobas Tsorona and Senafe, with emergency supplies of kerosene as firewood is not available for fuel and the areas are heavily land mined. (Starting date 21 August and completion date 20 November 2001)
7	MoH	Hospital equipment and furniture	Maeekel, Asmara	Health 28,000USD		28,000	2	At the height of the third offensive of May 2000, and the Ethiopian army advances deep into the territory of Eritrea, the MoH responded by deploying extra human power and other resources depleting its supplies of the hospitals in Asmara. After the cessation of fighting and peace talks, a return to normal routine activities resumed. But because of the shortage of supplies especially the hospital furniture and other items, the desired level of health services could not be maintained. Therefore, the MoH is seeking yet another assistance for the supply of hospital furniture and equipment. (Starting date 01 February 2002 and completion 31 March 2002)

CRIC Centro Redgionale d'Intervento per la cooperazione
APS Associazione per la partecipazione allo Sviluppo
CESVI Cooperazione E Sviluppo Onlus
ESCA Eritrean Solidarity and Cooperation Association

Annex 3 PoWER Programme

No.	Imp. Partner	Type of Intervention	Region/Sub-region Locality (ies)	Sector (s) & Cost per beneficiary	Beneficiaries	Total Budget USD	Months	Project Description & Notes
1	APS	Rehabilitation of 5 Schools and 4 Health Centers	Debub Region, Areza & Mai-Mene Sub-regions (Mai-Dima, Obel, Dabre, Areza, Mai-Mene)	Education 291,023USD 40USD/beneficiary Health 123,229USD 11USD/beneficiary	Education 4500 students Health 29,500 pop.	414,252	7	Rehabilitation of the elementary and middle schools in Mai-Dima, the elementary school in Dabre and the elementary and junior school in Mai-Mene including the provision of furniture, and school materials. In the health sector it aims to rehabilitate some health facilities in Areza, Mai-Dima and Obel and Dabre including the provision of medical equipment, furniture, drugs and technical assistance and training. (Starting date January 8, 2001 and completion date July 7, 2001)
2	APS	Strengthening MCHC inDebub zone	Debub region, Decemhare and Areza		3,450 residents of Decemhare and Areza	123,229		The project envisages providing technical assistance to the gynaecological and obstetric unit of Decemhare referral hospital. The project will implement also a module in Areza sub-zone aimed at enhancing the operational capabilities of Traditional Trained Birth Attendants (TTBAS) and health workers.
3	CESVI	Rehabilitation of 2 Schools	Gash-Barka Region, Guluj sub-region, Guluj and Gergef villages	Education 211,356USD 81USD/beneficiary	Education 2607 (students + teachers)	150,000	14	Rehabilitation of 2 schools in Guluj and Gergef including the supply of furniture, school materials and teaching items. (Starting date January 15, 2001 and completion date May 14, 2001; extended until March 15, 2002 due to additional work on water and fencing).
4	CESVI	Low Cost Housing Construction and research	Gash-Barka Region, Guluj and Tesseney	1. Housing 2. Multi-purpose center 3. Training 4. Testing and adopting	60 HH (houses)	504,761	12	This project aims at constructing 60 new housing units for the more vulnerable members of target communities. This shall be done through the construction of one large family room, an external kitchen, and an external pit latrine; all within a compound of 12.5m x 20m ⊠ 250 sq.m. An initial research on the prototype of the housing units will be tried by using conventional cement/sand hollow blocks for the wall and iron sheets supported by sawn timber for roofing. Such designs shall be revised to incorporate recommendations that may be made as a result of the linked parallel programme of research and development in low cost housing in rural areas. (Starting date March 1, 2001 and completion date 15 December 2001, completed in March 2002)

No.	Imp. Partner	Type of Intervention	Region/Sub-region Locality (ies)	Sector (s) & Cost per beneficiary	Beneficiaries	Total Budget USD	Months	Project Description & Notes
5	CESVI	Housing & public building rehabiliation	Gash-Barka Region, Sub-zoba Guluj, Omhajer	Rehabilitation of houses and market area 525.3USD/ beneficiary	400 HH	210,120	5	This project aims at the rehabilitation of houses and the market area; in which their roofs, windows, doors are removed and not severe damage is incurred on the wall. It will include the rehabilitation of residential houses and the market area. (Starting date September 15, 2001 and completion date December 15, 2001, completed in February 2002)
6	CESVI	Water Supply	Debub region, Senafe Sub-zone, Metera village and IDP's camp	Water 75,808		75,808	4	To rehabilitate the water supply system to the IDPs in the Metera camp and the village of Metera (Starting date August 8, 2001 and completion date November 7, 2001)
7	CONCERN	Agriculture & foot path	Debub region Adi-keih Sub-zone, Safira, Sibraso, Karibosa, Egila and Mesegelezula	Agriculture	1956	270,706	10	The project focuses on income generating activities for the community in the villages of Safira, Sibraso, Karibosa, Egila and Mesegelezula. The plan is to distribute 800 beehives to 400 families and to construct about 50kms of footpath. The community will also be trained on bee keeping. (Starting date October 1, 2001 and completion date May 31, 2002 extension until July 31, 2002)
8	COSV	Rehabilitation of 7 Schools	Gash-Barka region, Molki Sub-region, Molki, Endagaber, Derabush, Tukul, Maidoghalle, Adi-Tsetser and Jejah camp	Education 228,351USD 72USD/beneficiary	Education 3,160 students	228,351	6	Rehabilitation of 7 schools including the supply of furniture, school materials and teaching items. (Starting date January 15, 2001 and completion date July 14, 2001)
9	COSV	Rehabilitation of 2 Health Centers and Strengthening of 1 IDP camp Health Facilities	Gash-Barka region, Molki Sub-region, Molki, Derabush, Endagaber, and Jejah camp	Health 122,300USD 2.4USD/beneficiary	Health 51,000 pop + IDPs	122,300	6	Rehabilitation of 2 health centers in Molki and supply of health services in Jejah IDP camp. (Starting date January 15, 2001 and completion date July 14, 2001)
10	COSV	Upgrading of Akordot referral regional hospital and PHC facilities in Molki sub-zone	Gash-Barka region, Akordot & Molki Sub-zone	Health 113,300USD 0.6USD/beneficiary	191,000 residents of Akordat & Molki	113,300	8	To strengthen the existing health system in Gash-Barka focusing, the intervention in Akordot referral regional hospital and in the existing PHC facilities in Molki sub-zone. To restart of the activities of the surgical department in Akordot Hospital; to perform on-job training for medical staff; to provide technical assistance and to participate in epidemiological assessment in Molki sub-zone. (Starting date June 11, 2001 and completion date February10, 2002)

No.	Imp. Partner	Type of Intervention	Region/Sub-region Locality (ies)	Sector (s) & Cost per beneficiary	Beneficiaries	Total Budget USD	Months	Project Description & Notes
11	COSV	Rehabilitation and Extension of Schools	Gash-Barka region, Molki Sub-zoba, Mai-Dhogalle and Endagaber areas	Education 148,886USD 124USD/beneficiary	1200 students	148,886	5	The project aims to build 4 new classrooms in Endagaber and a dormitory (4 bedrooms) for teachers in Mai-Dhogalle as well as supplying furniture, educational and teaching materials. COSV has already rehabilitated the school in Endagaber but the returning IDPs have already increased the number of enrolment by 500 additional pupils and therefore new spaces are needed. Mai-Dhogalle, where COSV has already rehabilitated and furnished the schools, the living conditions in the village are rough and the teachers are occupying part of the classrooms to live in. (Starting date December 1, 2001 and completion date April 30, 2002)
12	COSV		Gash-Barka region, Akurdot Hospital	Health 10,815USD		10,815	3	In the original proposal approved by PoWER, the months/man for the expatriate anaesthetist in the Akordot Hospital were 2 months, given that by September 2001 a local anaesthetist would be available. As this condition has not been met, COSV is requesting to hire an expatriate to continue to supply technical support to the Akordot hospital at the surgical department.
13	COSV	PWDs rehabilitation project by a Mobile unit and technical assistance to Keren Orthopedic Workshop	Gash-Barka and Anseba		40,000	214,508	6	More than 100,000 people in Eritrea are suffering from various disabilities. Of these, more than 40,000 are estimated to be in need of orthopaedic appliances. (Starting date February1, 2002 and completion date July 31, 2002)
14	CRIC	Shelter	Debub Region, Adi-quala Sub-zoba, Geza Medabia villages	Shelter 271,127USD 2400USD/ beneficiary	113 HH	271,127	5	The overall objective of the operation is to support the reconstruction process by providing to war-affected communities building materials and technical support to construct their completely destroyed houses. At present part of the returnees of Geza-Medabai areas are living in temporary shelter (tents and plastic sheets as temporary roofing). This project is trying to combine low cost construction intervention with good technical input. (Starting date December 15, 2001 and completion date March 15, 2002)

No.	Imp. Partner	Type of Intervention	Region/Sub-region Locality (ies)	Sector (s) & Cost per beneficiary	Beneficiaries	Total Budget USD	Months	Project Description & Notes
15	Eritrean War Disabled Fighter's Association (AWDFA)	Reconstruction and Reinstallation of Barentu Bakery	Gash-Barka region	Support to disables 11 direct beneficiaries and indirectly 10,000 members of the EWDFA	More than 10,000	136,420	3	The bakery was completed by EWDFA in November 1998 but then destroyed in May 2000 by the Ethiopian invasion. The association aims to restore some capital funds of this disabled group in order to provide good quality bread to the Barentu town and neighbouring area. The bakery is supposed to have a net income of USD 7,000 per month that will be utilized for the repayment of the loan to the association, which will reinvest the capital in other activities. (Starting date August 1, 2001 and completion date October 31, 2001)
16	ERREC	Transportation of IDPs to place of origin	Gash-Barka & Debub	Transportation 450,000USD	About 200,000 IDPs	450,000	1-2	Contribution to the operation of transport of IDPs to their places of origin. (Starting date May 7, 2001 and completion date June 30, 2001)
No.	Imp. Partner	Type of Intervention	Region/Sub-region Locality (ies)	Sector (s) & Cost per beneficiary	Beneficiaries	Total Budget USD	Months	**Project Description & Notes**
17	GVC	Strengthening the Health Services in 3 IDP camps and distribution of essential NFI	Debub region, Adi-keih Sub-region (Zula, Soira camps) and Northern Red Sea region, Foro Sub-region (Buya camp, Ghinda)	Health & Sanitation 106,211 USD 18USD/beneficiary Relief 229,157USD 8USD/beneficiary	Camps 13,420 IDPs	335,368	5	To provide emergency relief to IDPs from the surroundings of Senafe providing essential NFI and improving health and sanitation facilities in the camps of Zula, Soira and Buya. (Starting date January 8, 2001 and completion date May 7, 2001)
18	InterSOS	Improvement of Shelter, Health and Sanitation conditions in the Deda camp	Debub region, Mai-aini Sub-region (Deda camp)	NFI 15,447USD Water & Sanitation 2,273USD Health 19,552USD Emergency Shelter 60,156USD Education 39,287USD	3,700 IDPs 1,100 students	136,715	3	Distribution of relief items (NFI) including educational materials and school furniture in Deda camp. (Starting date January 3, 2001 and completion date April 2, 2001)
19	InterSOS	Water and Sanitation	Debub region, Mai-aini Sub-region, Deda, Sesewe, Mebred, Ze-are villages	Water & Sanitation 374,707.83USD 86USD/beneficiary	4,355 pop.	374,707.83	9	Improve the water and sanitation facilities in the villages surrounding the IDPs camp of Deda to reduce social tension between IDP and hosting communities. (Starting date January 3, 2001 and completion date October 15, 2001)

No.	Imp. Partner	Type of Intervention	Region/Sub-region Locality (ies)	Sector (s) & Cost per beneficiary	Beneficiaries	Total Budget USD	Months	Project Description & Notes
20	InterSOS	Emergency Shelter	Gash-Barka region, Shambuko, Laelay Gash and Guluj	Shelter 408,000USD 340USD/beneficiary	1200	445,520	7	According to the Sub Working Group on Shelter and NFI at least 3,000 families of returning IDPs in Gash-Barka are in need of an emergency shelter. The SWG has decided that a suitable package would be composed by ronda structure with 20 grass mats (tonkebets) and plastic sheet per family. The ronda structure is a semi-temporary shelter produced in country (Dekemhare) that can be easily upgraded in the years to come to a more permanent house (by the construction of a wall to lift the structure from the ground) (Starting date 22 March 2001 and completion date 21 October 2001)
21	ISCOS MARCHE	Capacity building	Gash-Barka, Debub and Southern Red Sea regions	Capacity Building 300,000 212USD/beneficiary	700 Zoba and Sub-zoba staff	138,430	5	The Regional Administrations, especially the most war affected such as Gash-Barka and Debub, are facing an overwhelming challenge to track and coordinate the recovery intervention on their territories. The present pilot phase (3 month) aims to support those regions in order to give a variety of training courses to staff of the administration to upgrade their capacity to deal with their daily tasks (word processing and other basic software, finance, personnel management and accounting courses etc) To assist the planning and the administration of the above activities; To provide technical assistance to the Zobas to set up a GIS database (coordinating with OCHA)and to plan the human resources and training necessary for the year 2002 in order to sustain the data management without external assistance To plan for the year 2002 the human resources and the institutional set-up necessary to follow up the implementation of a collection of data from programmes to feed the above database To plan the resources and the training necessary to improve the project management of the Zoba Administration for the year 2002. (Starting date December 15, 2001 and completion date July 15, 2002)
22	MANITESE	Provision of water supply, sanitation, school and kindergarten activities and other social services and training to Mekete camp.	Northern Red Sea Region, Afabet Sub-region, Mekete camp	Education 143,988 USD 25USD/beneficiary Training and skill development 61,012USD 62.5USD/beneficiary	21,000 IDPs 2,000 students 800 women	205,000	8	Support to the social services in Mekete camp including management of water system, garbage disposal, health promotions, adult literacy campaign, support to the development of workshops and other skill development training (handicrafts). (Starting date January 10, 2001 and completion date September 9, 2001)

No.	Imp. Partner	Type of Intervention	Region/Sub-region Locality (ies)	Sector (s) & Cost per beneficiary	Beneficiaries	Total Budget USD	Months	Project Description & Notes
23	MANITESE	Training to women in home economics and traditional handcraft	Northern Red Sea region, Afabet area	Agriculture 57,604USD 360 Women + 600 school children 59USD/beneficiary	360 women and 600 school children	57,604	5	The project aims to benefit the host community of Afabet while MANITESE is still providing assistance to the IDPs Mekete camp through similar social activities especially for women. The request to extend these home economics activities to the host community came from the local branch of the Ministry of Agriculture while courses on traditional handcraft production originated from a request of the National Union of Women of Afabet. (Starting date May 1, 2001 and completion date August 31, 2001)
24	MANITESE	Support to food production & Socio-economic development Gash-Barka Sosona and Koita areas	Gash-Barka, Sosona & Koita	Water 35,919USD Agriculture 166,046USD Mill 13,499USD 37USD/beneficiary	5,800	215,494	8	In agriculture to open accessible land, to distribute farm animals, seeds and tools and initiate some poultry farming. Also to support the water system (2 pumps and 2 boreholes in Koita and the repair of the present pump in Sosona) and the establishment of a mill. (Starting date June 11, 2001 and completion date December 10, 2001)
25	MANITESE	Health and Education	Gash-Barka region Sosona and Koita	Health 166,667USD 24,118USD Education 161,667 46.4USD/beneficiary	7,474 population of the two areas	347,453	8	The activities are to construct a new health station (Sosona) and a new primary school (Koita) to benefit 2 of the poorest groups of the Eritrean population (Kunama and Nara) making access to primary education possible for small children (Koita). It is an integrated approach to upgrade social services by an organization, Manitese, which has show a high sense of responsibility in assisting war-affected communities in the Gash-Barka region to recover. (Starting date December 11, 2001 and completion date August 10, 2002)
26	Ministry of Education	Purchase of school library books and supplementary reading materials	Gash-Barka & Debub regions	Education 455,000USD 5.69USD/beneficiary	80,000 pupils of Gash-Barka and Debub regions	455,000	3	The MoE is requesting the funds to proceed to re supply 10 junior and 3 senior secondary schools and replaced their damaged school library books and supplementary reading materials, and also for the provision of education supplies for the total of 80,000 students affected by the war. (Starting date March 15, 2001 and completion date August 15, 2001)
27	Ministry of Health PMU	Supply of drug to war affected population of Gash-Barka	Gash-Barka region, Akordot, Tesseney and Barentu			750,000	2	This is an emergency request for the procurement of essential drugs made by the MoH to supply 2 regional drug warehouses. The procurement will be executed directly by PMU following UNDP rules and procedures for such thresholds. (Starting date October 1, 2001 and completion date November 30, 2001)

No.	Imp. Partner	Type of Intervention	Region/Sub-region Locality (ies)	Sector (s) & Cost per beneficiary	Beneficiaries	Total Budget USD	Months	Project Description & Notes
28	UNICEF	Child Friendly Centres Programme	Six IDP centres in Gash-Barka and Anseba, (Harena, Alba, Jejah, Mekete, Adikeshi and Toleganja)	Psycho-social support for unaccompanied children	3,092 separated children	275,000	12	This project was conceived as a result of an assessment conducted by the MLHW. The results indicated that the overwhelming majority of separated children are actually living in child-headed households. The project plans to create an environment that places high priority to the physical and psychosocial needs of separated children in IDP camps. It further aims to improve their current socio-economic situation by providing them with life skills they can utilize on their return home. (Starting date March 1, 2001 and completion date February 28, 2002 extended until June 30, 2002)
29	MOLG Gash-Barka					804,828		These projects aim at Generating Income thereby improving the earnings of war and drought affected people, IDPs, host communities and returnees. Project interventions are planned primarily in the areas of Soil and Water Conservation work, Maintenance of Feeder Roads and some activities in forestation and well/canal cleaning. The project is to provide cash for labour engaged in such public work activities and will have created competencies in the construction and management of such works. This project does benefit a large number of beneficiaries and produces assets that have a direct and positive impact on sustainable livelihoods of the communities in particular; and on the improvement of the environment in general. They fit the general philosophy and spirit of the PoWER programme in that they put some cash in the hands of the people but also result in outputs that enhance the environment, ultimately soil fertility and food production. (Starting date March 15, 2001 and completion date July 15, 2001)

No.	Imp. Partner	Type of Intervention	Region/Sub-region Locality (ies)	Sector (s) & Cost per beneficiary	Beneficiaries	Total Budget USD	Months	Project Description & Notes
30	MOLG Debub	Labour intensive projects in the war affected regions of Debub	Debub & Gash-Barka regions (368 villages)	Public Works/Intensive labour 13USD/beneficiary	125,000 Returnees, IDPs, War affected, Drought affected Communities	777,147	4	These projects aim at Generating Income thereby improving the earnings of war and drought affected people, IDPs, host communities and returnees. Project interventions are planned primarily in the areas of Soil and Water Conservation work, Maintenance of Feeder Roads and some activities in forestation and well/canal cleaning. The project is to provide cash for labour engaged in such public works activities and will have created competencies in the construction and management of such works. This project does benefit a large number of beneficiaries and do produce assets that have a direct and positive impact on sustainable livelihood of the communities in particular; and on the improvement of the environment in general. They fit the general philosophy and spirit of the PoWER programme in that they put some cash in the hands of the people but also result in outputs that enhance the environment ultimately soil fertility and food production. (Starting date March 15, 2001 and completion date July 15, 2001)
31	Ministry of Local Government Gash-Barka region	Rehabilitation of 12 schools	Gash-Barka region	Education 7,539 students 73USD/student	7,539 students	480,000	5	This is a direct execution by the MOLG Gash-Barka region, through the engineering and programme management department of a package of 12 schools in the region. PMU has designed the project together with the Gash-Barka administration and under the supervision of the planning department of the MoE. The cost estimation is based on the bill of quantities prepared by the zoba engineering department. (Starting date July 1, 2001 and completion date October 31, 2001)
32	MOLG Debub region	Shelter	Debub region, Senafe and Tsorona sub-zobas	Shelter 350,000USD 1000 beneficiaries 350USD/beneficiary	1000	350,000	3	This project aims to rehabilitate the houses damaged by the war; by providing roofing materials, doors and windows. (Starting date October 1, 2001 and completion date December 15, 2001)

No.	Imp. Partner	Type of Intervention	Region/Sub-region Locality (ies)	Sector (s) & Cost per beneficiary	Beneficiaries	Total Budget USD	Months	Project Description & Notes
33	MOLG Zoba Debub	Emergency Shelter Phase I and II	Debub region, Senafe and Tsorona sub-zobas	Shelter 921,569USD 307USD/ beneficiary	4,500	1,517,547	2	According to the Sub Working Group on shelter and NFI at least 5,000 families of returning IDPs in Debub are in need of an emergency shelter. The SWG has decided that a suitable package would be composed of corrugated iron sheets, rafter, purlins and materials for doors and windows. The MOLG zoba Debub will implement in covering the roofs of 2,000 houses in Tsorona area and 1,000 in Senafe area. (Starting date July 20, 2001 and completion date September 19, 2001; Netherland's funding)
34	MOLG Zoba Gash-Barka	Emergency Shelter Phase I and II	Laelay Gash, Shambuko, Gogne	Rehabilitation of houses destroyed by war	3,900	1.4 million		The SWG decided that a suitable package would be composed of corrugated iron sheets, rafter, purlins and materials for doors and windows. The MOLG zoba Gash-Barka will implement in covering the roofs of 3,900 houses. (Netherland's funding)
35	MOLG Zoba Gash-Barka	Assistance to war victims in Gash-Barka	Gash-Barka	Resettlement of Rural Deportees from Ethiopia 2.2 million USD	10,000	2.2 million	12	This project is aimed at settling the Rural Deportees from Ethiopia in areas suitable for agricultural activities and providing basic agricultural tools and necessities. (UNDP TRAC Funding)
36	MOVIMONDO	Rehabilitation and Equipment of 3 Health Structures and the Obstetric Dept. in Regional Hospital	Gash-Barka region, Tesseney sub-region (Tesseney), Guluj sub-region (Guluj, Gergef, Tebeldia)	Health 306,411.61USD 4.3USD/ beneficiary	71,000 pop	306,411.61	7	Structural and functional rehabilitation of the Health Center in Goluj and the Health Stations in Gergef and Tebeldia including the supply of drugs and medical equipment. Through also technical assistance, the project aims to reactivate the emergency obstetric dept in the referral hospital of Tesseney. (Starting date January 10, 2001 and completion date August 9, 2001)
37	MOVIMONDO	Shelter and Schools	Southern Red Sea region	Shelter 120,000USD Schools 70,000USD		190,000	3	The activities are focused on assisting the IDPs from Debai-sima and Musa-Ali in emergency shelter and NFI and rehabilitation of the water reservoirs and school. This can be achieved by providing 1 Agudo Structure and mats to cover it for each family, necessary NFI to each family and rehabilitating the water reservoirs and school. (Starting date December 15, 2001 and completion date April 14, 2002 extended until July 31, 2002)
38	MOVIMONDO	Upgrading of Infrastructure in Tesseney Hospital	Gash-Barka region, Tesseney & Guluj	Health 141,460USD 89,000 beneficiaries 1.59USD/ beneficiary	89,000 residents and 65,000 returnees	141,460	6	Project aims to reach a rapid strengthening of the potential and quality of the comprehensive health services offered to the population by Tesseney Hospital, the referral health facility in the Gash-Barka region. The project will focus on the minor rehabilitation, equipment, strengthening and technical assistance related to the; Operation Room (OR), Surgical examination area in the surgical block, radiology dept., Laboratory dept. (Starting date July 1, 2001 and completion date December 31, 2001)
39	MOVIMONDO	Health, water and sanitation	Gash-Barka, Goluj sub-zone, Gherset and Aklelet villages	Health 26,300 Water & Sanitation 23,700	10,000	50,000	4	This is a project aimed at improving health conditions of returnees from Sudan. The settlement areas are presently facing a serious emergency, both in terms of lack of health care and education; the water situation is under control in Gherset, but has to be supported in Aklelet. (Starting date August 1, 2001 and completion date February 28, 2002)

No.	Imp. Partner	Type of Intervention	Region/Sub-region Locality (ies)	Sector (s) & Cost per beneficiary	Beneficiaries	Total Budget USD	Months	Project Description & Notes
40	MOVIMONDO	Health	Gash-Barka region, Goluj sub-zone, Omhajer town	Health 350,000USD		350,000	9	Structural and functional rehabilitation of the Health Center in Omhajer including the supply of medical equipment and technical assistance. (Starting date September 15, 2001 and completion date July 15, 2002)
41	MOVIMONDO	Health	Gash-Barka region, Tesseney Hospital	Health 70,000 USD		70,000	4	The extension is requested as in Eritrea at present there is only one Orthopaedist (provided by Italian Co-operazione) and the hospital in Tesseney does not have this service available, considered by the MoH as essential.
42	OXFAM	Water & Sanitation improvement at Shelab camp	Gash-Barka region, Shelab Camp	Improvement of health and sanitation condition 46,714 USD 4.7USD/ beneficiary	10,000	46,714	4	This project aims to respond to the emergency needs to upgrade the water and sanitation conditions of the deportee camp in Shelab. It consists mainly of the provision of sanitation facilities, hygiene promotion and distribution of water storage equipment and the construction of bathing areas and building round 164 family latrines (group of 5/6 families sharing for a total of 850 families) (Starting date June 1, 2001 and completion date September 30, 2001)
43	REFUGEE TRUST	Integrated Relief and Recovery Programme	Debub Region, Adi-Quala sub-zone at Enda-Giorgis, Geza Hamle, Geza Medebai, Geza Keren villages	Multi sectoral NFI 122,073USD Agricultural & livestock 589,467USD	3,300 SFHH	711,540	12	This is a multi-sectoral project that starts with relief and ends with improved income of targeted female-headed beneficiary households (SFHH). The project aims, in its relief efforts, to distribute some essential household goods (utensils, blankets and clothing). In rehabilitation, the project plans to provide educational equipment and conduct psycho-social support activities; re-establish and improve agricultural activities through provision of tools, seeds and livestock; and promote sustainable community-based employment and income generation. (Starting date March 15, 2001 and completion date February 28, 2002)
44	REFUGEE TRUST	Water Supply	Debub region, Adi-Quala Sub-zone	Water 63,973 24.37USD/ beneficiary	2,625	63,973	6	In the two places there is a serious problem of lack of access to clean water; as a result many households are walking up to ten kilometers to fetch water while others are relying on contaminated water from unprotected water holes; some infected with water borne diseases such as bilharzias. The project is aimed to hand-dig in shallow well in Mai-Daero followed by a second, should water be insufficient for the target population, so as to provide clean, protected water for 5 villages with 2,625 residents. (Starting date September 15, 2001and completion date February 28, 2002)
45	UNDP	Direct payment/ procurement	All Regions	N/a	N/a	471,626 71,894 58,957 125,000 356,037 11,960		22 project vehicles 22 radios 2 ambulances for Molki & Goluj Transport of IDPs Support cost Sundries

No.	Imp. Partner	Type of Intervention	Region/Sub-region Locality (ies)	Sector (s) & Cost per beneficiary	Beneficiaries	Total Budget USD	Months	Project Description & Notes
45	UNDP	Direct payment/ procurement	All Regions	N/a	N/a	471,626 71,894 58,957 125,000 356,037 11,960		22 project vehicles 22 radios 2 ambulances for Molki & Goluj Transport of IDPs Support cost Sundries
46	UNDP/ERREC	Purchase of NFI	Debub, Gash-Barka and Southern Red sea regions	NFI 547,834.97		861,985		The NFI was procured by UNDP and given to ERREC for distribution to the beneficiaries. (USAID and Dutch funding)
47	WRD Assab	Water Supply	Southern Red Sea Region	Water supply 100,000 17,000 pop. of Assab 5.88USD/beneficiary	17,000	100,000	3	Assab water system is currently wasting huge resources because of a combination of leakages, old structures and poor management. Also most of the 15 boreholes out the of 18 in Harsile that are providing the water to the town are facing high salt sedimentation and the proposal suggests re-drilling at least 3 of them to supply fresh water.
48	ZOBA DEBUB Engineering Department	Emergency Rehabilitation Programme Debub zone Senafe & Tsorona sub-zobas	Debub Senafe & Tsorona	Education 700,000USD Over 9,000 students 78USD/beneficiary	9,000	700,000	5	This is a direct execution of the local government, through the engineer and programme management department of a package of 7 schools in the sub-region of Senafe and Tsorona. PMU is designing the project together with the Debub administration and with the supervision of the planning department of the MOE. (Starting date May 23, 2001 and completion date September 30, 2001)
49	MOLG	Water Supply	Gash-Barka	Water Supply		1.1 million		This is to supply 10 communities with clean and adequate water. The existing boreholes will be fitted with motorized pumps and the civil works will contine while the other new boreholes will be drilled. Gerenfit is part of this community.
50	MOVIMONDO	Health	Laelay Gash (Gerenfit) and Tesseney	Construction of prefab clinic in Gerenfit and the rehabilitation of MCHC clinic in Tesseney		228,851	8	Construction of a prefab unit and equipping it in Gerenfit settlement and the rehabilitation of Tesseney MCHC clinic and dissemination of PHC services.
51	COSV	Health and Education	Agordot & Gerenfit	Rehabilitation of Afordot Hospital and reposition of class rooms from Shelab to Gerenfit		219,390USD Health 36,000 USD Eduaction	8	This project was aimed at rehabilitating the Agordot hospital and moving the existing makeshift classrooms from Shelab to Gerenfit.

No.	Imp. Partner	Type of Intervention	Region/Sub-region Locality (ies)	Sector (s) & Cost per beneficiary	Beneficiaries	Total Budget USD	Months	Project Description & Notes
52	CESVI	Sustainable livelihoods	Gerenfit (Laelay Gash)	Distribution of chicks 929 women 158USD/beneficiary	929	147,037	6	This project was aimed at assisting the women headed households; so as to have some income generating activities. The first phase started while they were in Shelab camp, the second phase was in Gerenfit. They distributed chicks (24 in the first phase and 18 in the second phase per beneficiary), cage materials and feed 929 women headed families Training was also provided to the women.
53	MANITESE	Water harvesting	Molki area			141,591	6	The proposed project area is seriously affected by soil degradation, low and erratic rainfall and shortage of water sources, both for household and their livestock and it is the priority area of the MoA. The project aims to contribute to the soil and water conservation in the area; by harvesting runoff water and rehabilitating the eroded land.
54	ERREC	Transportation of Expellees	Shelab to Gerenfit		9,000	235,621	2	This is aimed at providing transport services to the expellees from Shelab to Gerenfit. and the transportation of expellees and IDPs from Korokon camp to Kotobia and Shambuko.
55	MoLWE/PMU	Purchase of hydrometrolocical instruments	In all war affected sub-zobas of Gash-Barka and Debub			240,000	2	This is for the replacement of the hydro metrological instruments which were looted or destroyed during the war. This budget is for all both war affected regions.
56	ERREC/UNICEF	Water and Sanitation	Gash-Barka, Omhajer	Construction of treatment plant	10,000	48,931.40		There is an existing water reservoir and a borehole with a yield of 6 l/s and safe bacteriological and chemical compositions, except slightly high Iron and Manganese contents; hence it is recommended that a treatment plant is necessary to remove the above impurities.
57	NUEYS	Mine Awareness	War-affected sub-zobas of Gash-Barka and Debub		25,000 children	58,442.85		This project is aimed at increasing the landmine awareness level among children and in turn decrease the rate of landmine caused injuries and deaths among them, Through Training youth as landmine awareness educators, preparation and production of color book and poster and awareness activities in 15 sites with in the TSZ.
58	COOPI	Health	Debub, Tsorona sub-zone	Health	40,000	134,152		The project will focus on Tsorona sub-zoba, Tsorona town, Endabastifanos (Endabastifanos and Gema'e camps), Genzebo (Maiwurai camp), Dekleafi and Ouna Andom villages. The health center, which was serving as a referral centre is destroyed by the war. Therefore, the NGO's aims to rehabilitate the existing health center and provide technical assistance, medicaments to the other health facilities.
59	GVC	Sustainable livelihood projects	Debub, Senafe, Adikeih, Tsorona and Maiaini	Poultry	1,800 women headed households	209,060.69		The project aims at the restocking of poultry in war affected areas of Zoba Debub. Through distribution of chicks, that is 25 chicks/beneficiary to 1,800 HH, distribution of chicks' feed and construction materials for the cage, training of beneficiaries and Rehabilitation of The Senafe poultry farm.
60	CRIC	Water and Sanitation	Debub, Adiquala sub-zoba (Kisad Ika, Adiquala and Ade Awhi)	Watsan	3,400	119,855		The project aims to cope with urgent needs in the water and sanitation sector for improving the actual condition of the facilities, the health status of the people and consequently for putting a base for further economical development. Rehabilitation of 4 hand dug water wells and 1 borehole and to equip them with manual pumping systems (1 hand pump in Kisad Ika, 2 in Adiquala and 2 in Adi Awhi).

No.	Imp. Partner	Type of Intervention	Region/Sub-region Locality (ies)	Sector (s) & Cost per beneficiary	Beneficiaries	Total Budget USD	Months	Project Description & Notes
61	REFUGEE TRUST	Water Supply	Debub, Adiquala sub-zoba, Maisagla village	Watsan		171,226		The project aims to provide clean water to the community of Maisagla village. It includes rehabilitation of the well, construction of distribution pipeline, construction of reservoir and public fountains, generator house construction and motorizing the system.
62	ISCOSE MARCHE	Capacity Building	Gash-Barka and Debub	Capacity building	42	72,164		The overall objective of the project is to allow the local administrations to keep full control of the recovery process in general and in specific food the security domain by better use of Information Technology tools.
63	MANITESE	Sustainable livelihood projects	Gash-Barka, Kotobia Camp	Different skills training	750	77,448.40	6	The project aims to train 750 women in different skills such as home economics, basic agriculture, sewing, hand looming and assistance to establish small businesses. It is targeting the rural expellees from Ethiopia in Kotobia camp and host communities.
64	MOVIMONDO	Sustainable livelihood projects	Gash-Barka, Laelay Gash, Ugumu village	Restocking	250	135,399	6	This project aims at the distribution of goats to rural expellees from Ethiopia who are going to be resettled in Ugumu area and the host communities of the Ugumu village.
65	MoLG Zoba Gash-Barka	Emergency Shelter	Gash-Barka, Laelay Gash, Gerenfit	Shelter	1,350	1,005,296	6	This project aims to assist the Rural Deportees from Ethiopia who are settled in Gerenfit village to construct their permanent shelter; through the provision of roofing materials (CIS, rafters, purlins) doors and windows. In addition it included the construction of prototypes which the farmers can use as model. (Netherlands Funding)
66	National Confederation of Eritrean Workers	Rehabilitation of Economic Infrastructure	Gash-Barka, Laelay Gash,			202,738		This project was for the rehabilitation of the Farmers Training center in Shemshmia, which was completely destroyed by the war. (Netherlands Funding)
67	MoLG Zoba Debu	Education	Debub region, Tsorona	School Rehabilitation		355,000		This project is aimed at the rehabilitation of the Tsorona Junior and Secondary school. By rehabilitating the school it will give a chance especially to girls who are not able to go to Adikeih and Dekemhare, to continue their education as it is far from their families. (Netherlands Funding)
68	MoLG Zoba Debu	Rehabilitation of Economic Infrastructure	Debub region, Tsorona	Rehabilitation of Tsorona Market	150	149,252.54		The overall objective of this project is to rehabilitate the Tsorona market, which was constructed in 1997 by the ECDF and completely destroyed by the war. It will benefit 150 women headed families. (Netherlands Funding)

Annex 4 First Joint Programme (November 2004 –March 2006)

No.	Type of Intervention	Region, Sub-region Locality (ies)	Sector (s) & Cost per beneficiary	Beneficiaries	Total Budget Expenditure USD	Project Description & Notes
1	Transportation of IDPs to villages of origin in Gash Barka	Gash-Barka region, Laelay Gash sub- zoba, Shilalo, Habela, Adi-Tsetser, Dembe-Dima, Tselale, Sheshebit, Adihakin, Maikokah, and Mukuti villages	Transportaion	19,000 IDPs 5,054 HHs	1,076,179.47	This component aims to return the IDPs and expellees from their present camps to their permanent villages so as to be able to initiate the rehabilitation process towards achieving normal life and ultimately attain self-reliance in their livelihoods. The transportation of the IDPs in Adi-Keshi camp to their villages of origin has been undertaken in February, 2005. UNDP, in collaboration with ERREC and other contributing agencies (ICRC, UNHCR and donors), shared the burden of transporting the returning IDPs. In this endeavour, UNDP's support was to extend financial assistance for the procurement of truck services, which would transport the IDPs, along with their personal belongings and animal farms, to the designated areas. UNHCR also contributed in kind by providing trucks for transporting IDPs with their personal effects.
2.	Sustainable Livelihood, support to agriculture	Gash-Barka region, Laelay Gash sub-zoba, Shilalo, Habela, Adi-Tsetser, Dembe-Dima, Tselale, Sheshebit, Adihakin, Maikokah, and Mukuti villages	Agriculture	5,054 HHs	496,023.04	During the year 2005, the returnee IDPs were assisted to build sustainable livelihoods through the provision of agricultural inputs and services. Each household has access to at least one hectare of farm plot. About 70% of the land was cleared through cash-for-work schemes and ploughed by tractors and oxen. This agricultural component aims to help the returnees to resume their active and productive lives in agriculture which is the main stay of the community. In this programme, 3556 Hectars of land was cleared, ploughed (by tractor and oxen) and sown. This task was accomplished by the regional office of the Ministry of Agriculture.
3	Construction of permanent Water Supply Systems	Gash-Barka region, Laelay Gash sub-zoba, Shilalo, Sheshebit, Dembe-Dima, Maikokah, and Mukuti villages	Water		382,440.69	In some of the villages the water wells were fitted with motorized pumps while in other villages they were fitted with hand pumps. Prior to the initiative of establishing water points in each of the villages the communities were fetching water by walking up to 4km to the sites of the wells. This prompted the need to construct distribution points and reservoirs with the necessary fittings so that the communities could access water within their villages. The work started in July 2005. The physical digging of the lines for pipes was completed in September 2005 in Shilalo, Sheshebit and Mukuti. Other activities such as the construction of public fountains (water points) and reservoirs are expected to be completed by the end of May 2006.
4	Permanent Shelter	Gash-Barka region, Laelay Gash sub-zoba, Sheshebit, Maikokah, Shilalo, Adihakin and Mukuti villages	Shelter	2200 HHs	430,180.36	UNDP provided 2200 shelter kits (comprising corrugated iron sheets, purling, rafters, nails and hinges) and cash for labour costs. UNDP had to adopt a flexible approach, that is, provision of the shelter kits, plus additional cash equivalent contribution to the cost of constructing 5m x 5m stabilized soil block walls for each household. The households were given the option of deciding the type of walls they wanted. The extra cost beyond the UNDP's contribution was to be covered from the individual household's own resources or other sources to be identified by Gash-Barka administration.

No.	Type of Intervention	Region, Sub-region Locality (ies)	Sector (s) & Cost per beneficiary	Beneficiaries	Total Budget Expenditure USD	Project Description & Notes
5	Food Aid	Gash-Barka region, Laelay Gash sub-zoba, Shilalo, Habela, Adi-Tsetser, Dembe-Dima, Tselale, Sheshebit, Adihakin, Maikokah, and Mukuti villages		5,054 HHs		As a continuation of previous emergency relief, WFP continued the distribution of food assistance to the IDPs who returned from Adi Keshi to their villages of origin.
6	Non Food Items	Gash-Barka region, Laelay Gash sub-zoba, Shilalo, Habela, Adi-Tsetser, Dembe-Dima, Tselale, Sheshebit, Adihakin, Maikokah, and Mukuti villages				Non-food items Mosquito nets, Metal oven (Griddles), Blankets, Soap, Sickles, Plough, Axes, Spades, Hoe and Kitchen sets were also distributed to the returned IDPs by different agencies: UNHCR, ICRC, the Eritrean Red Cross Society and the government beginning February 2005.
7	Education Construction of 30 makeshift and 18 new class rooms and 18 new teachers' residence	Gash-Barka region, Laelay Gash sub-zoba, Shilalo, Adi-Tsetser, Dembe-Dima, Mukuti and Maikokah villages	Education			During the summer of 2005, 30 classrooms from Adi-Keshi camp were dismantled and re-erected in the different villages of return/ resettlement. An additional 18 new classrooms and 18 residences for teachers have also been constructed.
8	Rehabilitation of a Health Station	Gash-Barka region, Laelay Gash sub-zoba, Shilalo village	Health			This health station was rehabilitated prior to the arrival of the IDPs and became fully functional. However, it is the only health facility serving about 20 villages including 9 villages of return. Since, some of the villages are remote from Shilalo, many people are finding it difficult to access the health services.

Annex 5 Expanded Joint Programme (May 2006-December 2007)

No.	Type of Intervention	Region, Sub-region Locality (ies)	Sector (s) & Cost per beneficiary	Beneficiaries	Total Budget Expenditure USD	Project Description & Notes
1	Transportation of IDPs to villages of origin or re-settlement	Debub region, Sub-Zobas, Tsorona and Senafe, Hadish Adi, Lhiyo, Meshal and Endeli (Metkel Abet) areas.	Transportation	2,188 HHs	1,126,435.13 (for both regions)	This component aims to return the IDPs and expellees from the present camps to their permanent villages so as to be able to initiate the rehabilitation process towards achieving normal life and ultimately attain self-reliance in their livelihood. The transportation of the IDPs in emergency camps in Debub namely, *Mai Wurrai, Metera, Afoma and Hahaile,* a total of 9344 persons, have been returned to their villages of origin or re-settlement in **May 2006.** The regional administration has established an elaborate and efficient ad-hoc structure to undertake the safe movement of people and goods. A large number of buses and trucks were mobilized; Ambulances were dispatched for emergency first aid services and emergency food and water supply were made available; and means of transport for the IDPs and their belongings were provided.
2	Transportation of IDPs to villages of origin or re-settlement	Gash-Barka region, Sub-Zobas, Shambuko and Molki, Girme, Ellala, Sheh'ate and Folina villages	Transportation	2,891 HHs		This component aims to return the IDPs and expellees from the present camps to their permanent villages so as to be able to initiate the rehabilitation process towards achieving normal life and ultimately attain self-reliance in their livelihood. The transportation of the IDPs in emergency camps in Gash-Barka namely, *Bimbina, Ade baare,* Shambuko, *Koroken, Dembe-Doran,* a total of 11,298 persons, have been returned to their villages of origin or re-settlement during the period of **11 May to 7 June 2006**. The regional administration has established an elaborate and efficient ad-hoc structure to undertake the safe movement of people and goods. A large number of buses, trucks were mobilized; Ambulances were dispatched for emergency first aid services and emergency food and water supply were made available; and means of transport for the IDPs and their belongings were provided.
3	Transportation of IDPs to villages of origin or re-settlement	Gash-Barka region, Sub-Zobas, Guluj (Tebeldia, Gergef, Sabunait, Goluj, Driesa and Aklalat); Shambuko (Bimbina, Tologamja, Anagulu and Adi-Maelel) And Omhajer and lyteref villages	Transportation	2,624 IDP HHs from camps 2,409 IDPs(10,910 persons) From host communities	548,223.38	This component aims to return the IDPs and expellees from the present camps to their permanent villages so as to be able to initiate the rehabilitation process towards achieving normal life and ultimately attain self-reliance in their livelihood. The transportation of the IDPs in emergency camps in Gash-Barka namely, Koitobia,*and Ade bare,* a total of 9,982 persons, have been returned to ten existing localities during the period of **April/May 2007.** Besides, the Government with the support of the UN and its partners returned 2,409 HHs (10,910 persons) who were living in host communities in Gash-Barka, to their places of origin in Omhajer and lyteref villages. The transportation included the people's personal belongings and their animals.

No.	Type of Intervention	Region, Sub-region Locality (ies)	Sector (s) & Cost per beneficiary	Beneficiaries	Total Budget Expenditure USD	Project Description & Notes
4	Sustainable Livelihood, support to agriculture (land surveys, land clearing, ploughing/ planting, provision oxen, and provision of agricultural inputs such as seeds)	Gash-Barka region, Sub-Zobas, Laelay Gash, Shambuko and Molki, Girme, Ellala, Sheh'ate and Folina villages	Agriculture		3,063,215.19 (for both Zobas)	The returnee IDPs were assisted to build sustainable livelihoods through agricultural support. In **2006**, in order to allocate one-hectare cropland for each of the new IDP/Expellee Households, 1,376 Hectares of new cropland surveys were undertaken in the villages of Girme, Ellala and Sheh'ate. Whereas, for those who have returned to their villages of origin and have their own plots of land an assistance was made in land clearing and ploughing. Ploughing and planting activities have been carried out in all return areas in sub zones of Shambuqo, Molki, and Lalai Gash. These activities mostly have been conducted with tractors in Lalai Gash and Molki and in some areas with oxen in Shambuqo and Molki sub zones. The planting activity has been done following first phase ploughing on 1,363 hectares while the remaining of the farmlands 3,467.75 hectares were planted without the first preparatory ploughing. 2,263 oxen to 12 beneficiary villages in sub zones of Lalai Gash, Shambuqo, and Molki. The beneficiaries (2263 HHs) were vulnerable households and mostly female-headed households. 1,650.55 Quintals of cereal seeds have been distributed to returnee farming households and crops have been sown successfully. This task was accomplished by the regional office of the Ministry of Agriculture.
5	Sustainable Livelihood, support to agriculture (land surveys, land clearing, ploughing/ planting, provision oxen, and provision of agricultural inputs such as seeds)	Debub region, Sub-Zobas, Senafe (Lahyo, Enghebeto, Ahiz, Meshal, Ham, Enta, Unawelesti, Adimereta, Fihe, Aregen and Aditelae) and Tsorona (Hadish Adi, Kinto, Adimesgene, Hashaso, Adishehu, Kinn, Gherghera, Selim kelay and Dembe Haysh), Endeli	Agriculture			During the year **2006**, the returnee IDPs were assisted to build sustainable livelihoods through agricultural support. The support to agriculture in Zoba Debub consisted mainly in land development and clearing, terracing and tree planting through cash-for-work programmes, procurement and distribution of agricultural hand tools and provision of resources for the purchase of oxen for distribution to vulnerable IDPs in areas of return/resettlement. 4,659 sets of agricultural tools of each type of tools have been distributed to returnee IDPs who have returned to their places of origin or resettled in new areas while 1,553 households have received cash assistance to purchase one ox each in Tsorona, Senafe and Endeli. 74.38% of the agricultural hand tool beneficiaries were female-headed households. In Tsorona, a tractor service support for about 700 ha. was given. Besides, 240 quintals of *Teff seed was offered* for the 566 households who resettled in Una Argena.

No.	Type of Intervention	Region, Sub-region Locality (ies)	Sector (s) & Cost per beneficiary	Beneficiaries	Total Budget Expenditure USD	Project Description & Notes
6	Sustainable Livelihood, Environmental Intervention	Gash-Barka region, Sub-Zobas, Laeylay Gash (Shilalo, Adi-Tsetser, Sheshebit, Adi-Hakin, Mukuti, Maikokah and Habela); Shambuko (Sheh'ate, Girme, and Dembehimbrti (Ellala) and Molki, , (Folina and Sifra Genet)	Environment	400 women trained on installation of improved Mogogo 4000 women HHs provided with improved Mogogo	70,000	In **2006**, the Component on environmental intervention started procuring the necessary materials for energy saving devices; beneficiaries have been identified and a training programme finalized in consultation with the Ministry of Mines and Energy. The Implementing Partner in Gash Barka is the National Union of Eritrean Women Branch office in Barentu. This component envisages the introduction of improved Mogogo and related training; the provision of community solar PV. Activities related to terracing, and planting of trees and shrubs to enhance environmental conservation have also started. The Environment subcomponent of the SLH activities, which is funded from the UNDP Trac II resource, has also recorded a remarkable accomplishment. Part of the core resource was allocated to install improved Mogogos within the IDPs areas of return and resettlment. NUEW, GB branch has carried out the procurement of improved Mogogo materials, conducted training sessions on how to install and use the system and provided 4,000 improved Mogogs to vulnerable female headed beneficiary households.
7	Sustainable Livelihood, support to agriculture (land development, land clearing, ploughing/ planting) Provision of agricultural inputs and improved seeds	Gash-Barka region, Sub-Zobas, Laelay Gash, Shambuko, Molki and Barentu.	Agriculture		1,606,784.10	A total of 9,638 hectares of land was ploughed and planted in the 2007 crop production season. The returnee farmers in Gash-Barka have conducted most of the land clearing activity manually on a cash-for-work basis. 2,144 shovels, 3,663 iron plough tips, 2,500 hoes and 7,472 sickles were distributed to returnee families. A total of 2,076 qt. of cereal crop seeds and 300 qt. of chickpea were distributed to about 140 HHs.
8	Sustainable Livelihood, support to agriculture land development (through the promotion of soil and water conservation); provision of improved seeds and restocking for the resource poor female headed HHs	Debub region, Sub-Zobas, Senafe and Tsorona	Agriculture		560,904.20	During the year 2007, in Debub region different land development activities such as construction of terraces, check dams, soil embankment and diversion; land levelling; stone collection and road construction and road maintenance. 676 qt. of improved seeds of different types of crops distributed to 3,281 HHs in Tsorona. 1,003 resource poor and women headed HHs have received cash assistance for the purpose of restocking (one ox per each HH).

No.	Type of Intervention	Region, Sub-region Locality (ies)	Sector (s) & Cost per beneficiary	Beneficiaries	Total Budget Expenditure USD	Project Description & Notes
9	Sustainable Livelihood, Environmental Intervention Provision of fuel saving improved stoves Soil and water conservation	Gash-Barka region, Sub-Zobas, Shambuko, Goluj, Laelay Gash, Molki and Gogne	Environment	2,200 women HHs	35,000	In 2007, improved stoves were distributed to 2,200 resource poor and women headed households among the returnee/resettled communities of Shambuko and Goluj. The beneficiaries also received training on the construction and use of the improved stove. Soil and water conservation activities such as hillside terracing and construction of check dams were done by the returned/resettled IDPs in Laelay Gash, Molki, Shambuko and Gogne. Different species of trees that are proven to be suitably grown in various areas of Gash-Barka region were distributed to families in returnee/ resettlement sites of sub-zobas Molki, Goluj, Laelay Gash and Gogne for planting in the homestead areas.
10	Construction of permanent Water Supply Systems	Gash-Barka region, Sub-Zobas, Shambuko and Molki, Girme, Ellala, Sheh'ate, Tselim kelay, Adi Maelel and Folina pevillages	Water		537,377.32	Water supply wells have been drilled by ECDC in Girme, Ellala, She'hate, Tselim Kelay, Adi Maelel and Folina. The Girme Water Supply system includes so far the installation of a submersible pump, a 10 Meter Cube bladder, faucets and pipeline (50mts), hydrant, hand pump and an initial supply of fuel for the generator.
11	Construction of permanent Water Supply Systems	Debub region, Sub-Zobas, Senafe and Tsorona (the project sites are in Adimereta, Adishehu- Adimesgene, Ahiz, Aregen, Cheanadug, Fihe-Muguo, Hadish Adi- Hashaso, Ham, Kinto, Lahyo, Tahtay Fihe, Unanazo-Kudoweiba)	Water			In Debub the return villages are located in most cases on the top of the mountains. The water sources are in the nearby riverbeds. The budget allocated for Debub is 225,000 USD which is very little compared to the challenge of finding a source and laying down the water supply system. So far, the design works of the water supply schemes for 12 IDPs return villages has been completed.
12	Construction of permanent Water Supply Systems	Debub region, Sub-Zobas, Senafe and Tsorona (the project sites are in Adimereta, Adishehu- Adimesgene, Ahiz, Aregen, Cheanadug, Fihe-Muguo, Hadish Adi- Hashaso, Ham, Kinto, Lahyo, Tahtay Fihe, Unanazo-Kudoweiba)	Water	Borehole based 996 HHs Masonary Dam based 223 HHs Recharging Scheme 154 HHs Spring based 124 HHs Earth Dam based 275 HHs		In Debub, sub-zobas Senafe and Tsorona, 15 water supply schemes are being constructed in the return villages in 2007. Seven bore hole based water schemes (Adimereta,, Ahiz, Tahtay Fihe, Unanazo-Kudoweiba, Unawelesti and Inta villages) Three micro-dams in Hadish-Adi, Kinito and Ham villages (the micro-dam in Ham not completed). Components of the water supply schemes, such as water reservoirs and public fountains have been constructed

No.	Type of Intervention	Region, Sub-region Locality (ies)	Sector (s) & Cost per beneficiary	Beneficiaries	Total Budget Expenditure USD	Project Description & Notes
13	Construction of permanent Water Supply Systems	Gash-Barka region, Sub-Zobas, Shambuko and Molki, Girme, Ellala, Sheh'ate, Tselim kelay, Adi Maelel and Folina villages	Water	1,117 HHs		In 2007, the water supply system construction of Folina, Ellala and Adi-maelel are almost completed. Rehabilitation works of Omhajer water supply project has been completed. Three bore hole- bases have also been completed in 2007in the returnee villages of Mukuti, Sheshebit and Dembedima.
14	Permanent Shelter	Debub region, Sub-Zobas, Senafe (Lahyo, Enghebeto, Ahiz, Meshal, Ham, Enta, Unawelesti, Adimereta, Fihe, Aregen and Aditelae) and Tsorona (Hadish Adi, Kinto, Adimesgene, Hashaso, Adishehu, Kinn, Gherghera, Selim kelay and Dembe Haysh), Endeli	Shelter	1,907 HHs	1,409,421.98	The proposal was cash assistance in three instalments to be provided to the returnees for the construction of permanent shelter with a minimum area of 4x5 = 20 meter square for one HH. Accordingly, the Debub administration has disbursed the first and second instalment of funds to 1907 HHs (at a rate of 12,000 Nakfa per HH; 4,000 being the first instalment and 8,000 being the second instalment, respectively) towards the erection of one multi-purpose room.
15	Permanent Shelter	Gash-Barka region, Sub-Zobas, Shambuko (Sheh'ate, Girme, Tsibra and Dembehimbrti (Ellala) and Molki, , (Folina and Sifra Genet)	Shelter	1,643 HHs	2,201,665.41	The Gash Barka Regional Administration has disbursed the first and the second instalment of funds to 1,643 HHs (at a rate of 5,000 and 8,000, i.e. a total of 13,000 Nakfa per HH respectively) so as to enable them to erect a permanent one-room shelter with the minimum area is 4x5 = 20 meter square.. The amount of cash assistance per beneficiary HH is 23,000 Nakfa. In Gash Barka among the beneficiaries of the shelter programme 64.6% constitute women headed households.
16	Permanent Shelter	Gash-Barka region, Sub-Zobas, Shambuko (Sheh'ate, Girme, Tsibra and Dembehimbrti (Ellala) and Molki, , (Folina and Sifra Genet)	Shelter	1,643 HHs 2,681 HHs 441 HHs		The Gash Barka Regional Administration has disbursed the third instalment of funds to 1,643 HHs. Accordingly, these HHs fully completed the shelter construction in 2007. An Additional 2,681 HHs received the first installment cash assistance. Among those who received shelter kits to construct their permanent houses, 441 HHs have received cash assistance to cover their loabour cost.

No.	Type of Intervention	Region, Sub-region Locality (ies)	Sector (s) & Cost per beneficiary	Beneficiaries	Total Budget Expenditure USD	Project Description & Notes
17	Permanent Shelter	Debub region, Sub-Zobas, Senafe (Lahyo, Enghebeto, Ahiz, Meshal, Ham, Enta, Unawelesti, Adimereta, Fihe, Aregen and Aditelae) and Tsorona (Hadish Adi, Kinto, Adimesgene, Hashaso, Adishehu, Kinn, Gherghera, Selim kelay and Dembe Haysh), Endeli	Shelter	1,907 HHs		The Debub Regional Administration has disbursed the third instalment of funds to 1,907 HHs. Accordingly, most of these HHs fully completed the shelter construction in 2007.
18	Health and Nutrition					Reducing acute malnutrition of children 6 to 59 months in resettlement communities. Access to health services and immunization.
19	Education					Access to safe learning spaces in Gash-Barka. Access to Sanitary (latrine) facilities in Debub. Capacity Building of Teachers.
20	Child Protection and Non-food Items					Mine Risk Education (MRE). Non-food Items Distribution and Income Generation Assets.

ANNEX 6. - ANNOTATED BIBLIOGRAPHY

Alden Chris. *Making Old Soldiers Fade Away: Lessons from the Reintegration of Demobilized Soldiers in Mozambique.*
Accessed at: www.jha.ac/articles/a112.htm
On 10/08/2008.

This article outlines the demobilisation and reintegration programme in Mozambique and conducts an investigation into the particulars of the internationally-funded approaches to reintegration and the concomitant difficulties experienced in the course of implementation. Furthermore, it analyses the outcomes of the reintegration experience in Mozambique and assesses the lessons learned for other reintegration programmes.

Buse Margaret. *RONCO Executives Talk About Demining Integration and the IMAS Contract: An Interview with Lawrence Crandall, Stephen Edelmann and A. David* Lundberg, Journal of Mine Action, "Deminers, Manual Demining and their Personal Protective Equipment," Issue 4.2, Summer 2000, p. 69.

In this interview A. David Lundberg from RONCO talks about some of the challenges in setting up a successful demining program. There is lack of trained in-country personnel in most of the developing world and the biggest challenge is building and developing indigenous capacity. He also discusses the stereotypes they face in different countries with different cultures and beliefs. Therefore, building a successful demining programme requires not only training but also attitudinal changes.
Buse Margaret. The Role of the United Nations in Mine Action: An Interview with Ian Mansfield," Journal of Mine Action, "National Mine Action Programs," Issue 6.1, Winter 2002, p. 6.

In this interview Ian Mansfield of the United Nations Development Programme talks about the various mine action offices in the UN, how the UN organizes mine action, the role of host governments, donors, and the successes and challenges of coordinating integrated mine action activities with infrastructure development and capacity building.

Catley A, 1995. *The livestock component of the PROFERI Pilot Project: final report to Christian Aid, Oxfam UK/Ireland and the Overseas Development Administration (UK).*

This report details the progress of the livestock component of the Programme for Refugee Reintegration and Rehabilitation of Resettlement Areas in Eritrea (PROFERI) Pilot Project. It assesses the importance of the provision of livestock to the returnees and its implementation by the Ministry of Agriculture (MoA) working with the Commission for Eritrean Refugee Affairs (CERA) and the local government. Furthermore, it highlights some of the major flaws made in the design of the livestock component of the PROFERI and offers suggestions for possible improvements to the project in later phases.

Catley, A. and Blakeway, S. 1997. *Donkeys and the Provision of Livestock to Returnees: Lessons from Eritrea.* http://www.atnesa.org/donkeys/donkeyscatley-returnees-ER.pdf (10 June 2008).

Outlines the provision of livestock to returnees as part of a large-scale, integrated resettlement project in Eritrea. Before procurement of livestock, returnees were interviewed to understand their preferences for different livestock types. Based on the results of the interviews, the number of donkeys provided by the project was increased by up to 7.3 times the number in the original project plan. Both female and male-headed households opted to receive donkeys. The authors discuss the role of donkeys in 'restocking' projects and advocates participation of beneficiaries in the identification of appropriate livestock inputs.

This article illustrates a case example of a livestock intervention that aims to restore a sustainable livelihood system for Eritrean refugees. It demonstrates the importance of input from participants in planning livelihood interventions and the use of monitoring and evaluation in assessing the impact of livelihood interventions.

Chris Horwood, Team Leader of the External Evaluation, and Michel Le Pechoux, Children Affected by Armed Conflict Project Officer, UNICEF Cambodia, *The Children's Plight in Cambodia,* Journal of Mine Action, "Landmines in Asia & the Pacific," Issue 5.1, Spring 2001, p. 59.

Cambodia Mine action agencies in Cambodia continue to face a major challenge. In the past decade they have only been able to partially address the vast mines and UXO problem. This article seeks to show that despite this sobering context there are positive and important lessons to be learned from the Cambodian experience that need to be shared with the global mine action community as models for progress.

Specifically, this article represents some lessons learned from UNICEF's mine action involvement in Cambodia, as highlighted in a recent external evaluation conducted for UNICEF.

Fiederlein Suzanne. Potential Value of Mine Victims Needs Assessment. Posted on 6/27/2007. Mine action information centre

This information is posted by a senior research associate of the Mine Action Information Centre (MAIC) in the lessons learned mine action window. It talks about the potential value of Mine Victims Needs Assessment. Conducting a mine victims needs assessment can provide valuable information for defining the extent of the need for services and the particular types of medical and rehabilitation services required.

These detailed surveys generally focus on landmine/UXO survivors but can also gather information on other victims, such as family members of those injured or killed in accidents. The data collected can augment the accident data collected by a mine action center and thus also be of use to those working in mine clearance and MRE activities.

Hadgu A, Ghiorgis D, Teclemarium E and Blakeway S, 1995. *Evaluation of the agricultural component of the pilot phase of PROFERI, December 1995.*

The evaluation of the agricultural component of the pilot phase of PROFERI reviews the implementation of the agricultural package which comprises of access to land with food for work for communal clearing, tractor plowing, provision of seeds, tools and fertilizers; agricultural extension services; livestock provision and veterinary services. Based on the result of the evaluation, the team proposes a list of recommendations for the consecutive phases of the programme.

Hamid E. The importance of donkeys in a restocking programme in Eritrea. Ministry of Agriculture, Gash-Barka Zone, Eritrea. http://www.atnesa.org/donkeys/donkeys- ezedeen-restocking-ER.pdf (10 June 2008).

There are three breeds of donkey in the western lowlands of Eritrea, namely Mekadi, Atbawi and Reef. The donkey is an important livestock species that is well adapted to the different environments of Eritrea. It serves for riding, as a pack animal for short distance transport, and as a draft animal. Because of its importance the donkey was included in a restocking programme which aimed to overcome the shortage of agricultural power encountered by returnee farmers.

A study showed that owning a donkey reduces the work load of women and at the same time increases time spent on other income generating activities. Lack of farmers' knowledge of appropriate harnesses and management is a limiting factor in the more efficient use of donkeys. There is a potential for the greater use of donkeys in the rural economy of Eritrea and by returnees. Realisation of this potential depends on technical and social changes for which a research and extension programme is needed.

JJ Scott, *The Kosovo MACC: The Most Successful Mine Action Program Ever,* Journal of Mine Action, "National Mine Action Programs," Issue 6.1,Winter 2002, pp.26-27.

This article details the organization and principles of the Kosovo Mine Action Coordination Centre. It gives detailed analysis of the four pillars of the Mine Action Program which are mine clearance, mine awareness, victim assistance and advocacy. Furthermore, it highlights the lessons learned from the country's experience and the future of mine action.

Nevertheless, it underscored that success could not be easily replicated from one country to the other, that is, mine action programmes to be successful need to devise demining methods appropriate to their unique situations.

Keeley R. and Haile T. 2008. *Independent Final Evaluation of the Eritrean Mine Action Capacity Building Programme (MACBP) 2002 – 2006.* Evaluation Report.

This report documents the evaluation of the Mine Action Capacity Building Programme (MACBP: 2002-2006) initiated by UNDP in consultation with the Government of Eritrea and relevant stakeholders. The objective of the MACBP was to expand national capacity for mine action. This evaluation report discusses the progress of the MACBP and identifies some lessons learned and possible ideas for re-engagement in the mine action sector in Eritrea.

Kibreab G. 1998. Evaluation of the USAID Portion of the Pilot Program for Reintegration and Rehabilitation of Resettlement Areas in Eritrea (PROFERI)

USAID's inputs in the pilot phase of the PROFERI has three components namely agriculture with four packages such as provision of seeds, hand tools, livestock and tractor hire service; institutional strengthening relating specifically to staffing and operations of CERA and feeder road construction and rehabilitation. This evaluation report shows the assessment of whether the program remained consistent with its stated goal of assisting the reintegration of returnees; whether planned results were met and to explain why and why not; and whether the emergency needs of the settled returnees were met; the effectiveness of institutional strengthening to CERA (later ERRA). It also distills lessons that might be of use for future interventions.

Matos M. Elizabeth. 1998. Seed and Plant Genetic Resources Restoration in Disaster and Conflict Situations In Angola: Some Experiences From Over 20 Years of Conflict Situations, Case Study.

This case study articulates the nature of conflict in Angola in relation to seed supplies and Plant Genetic Resources (PGR) conservation. It explores the plant genetic resources in Angola and considers the seed and tool distributions to displaced people post 1992. Moreover, it identifies the requirements of the displaced and returnee farmers to increase crop and seed production.

Mehreteab A. 2000. Reintegrating Returnees and Ex-Fighters in the Process of Reconstruction in Post-Conflict Eritrea. PhD Thesis (unpublished)

With independence and the return of peace there was an opportunity as well as a need to repatriate the refugees, demobilize the fighters and re-integrate them in to mainstream society. This thesis examines the re-integration of returnees in Eritrea within the context of rehabilitation and reconstruction process. The analytical models followed are the economic, social, cultural and socio-psychological re-integration which are interrelated and interdependent. It identifies and analyzes the variables that influence re-integration.

Furthermore, comparisons are made between ex-refugees and ex-fighters by analyzing the variables. After placing the policies and programmes that have been developed to address the problems of re-integrating returnees, the thesis analyzes the effectiveness of the various approaches. Moreover, the roles of different internal and external actors are examined. In conclusion, policy recommendations are proposed to show how re-integration policies and programs could be further improved in the future development of the country.

Mehreteab A. 2002.A Comparative Study on Two Demobilization and Reintegration Exercises in Eritrea, Bonn International Center for Conversion (BICC), Bonn.

This paper compares the two demobilization and reintegration exercises practiced by Eritrea under different contexts.

The first was the demobilization and reintegration of the freedom fighters and the second is the current demobilization and re-integration of the ex-soldiers who were mobilized during the 1998-2000 border war with Ethiopia. It presents a thorough study on the past experience and compares it to other experience in Africa and elsewhere and draws necessary lessons from this exercise.

Mengistu G., Pardeshi P., Salmarshe D., and Maria de Vita G., 2002. The UNDP/BCPR Transition Recovery Response: Mid-Term Review, Eritrea.

This mid term evaluation is primarily concerned with understanding how the Transition Recovery Concept (TRC) was applied in response to the post-conflict situation in Eritrea from 2000 to 2002. Its principal objective is to assess how the Transition Recovery Programme has assisted the Government of Eritrea and other key humanitarian and developmental stakeholders negotiate the transition from relief to recovery.

A subsidiary objective is to draw lessons for the future application of the approach. The means by which the evaluation goals have been met has been through the examination of 21 projects spread across the sectors of shelter, social infrastructure and livelihoods in the two war effected regions of Eritrea. In addition a number of interviews have been undertaken with government officials and other relevant individuals. The report also describes the relief to recovery process from project, strategic and institutional perspectives so as to shed light on the management of the recovery phase and the transition to longer term development modalities.

Michael A. Boddington, Sustainability of Prosthetic and Orthotic Programs, Journal of Mine Action, "Victim and Survivor Assistance," Fall 1999, Version 3.3, p. 23.

This paper examines the overall incidence of disability, and specifically of motor-disability, in low-income countries of the world. It observes the attitude of society toward those suffering from disabilities, and argues that there is a need for long term support for services to the motor-disabled by the international community.

In order to generate this support, low-income countries must develop highly efficient services that minimize the call on international resources. Such services are likely to be outside government. They will be within private nonprofit organizations; ring fenced, transparent, and capable of regular audit.

Nagoda Sigrid de Barbentane. and Fowler Cary. Seed Relief after Hurricane Mitch in Honduras: A Critical Analysis of Institutional Responses. http://www.jha.ac/articles/a114.htm#_ftnref1

This paper is based on interviews with people working in the local, national and international organizations involved in emergency agricultural restoration following Hurricane Mitch in Honduras.

Coordination between relief organisations and local communities was weak among most seed relief programs. Eschewing diversity, the programs distributed a small number of improved varieties.

Most organizations found it less time consuming and risky to distribute varieties already certified and promoted as having broad adaptation in marginal areas than to multiple and distribute local varieties. However, many institutions designed their interventions without a serious assessment of local seed security or seed management practices.

The varieties distributed did not always respond to the considerable variations in ecological, economic and social conditions found in Honduras. Seed supply, rather than seed demand, may have been the driving force behind seed activities.

Praxis Group, Ltd. 2002."Willing To Listen" An Evaluation of the United Nations Mine Action Programme in Kosovo 1999-2001. Riverside/Geneva.

This report addresses the initial threat assessment and response of the United Nations as well as the first steps taken by various donors, the establishment of a United Nations mine action coordination capability within the framework of the United Nations Interim Administration Mission in Kosovo (UNMIK), the implementation and the effectiveness of the resulting mine action programme, the nature and scope of donor support to - and participation in - the programme, and the handover of expertise and responsibilities to the new governance structures in Kosovo.

PROFERI. 1995. 'Phase 1 Operational Plan 1995', Government of Eritrea Commission for Eritrean Refugees Affairs (CERA).

This operational plan documents the plan for the implementation of phase one of the PROFERI which has eleven components identified for the repatriation and reintegration activities for 100,000 refugees from Sudan to 50 sites in the five provinces of Eritrea. Each component provides an objective, a strategy, activities, inputs/costs and implementation arrangements based on an implementation schedule.

UNDP.2005. National Commission for the Demobilization and Re-integration Programme (NCDRP): United States Agency for International Development (USAID) Technical Assistance Programme Executed by the United Nations Development Programme (UNDP), Terminal Report.

This report provides an overview of the progress of the USAID funded Technical Assistance Programme (TAP) provided by the UNDP. The aim of the TAP was to plan and facilitate the efficient implementation and management of the NCDRP training activities related to social and economic reintegration interventions.

The report details the achievement of the commissioned consultancies and assesses the impact TAP has had on the NCDRP and on the overall demobilization programme.

ANNEX 7 – UNDP RECOVERY PROGRAMMES IN ERITREA: Resources Mobilized

Programme/Project		Budget	Donor
Post Liberation/Pre-referendum Project - PRP (1992 1993)		6,000,000	UNDP
Sub Total		**6,000,000**	
PROFERI (1995-1997)		9,305,873	UNDP
		2,054,795	Swedish Trust fund (managed by UNDP)
	Sub Total	**11,360,668**	
Pre-PoWER (July 2000-March 2002)	Emergency Assistance	1,334,661	Italy
	Emergency Assistance	314,150	USAID
	Sub Total	**1,648,811**	
PoWER (November 2000-October 2004)	PoWER I (Nov. 2000-Dec.2001)	14,934,882	Italy
	PoWER II	2,177,056	Italy
	Emergency shelter & HH Items	5,336,156	Netherlands
	Capacity Building Mine Action	4,035,193	Norway, Netherlands, EU, UK, Canada
	Preparatory Assistance Demobilization	200,000	UNDP
	TA for Demobilization	580,000	USAID
	Sub Total	**27,263,287**	
IRP *(2003-2004)*	Jumpstart IRP	226,000	UNDP/BCPR
	Sub Total	**226,000**	

First Joint Programme **(*November 2004-March 2006*)**	Pooled Funding	1,000,000	UNDP
		2,061,088	Norway
		1,111,000	Netherlands
		1,000,000	USAID
		240,000	UNICEF
		829,384	Italy
	Parallel funding	3,030,000	WFP (In-knid)
		2,370,000	Norway (NGOs)
		1,300,000	Government (In-kind)
	Sub Total	**12,941,472**	
Expanded Joint Programme *(April 2006-December 2009)*	Pooled Funding	2,400,000	UNDP
		11,788,113	Norway
		904,000	Netherlands
		3,875,171	USAID
		1,600,000	Norway (transferred funds from Mine Action to IDPs)
		996,000	CERF
		240,000	CERF to IDPs
		240,000	CERF to Mine Action
		400,000	CERF to IDPs
		15,741,400	EC
	Parallel funding	300,000	UNICEF
		70,500	UNHCR
		In-kind	UNHCR
	Sub Total	**38,555,184**	
Transition and Early Recovery Programme - TER (January 2010-December 2012)		20,647,943	UNDP Norway EC CERF IFAD
	Sub Total	**20,647,943**	
	Total	**119,990,669**	

Annex 8 - Food Production Zoba Debub 2006 and 2007

Description	Sub- Zoba Tsorona						Sub- Zoba Senafe					
	2006			2007			2006			2007		
	Area Sown (ha)	Production (qt)	Yield (qt/ ha)	Area Sown (ha)	Production (qt)	Yield (qt/ ha)	Area Sown (ha)	Production (qt)	Yield (qt/ ha)	Area Sown (ha)	Production (qt)	Yield (qt/ ha)
Cereals												
Sorghum	1600	7680	4.80	3500	57330	16				300	2400	8
Wheat							4135	4465.8	1.08	4700	36660	7.8
Maize	920	6182.4	6.72	1870	62327	33				200	2100	11
Barley				250	6075	2.70	3003	6006	2.0	2300	19550	8.5
Taff	3000	15900	5.30	2824	27760	9.80				100	500	5
Pearl millet												
Hanfez										1000	8000	8
Dagusha	1400	11704	8.36	600	9828	16				150	1050	7
Other food crops												
Peas										80	880	11
Chick peas	1000	15400	15.40									
Horse beans (baldonga)										200	2060	10.3
Lentils										250	950	3.8
Linseed										250	650	2.6
Horticulture												
Tomatoes	38	4560	120	72.1	8652	120	50	6000	120	71.25	8550	120
Pepper	15	1200	80	9.25	740	80	34	2720	80	43.5	3480	80
Potatoes	1	120	120	13.45	1614	120	6	720	120	104.5	12540	120
Onions	19	1235	65	15	975	65	24	1560	65	34.75	2258.75	65
Cabbage	4	600	150	3.9	585	150	20	3000	150	57.25	8587.5	150
Green leef veg	8	800	100	8.85	885	100	28	2800	100	58.5	5850	100
Salad veg	19	2090	110	6.78	745.8	110	22	2420	110	54.5	5995	110
Carrot	1	120	120	0.5	60	120	4	480	120	10	1200	120
Zucchini	0	0	100	0.83	83	100	0	0	100	3	300	100
Garlic	0	0	60	0	0	60	3	180	60	15.75	945	60

Source: MoA Annual Reports 2006 and 2007.

Annex 9 - Food Production - ZOBA DEBUB

Sub-zoba	Adm. Area	Village	No of HHs	No of Persons	Area of farm land (Ha)	Production	Yield per Ha
Tsorona	Dibi	Debasit	74	286	128.24	160.3	
		Dibi	78	333	44.00		
		Egri-Mekel	86	312	31.75		
		Enda-Sherif	56	222	27.62		
		Gemae	86	355	70.12		
		Hatako (expellees from Tigray)	22	85	-	-	
		Kurbeli	49	185	36.25		
		Mehradchele	99	360	73.62		
		Qolomia	36	143	31.37		
		Sub-total	**586**	**2281**	**442.97**		
	Endabaestifanos	Aiba	190	766	282.00		
		Berik-Hussa	99	451	93.00		
		Endabaestifanos	32	130	16.25		
		Enda-Haji	37	162	46.25		
		Ferashit	50	193	-	-	
		Gefafin	30	123	127.00		
		Godofai	53	321	48.50		
		Kormedeguzai	38	169	40.75		
		Selolo	58	204	60.75		
		Unkurai	27	107	-	-	
		Sub-total	**614**	**2626**	**714.50**		
	Hadish-Adi	Adi-Mesgene	187	405	18.75	23.45	
		Adi-shuhu	106	400	94.00	117.50	
		Hadish-Adi	143	567	61.12	76.40	
		Hashaso	182	706	123.25	154.10	
		knito	132	606	64.50	80.65	
		Sub-total	**750**	**2684**	**361.62**	**452.10**	
	Tsorona	kudoweiba	226	939	127.25		
		Una-nazo	144	558	205.26		
		Sub-total	**370**	**1497**	**332.51**		

		Ambeset			22.5	-	
	Ambesete Geleba	Lailay-Geleba			37.0	-	
		Maekelay-Geleba			24.5	-	
		Sub-total	**796**		**84.00**		
		Ased			29.00	25.00	
	Degogolo	Moko			56.00	97.00	
		Sub-total			**85.00**	**122.00**	
		Melhin-Dega			160.00	92.00	
	Golo	Merbed			179.00	124.00	
		Sub-total			**339.00**	**216.00**	
		Aregen			162.50	131.00	
		Ahiz			235.00	183.75	
		Ham-Cheanadug			136.00	152.00	
	Lahiyo	Lahiyo (Egri-Abew)	91	400	76.50	62.80	
		Fihe			83.00	56.00	
		Sub-total			**693.00**		
		Adi-Mereta	48	236	37.50	-	
		Adi-Telae	104	382	52.00	-	
		Engebeto	197	712	101.25	-	
	Meshal-Akran	Enta	112	347	53.50	-	
		Meshal-Akran	234	897	180.75	-	
		Una-Welesti	54	287	23.50	-	
		Sub-total	**749**	**2861**	**448.5**	-	
		Narea			43.00	-	
	Telhanarea	Geredef			12.00	-	
		Sub-total			**55.00**	-	
	Hakir	Tisha	**260**		23.00	20.00	
		Endeli∞	408				
		FekeMereh∞∞∞	425				
Total							

Annex 10 - Food Prices in Nakfa

Description							
		Sub-Zoba Tsorona			Sub-Zoba Senafe		
Cereals	**Unit**	**2006**	**2007**	**2008**	**2006**	**2007**	**2008**
Sorghum	qt	810	1650	2700	920	915	2450
Wheat	qt				1255	1670	4080
Maize	qt	870	1170	2850	1205	1130	4330
Barley	qt				1040	1050	3915
Taff	qt	1200	1740	3900	1745	2205	4360
Finger millet	qt	1350	2010	3900	850	1165	2280
Hanfez	qt				965	1070	3915
Other food crops							
Peas	qt				2280	1855	3640
Chick peas	qt	2100	2550	3080			
Horse beans	qt				1825	1840	3640
Lentils	qt				2340	1640	2850
Linseed	qt						
Hoticultural products							
Onions	kg	21	16	24	11	12	16
Potatoes	kg	18	17	18	12	14	15
Tomatoes	kg	24	20	25	8	8	10
Pepper	kg	28	28	28	20	22	24
Cabbages	kg	5	4	5	9	7	8
Bamia	kg	8	9	10			
Livestock							
Ox	no				7500	6000	6000
Goat	no	800	750	700	1050	900	775
Sheep	no	800	750	700	900	800	700
Donkey	no	1500	1500	1800	1250	1300	1400
Camel	no			15000			
Source: MoA in the sub-zobas, November 2008							

Annex 11: SOCIAL AND ECONOMIC REINTEGRATION OF DEMOBILIZED SOLDIERS - LIST OF ACTIVITIES COMPLETED UNDER THE TECHNICAL ASSISTANCE

As indicated in the original TAP proposal, some assignment were split into multiple and related missions – especially in respect of senior international consultants appointed. All assignments have been completed and reports completed. The consultancies listed below are those which were ultimately agreed to for inclusion in the TAP between the NCDRP and the UNDP.

M3: Senior strategic reintegration planning consultant

All Assignments have been successfully concluded.

M5: Senior information and sensitisation consultant

All missions have been successfully concluded..

M6: Senior training programme consultant

It was decided to combine this mission with that of the senior training design and planning consultant (S2) to facilitate coordination during the planning and implementation stages. All assignments under both terms of reference have been successfully concluded and several reports with recommendations for implementation have been completed.

Several workshops were conducted in conjunction with the line ministries and relevant NCDRP staff, where appropriate, to provide feedback on recommended actions, policy matters and the overall improvement and strengthening of access to training opportunities for DS. Meetings with implementing partners were held at several junctures to urge progress with the implementation of the recommendations. The endemic lack of capacity in the line ministries however continues to frustrate implementation.

The coordination and integration of several consultants' activities, i.e. job attachments, apprenticeships, the public works programme, architectural requirements for the refurbishment of SDC's, costing of training and training of trainers was also effected during the missions.

Terms of Reference for a consultant to develop capacity for the recognition of prior learning became a necessity and were developed. A consultant was appointed and has completed the first mission. Additional missions will be required during 2004. This will enable DS to receive formal recognition for experience, skills and knowledge gained during the mobilization and thus accelerate access to economic opportunities.
A key challenge is to ensure that the training component is supportive of the NCDRP's rural and entrepreneurship strategies and that labour market demands are incorporated.

M8: Senior social reintegration consultant

Component substantially developed, particularly in respect of psycho-social aspects that are ready for implementation. Over 600 persons as para-psycho-social advisers have been trained in zobas in preparation of the services indicated in this component. Medical and physical rehabilitation components have not been suitably developed. This is currently being followed up with the Ministry of Health.

The contracted assignment of this consultant comes to an end mid of 2004

M9: Senior rural development consultant

The initial assignment has been completed and the reports produced to provide an overall rural development strategy. Due to elements of the report considered unsuitable to the NCDRP, terms of reference for further consultancies were compiled and appointments made. The final report was completed during December 2003. The primary tasks of this second appointment were to review and validate the findings and designs of the thematic experts and ensure that they are consistent with the rural strategy developed and the refinements made by the NCDRP.

Senior training design consultant (on-the-job training)

All tasks have been successfully concluded. Systems for the implementation of Attachment Programmes were developed including identification criteria for the selection of Implementing Agencies and Implementing Partners. The first mission also provided the framework for the T4 consultant to research the specific on-the-job training, apprenticeships, public works and job placement opportunities (in all sectors and at all levels) for possible NCDRP interventions.

It also suggested an integrated approach to employ Implementing Agencies who would facilitate job attachments in the market. The second mission focused on the research data and suggested strategies to roll-out attachment opportunities for DS in conjunction with the IA's and IP's. These recommendations were integrated by the M6 consultant into the overall menu of training opportunities.

S2: Senior design and planning consultant (skills training facilities)

All missions (5 in all) have been successfully concluded. This includes the investigation into the feasibility of regenerating Sawa as a multi purpose training centre which was not originally provided for under the TAP.

The recommendations in all the reports are in the process of implementation although capacity problems within the line ministries have delayed this substantially. These include the redesign and refurbishment of the skills training facilities (T10), prioritisation of training courses to be provided (T5), integration of training activities with business development and rural development imperatives, the development of emergency responses to DS training needs through training contracts with IP's (T6) and synchronisation with job attachments (T4), training of trainers (T9), as well as mobile training and aftercare (S3).

The overall coordination function under M6 was facilitated by this integrated approach and simplified the overall synchronisation of the training component and related recommendations.

S3: Senior training design consultant (Mobile Training)

See S2 and M6

Senior labour market systems design consultant

All targets under this category have been completed. The initial focus was concerned primarily with the initial design of the labour market information system to be implemented and subsequently to the development of reporting systems and updating data collection.

The system has been designed for implementation at regional level with a roll-up nationally to ensure that NCDRP interventions respond directly to localised needs. Information was to be updated quarterly. Weaknesses in the system have been identified and feedback received from the M6 consultant would indicate that not enough has been done to integrate the labour market forecasts with national economic priorities such as the "crash programme" for exports. This observation received attention from the NCDRP in conjunction with line ministries.

Senior Monitoring and Evaluation consultant

The M&E consultant has completed her assignments and recommendations have been submitted to the NCDRP to implement systems. A Monitoring and Evaluation Guide has been developed. It introduces monitoring and evaluation and focuses on concepts, principles and methodology. The second volume contains a Strategic Results Framework (SRF) which was constructed with five phases and a step-by-step guide for conducting monitoring and evaluation of NCDRP Sub-Projects and Activities. The indicators for M&E are based on generally accepted international practise in this regard and include, relevance, effectiveness, efficiency, impact and sustainability. Management and MIS staff of the NCDRP have been trained in the implementation modalities of M&E.

Job Attachments expert

(Note: Previously called On-the-job training, apprenticeships, public works and job placement experience). Instead of three consultants being appointed as planned, one consultant with an increased ToR was identified and appointed.

The consultant, with the guidance of the Senior Consultant has completed the identification of specific on-the-job training, apprenticeships, public works and job placement opportunities (in all sectors and at all levels) for possible NCDRP interventions. Interviews with over 330 possible implementing partners and employers have been conducted in all the Regions.

The raw data has been captured and has been interpreted and recommendations made around the utilisation of these opportunities and synchronising/integrating them with other training interventions. The final report was completed and recommendations integrated into Senior consultant report and ultimately in the Senior training programme strategies.

Training facility (strategic and operational planning) expert

The assignment has been completed and integrated into the reports of the Senior design and planning consultant (skills training facilities) and Senior training programme consultant. The regeneration needs of the Skills Development Centres have been assessed in conjunction with the Senior Consultant and recommendations have been made in a report dated 21st August 2002. Broad sectoral training priorities have also been established.

The training needs of the NCDRP as indicated in planning documentation have been finalised and were under a continuing process of refinement as more relevant and recent data became available. This process was expected to continue throughout the programme. Recommendations on the numbers to be trained in each centre have been finalised and recommendations made to the Ministry of Education, which was responsible for the implementation of the recommendations. Reports dated April and November 2002 were produced.

Training (provider assessment and capacity building) expert

All assignments have been completed and reports submitted. The consultant has completed the field work to compile a database of private training providers in Eritrea which details the training programmes (scale, sectors, content, curricula, duration) that they offer. The report highlights substantial institutional bottlenecks and recommendations including the development of pro-active projects by the NCDRP, based on labour market projections and demands from the DS, which will require stimulating the establishment and expansion of private training providers through invitations to participate in creating training opportunities.

Entrepreneurship training, research and design expert

An Entrepreneurship training, research and design expert was appointed to carry out the necessary studies in conjunction with the Senior training design consultant.

Labour market needs research expert

The assignments have been completed although weaknesses were experienced with the relevance and accuracy of information provided. This resulted in the consultant requesting an extension to the contract to conduct an enterprise survey of 200 Eritrean enterprises to verify and refine the data gathering processes. Labour market profiles of all Regions have been compiled. In addition, the expansion of the labour market system on a sustainable basis was discussed with the Ministry of Labour and Human Welfare and appropriate steps were taken to transfer the system to the MoLHW. An agreement was reached between DRP and Ministry of Labour and Human Welfare, that the Labour Department of the MoLHW come out with a new registration or list of all enterprises in country and then conduct enterprise survey by the same consultant. With the completion of the task of registering all private establishments by the Labour Department and the consultant was given the go ahead to the survey

Training of trainers pedagogy programme expert

The Consultant on training of trainers pedagogy programme has completed the assignment and conducted a pilot project to train a group of selected trainers in technical fields and in training methodologies during January 2004. Adjustments to the training methodologies were also incorporated after completion of the pilot project.

Architectural expert

The consultant completed his assessment of the Skills Development Centres during the first phase. Arising from this assessment the architect drafted basic plans of the existing structures since such plans were unavailable at the Ministry of Education or at the SDC's. The second phase of the task was to incorporate the recommendations of the Senior design and planning consultant (skills training facilities) reports, which specify the courses and number of trainees to be trained in each centre. The refurbishment needs were also identified and are contained in the architectural workplans and bills of quantities developed and submitted to the ministry of education.

Recognition of prior learning (RPL)

Subsequent to an exposure visit to South Africa by the NCDRP Programme Manager and Training Specialist, the importance of developing modalities for the recognition of prior learning was identified. A Consultant has completed and a report dated August 2003 was prepared. Arising from the recommendations, two further studies were required to finalise the development of a RPL system in Eritrea. The consultant is expected to develop a system for certifying skills acquired out of the context of a formalized training programme that could initially be used to certify acquired skills of demobilized soldiers – thereby reducing the quantum of longer term training interventions to be implemented by the NCDRP. The systems developed will initially be related to construction and related trades and will form the basis of an incipient system to be implemented on a larger scale by the MoE in the future.

Demobilized soldier benefits (DSB)

Proposals regarding the nature of benefits were developed that demobilised soldiers could expect when taking part in training opportunities provided by the NCDRP. This included the development of a policy regarding the nature of stipends, transport benefits, duration of assistance, start-up kits or tools after training, duration of training programmes etc. The proposal also includes draft contracts that could be signed between the demobilised soldiers and implementing agents as well as with the NCDRP detailing the rights and responsibilities of the three parties. An analysis of the benefits policy report indicates that the report requires substantial revision and change. A process has been recommended to the NCDRP to facilitate this in conjunction with the consultant and the UNDP. Subsequently, another consultant has submitted his revised report.

Annex 12 - REPORTS PRODUCED FOR THE ECONOMIC AND SOCIAL REINTEGRATION OF DEMOBILZED SOLDIERS

<table>
<tr><th>This document section/strategy component</th><th>This document content or Sub-component/ activity description</th><th>Available support documentation for reference purposes</th></tr>
<tr><td>1. Introduction</td><td>General overview</td><td rowspan="5"><ul><li>Progress report 1st Quarter 2005</li><li>NCDRP Operations manual</li><li>Project proposals for the Social and Economic Re-integration Programme (Donors conference September 2001)</li><li>Technical Assistance Programme Proposal (March 2002)</li><li>Various technical annexes produced in World bank appraisal missions – January to June 2001</li><li>Workshop on Planning the Re-integration Programme (Selam Hotel August 2001)</li><li>TA Report for NCDRP Project implementation plans (PIP)</li><li>Draft Policy on -Capacity Building of Providers to the NCDRP</li></ul></td></tr>
<tr><td>2. Summary of overall strategy</td><td>General overview</td></tr>
<tr><td>3. Demobilisation component</td><td>Procedures and policies</td></tr>
<tr><td>4. Reinsertion component</td><td>Procedures and policies</td></tr>
<tr><td>5. social and economic reintegration component</td><td>General overview, framework and guiding principles</td></tr>
<tr><td rowspan="4">6. Social reintegration sub-component</td><td>Introduction and general approach</td><td><ul><li>Project proposals for the Social and Economic Re-integration Programme (Donors conference September 2001)</li><li>Various technical annexes produced in World bank appraisal missions (Social reintegration as well as economic reintegration)</li><li>Workshop on Planning the Re-integration Programme (Selam Hotel August 2001)</li></ul></td></tr>
<tr><td>Information and sensitisation</td><td><ul><li>Report on Information and Sensitisation (Mark Jeffries)</li><li>World Bank Appraisal Mission January 2001 (Technical annex on Information and Sensitisation)</li></ul></td></tr>
<tr><td>Counselling</td><td><ul><li>Capacity analysis concerning the social re-integration of Demobilised Soldiers; Dr Tesfai Aradom</li><li>Psycho-social Intervention for Vulnerable Populations: Traumatised Individuals, Internally Displaced People, returnees and Deportees Dr Tesfai Aradom</li><li>Progress Report - Social Reintegration Component, Dr Tesfai Aradom</li><li>Various presentations, reports and occasional documents</li><li>World Bank Appraisal Mission January 2001 (Technical annex on Counselling)</li></ul></td></tr>
<tr><td>Medical rehabilitation</td><td><ul><li>World Bank Appraisal Mission January 2001 (Technical annex on Medical Rehabilitation)</li></ul></td></tr>
</table>

7. Economic reintegration sub-components	Introduction and general approach			• Project proposals for the Social and Economic Re-integration Programme (Donors conference September 2001) • Various technical annexes produced in World bank appraisal missions (Social reintegration as well as economic reintegration) • Workshop on Planning the Re-integration Programme (Selam Hotel August 2001)
	Training	Job attachments	Formalise on-the-job training and apprenticeship programmes	• Systems for the implementation of attachment programmes. Teddi Sander and Woldegabriel Tesfamariam (December 2002)
			Develop Public Works on-the-job training	
			Provide job placement and experience for graduates	
		Training capacity	Regenerate the skills development centres	• Mission report – Brian Stewart (November 2002) • Regeneration of SDC's in Eritrea – Brian Stewart (August 2002) • Report on the present stage of the regeneration of the 5 SDC's – M and Y consulting architects Engineers and Planners (December 2002) • Costing model for training provision at SDC's – Dr Tesfai Haile (December 2002) • Draft capacity building policy – (December 2002)
			Develop mobile training capacity	• Regeneration of SDC's in Eritrea – Brian Stewart (August 2002) • Regeneration of SAWA Training Centre - Brian Stewart (November 2003)
			Expand private provision	• Capacity building of private providers - Dr Tesfai Haile (March 2003)
			Enhance intermediate and advanced training provision	• No available report
			Train TVET trainers	• Mission report – Brian Stewart (November 2002) • Regeneration of SDC's in Eritrea – Brian Stewart (August 2002) • Training of Trainers report – Dr. Tesfai Haile December 2003
		Training systems	Systems are developed ensure that training is responsive to market needs	• Labour Market Information Systems - Jorgen Billetoft and Tesfamariam • Interpretive Report on Labour Market Information –Brian Stewart (November 2003) • Technical Note on Employment Opportunities and Skill needs in the short term: Tesfaymariam • Regeneration of SAWA Training Centre - Brian Stewart (November 2003)
			Establish a system for the recognition of skills acquired during military service	• Mission report for the recognition of prior learning—Paul Farrelly August 2003 • Regeneration of SAWA Training Centre - Brian Stewart (November 2003)
			Develop the capacity to design appropriate learning materials for basic and specialised training	• Mission report – Brian Stewart (November 2002) • Regeneration of SDC's in Eritrea – Brian Stewart (August 2002) • Training of Trainers report – Dr. Tesfai Haile December 2003
		Training costs	Fund the training costs	• NCDRP Operations manual • Costing model for training provision at SDC's – Dr Tesfai Haile (December 2002) • Systems for the implementation of attachment programmes. Teddi Sander and Woldegabriel Tesfamariam (December 2002) • The formulation of DS benefits policies (Revised draft)
	Business development		Include business information and awareness in NCDRP information and sensitisation programmes	• Project proposals for the Social and Economic Re-integration Programme (Donors conference September 2001) • Various technical annexes produced in World bank appraisal missions (Social reintegration as well as economic reintegration) • Workshop on Planning the Re-integration Programme (Selam Hotel August 2001) • Draft Business development strategy and relationship between SMCP and NCDRP • Regeneration of SAWA Training Centre - Brian Stewart (November 2003)
			Include business information and awareness in pre-discharge orientation	

			Provide an entrepreneurship orientation to basic training	
			Facilitate business training courses for selected DS wishing to develop their own income generating projects or small and micro businesses	
			Facilitate DS access to and refer selected DS who require business development services and credit to appropriate organisations	
			Advocate for changes in the operating and regulatory environment for small and micro businesses	
			Develop working relationships and MoUs with organisations providing business information, business development services and micro-finance	
	Rural development		Provide basic and relevant information materials on available opportunities and services	• Rural Development Strategy paper and draft implementation plan (including annexes) July 2002 • Rural Development Strategy- Maija Tsegai December 2003 • Agricultural development and serviced land for demobilised soldiers – (April 2003)
			Increase household food security	• Rural Development Strategy paper and draft implementation plan (including annexes) July 2002 • Rural Development Strategy- Maija Tsegai December 2003
			Promote non-agricultural income generation activities	• Rural Development Strategy paper and draft implementation plan (including annexes) July 2002 • Non-Agricultural income generating activities – Dr Tesfai Haile (November 2003) • Rural Development Strategy- Maija Tsegai December 2003 • Regeneration of SAWA Training Centre - Brian Stewart (November 2003)
			Establish Agricultural Development Areas	• Rural Development Strategy paper and draft implementation plan (including annexes) July 2002 • Agricultural development and serviced land for demobilised soldiers – (April 2003)
			Promote fisheries and Seawater Farming	• Rural Development Strategy paper and draft implementation plan (including annexes) July 2002 • Job Opportunities Programme Design for Demobilised Soldiers under Fisheries and Sea Water Farming – Dr Frewengel (April 2003)
8. Management of the NCDRP	All aspects of managing the NCDRP			• Operations manual • Monitoring and Evaluation Guidelines • Strategic Results Framework: Step-by-step Guide for conducting Monitoring & Evaluation of NCDRP Sub-Projects and activities (April 2003) • Various financial and administration reports regarding internal procedures • Annual Programme Implementation Plans
9. Project cycle modalities	Project cycle management			• Operations manual • Monitoring and Evaluation Guidelines

Annex 13 – Demographic Information and Characteristics

13.1 Summary of Demographic Information of IDPS in Camps

Current Settlement			From 6 to 60		children<5		Elderly>65		Total						
Sub Zoba	Villages	Camp	Male	Female	Male	Female	Male	Female	Population	M.HH	F.HH	T.HH	%fhh	%females	HH.size
Gash Barka															
Barentu	Barentu		1	2					3	1	1	2	50%	66.7	1.5
Gogne	Adi Keshi		5521	6340	1557	1366	472	324	15580	1093	2976	4069	73%	51.5	3.8
Goluj	Gergef		512	513	104	112	48	11	1300	154	124	278	45%	48.9	4.7
	Goluj		1631	1853	386	401	119	75	4465	411	651	1062	61%	52.2	4.2
	Sabunait		30	27	13	7	6	2	85	10	13	23	57%	42.4	3.7
	Tebeldia		403	501	105	118	51	13	1191	120	214	334	64%	53.1	3.6
Haikota	Alebu		4	5	1	3	1		14	2	1	3	33%	57.1	4.7
Logo Anseba	Liban			1					1		1	1	100%	100.0	1.0
Molqui	Dembe Asmara		1	2	1	2			6		1	1	100%	66.7	6.0
	Dembe Doran		742	992	280	259	77	50	2400	173	428	601	71%	54.2	4.0
	Dembe Hahoto		3	5	2	1			11	1		1	0%	54.5	11.0
	Dembe Kuakito		23	31	9	8	2		73	5	14	19	74%	53.4	3.8
	Dembe Tsaeda		1					1	2	1		1	0%	50.0	2.0
	Dembe Yarega		2	2					4	1		1	0%	50.0	4.0
	Maigaba		5	6	1	2			14		2	2	100%	57.1	7.0
Shambuko	Binbina		218	284	60	75	24	9	670	36	135	171	79%	54.9	3.9
	Bushuka		1	1					2	1		1	0%	50.0	2.0
	Dembe Himbrti		3	1		1			5	1		1	0%	40.0	5.0
	Korekon		2134	2523	664	632	234	147	6334	517	1129	1646	69%	52.1	3.8
	Shambuko		633	779	175	149	75	43	1854	122	326	448	73%	52.4	4.1
Tesseney	Tesseney		341	354	62	55	19	9	840	84	72	156	46%	49.8	5.4
Sub Total			12209	14222	3420	3191	1128	684	34854	2733	6088	8821	69%	51.9	4.0
Debub															
Adi Keih	Adi Keih		4	3	2	2	1		12	1	2	3	66.67	41.7	4.00
	Egela			2	1	1			4		1	1	100	75.0	4.00
Adi Quala	Adi Wesen		1	2	1				4	1	1	2	50	50.0	2.00
	Awsran		2	2	1	1			6		1	1	100	50.0	6.00
	Endaesh		157	237	63	60	18	21	556	55	107	162	66.05	57.2	3.43
	Harish Kofono		3	4	2	1			10		3	3	100	50.0	3.33
Areza	Adi Gurdi		1	1					2		1	1	100	50.0	2.00
	Adi Tekualu		1	1					2		1	1	100	50.0	2.00
	Maidma			1					1		1	1	100%	100.0	1.0
Mai Aini	Adi Oka		12	14	7	7	1		41	7	1	8	12.5	51.2	5.13
	Adi Ontura		26	30	8	9	2	1	76	11	9	20	45	52.6	3.80
	Adi Shaki		30	27	10	6	2	1	76	9	9	18	50	44.7	4.22
	Eduf		30	40	8	8	6	1	93	13	12	25	48	52.7	3.72
	Enko Walaka			2					2		1	1	100	100.0	2.00
	Hamto		2	2					4		1	1	100	50.0	4.00
	Keih Kewhi		67	83	29	25	8	2	214	25	26	51	50.98	51.4	4.20
	Keih Walako			2					2		1	1	100	100.0	2
	Oduf		7	9		1			17	1	2	3	66.67	58.8	5.67
	Ona Gobay		36	54	17	18	5	4	134	12	31	43	72.09	56.7	3.12
	Ona Watot		457	527	169	167	35	39	1394	131	258	389	66.32	52.6	3.58
Sena'fe	Adi Ageb		1	1	1	1			4		1	1	100	50.0	4

Current Settlement		From 6 to 60		children<5		Elderly>65		Total						
	Adi Mereta	32	30	9	2	6	2	81	10	6	16	37.5	42.0	5.06
	Afoma	222	403	131	133	7	19	915	48	230	278	82.73	60.7	3.29
	Akeb Gorzo	178	210	50	54	25	34	551	36	105	141	74.47	54.1	3.91
	Ambakom		2	1				3		1	1	100	66.7	3.00
	Angebeto	51	65	11	17	11	8	163	28	14	42	33.33	55.2	3.88
	Aromo	374	572	151	138	77	69	1381	128	239	367	65.12	56.4	3.76
	Ased	2	4	3	1			10		2	2	100	50.0	5.00
	Awlie Hahaile	1213	1556	525	468	128	123	4013	247	616	863	71.38	53.5	4.65
	Chea	91	135	36	21	13	14	310	21	57	78	73.08	54.8	3.97
	Enta	16	21	3	2	8	1	51	7	7	14	50	47.1	3.64
	Ger'ana	31	38	4	7	6	5	91	8	14	22	63.64	54.9	4.14
	Hariena	4	6					10	1	3	4	63.23	60.0	2.50
	Kolet	268	362	91	92	51	40	904	82	141	223	82.98	54.6	4.05
	Ksad Agruf	48	78	29	21	6	8	190	8	39	47	72.28	56.3	4.04
	Ksad Emba	331	464	108	113	51	60	1127	84	219	303	70.16	56.5	3.72
	Megedi'erfi	130	184	43	50	34	27	468	37	87	124	50	55.8	3.77
	Merber	3	4	2	4			13	1	1	2	100	61.5	6.50
	Mereta	3	2	1	1			7		2	2	49.28	42.9	3.50
	Mesehal	83	97	13	16	24	19	252	35	34	69	100	52.4	3.65
	Mesraha	1	1		1			3		1	1	72.58	66.7	3.00
	Metera	1517	2077	548	477	157	169	4945	309	818	1127	100	55.1	4.39
	Obuk	1	2					3		1	1	100	66.7	3.00
	Saloda	1	4					5		1	1	65.52	80.0	5.00
	Sena'fe	55	55	13	17	2	2	144	10	19	29	100	51.4	4.97
	Shea	4	6	2				12		3	3	0	50.0	4.00
	Tisha	5	3	2	2			12	2		2	68.79	41.7	6.00
	Zekolo	183	271	50	42	30	33	609	49	108	157	#REF!	56.8	3.88
Tsorona	Adi Shaho		1	2				3		1	1	100	33.3	3.00
	Dbi	5	8				1	14	1	4	5			2.80
	Endaba Stifanos	333	412	116	132	41	26	1060	102	181	283			3.75
	Gemae	227	312	100	116	25	16	796	72	166	238	69.75	55.8	3.34
	Mai Wuray	1337	1898	457	433	154	151	4430	326	998	1324	75.38	56.0	3.35
	Mhrad Chele	1	2					3	1		1	0	66.7	3.00
	Ona Welesti	31	29	8	12	6	3	89	13	7	20	35	49.4	4.45
	Tsorona	330	446	123	100	45	34	1078	70	216	286	75.52	53.8	3.77
Sub Total		7948	10804	2951	2779	985	933	26400	2002	4811	6813	70.62	55.0	3.87
Northern Red Sea														
Ghelalo	Adi Gada	4	2					6	1		1	0	33.3	6.00
	Ed Ahlaf	2	1	1	1			5		1	1	100	40.0	5.00
	Guridega	2						2	1		1	0	0.0	2.00
	Mogale	3	1					4	1	1	2	50	25.0	2.00
	Oridaga		1		1			2		1	1	100	100.0	2.00
Ghindae	Ghindae	117	132	57	44	9	2	361	40	45	85	52.94	49.3	4.25
Massawa	Massawa	1						1	1		1	0	0.0	1.00
Sub Total		129	137	58	46	9	2	381	44	48	92	302.9	247.6408	4.14
Grand Total		20286	25163	6429	6016	2122	1619	61635	4779	10947	15726	374.2		
Source: ERREC Statistics Department														

13.2 Rural Expellees Distribution - October 31,2002

Zoba Gash Barka

Current Place		Family heads			Individuals					
Sub Zoba		**Male**	**Female**	**Total**	**Male**	**Female**	**Total**	**% fhh**	**% females**	**HH. size**
Gogne	Adi Keshi	438	302	**740**	1350	1264	2614	0.41	48	3.53
Molqui	Dembe Doran	3	1	**4**	8	4	12	0.25	33	3.00
	Tukul		1	**1**		1	1	1.00	100	1.00
Shambuko	Korekon	10	18	**28**	77	68	145	0.64	47	5.18
	Kotebia	683	744	**1427**	2495	2737	5232	0.52	52	3.67
	Shambuko		1	**1**		2	2	1.00	100	2.00
	Tokombia		1	**1**		1	1	1.00	100	1.00
Mensura	Shelab	1130	1458	**2588**	4002	4540	8542	0.56	53	3.30
Lae'lay Gash	Shelalo	1		**1**	1		1	0.00	0	1.00
Total		**2265**	**2526**	**4791**	**7933**	**8617**	**16550**	**0.53**	**52**	**3.45**
Zoba Debub										
Adi Quala	Enda Eshe	32	29	**61**	121	102	**223**	0.48	46	3.66
Dubarwa	Sefea	1	0	**1**	1	3	**4**	0.00	75	4.00
Senafe	Hahaile	0	1	**1**	1	1	**2**	1.00	50	2.00
	Metera	20	41	**61**	88	128	**216**	0.67	59	3.54
	Senafe	3	5	**8**	15	18	**33**	0.63	55	4.13
Tsorona	Afoma	2	1	**3**	3	1	**4**	0.33	25	1.33
	Gemae	2	1	**3**	2	1	**3**	0.33	33	1.00
	Mai Wuray	1	0	**1**	1	4	**5**	0.00	80	5.00
	Mihrad Chele	0	1	**1**	3	2	**5**	1.00	40	5.00
	Tsorona	1	0	**1**	3	1	**4**	0.00	25	4.00
Total		**62**	**79**	**141**	**238**	**261**	**499**	**0.56**	**52**	**3.54**
Northern Red Sea										
Ghindae	Ghindae	7	4	**11**	23	19	**42**	36	45	3.82
Total		**7**	**4**	**11**	**23**	**19**	**42**	**36**	**45**	**3.82**
Grand Total		2334	**2609**	**4943**	**8194**	**8897**	**17091**	**0.60**	**52**	**2.09**
Source: ERREC Statistics Department										

13.3 Distribution of IDPs in Camps in December 2000

Region	Sub-region	IDP Camp	Households	Population	Children<5	Percent
Debub	Tsorona Mai Aini	Alba Deda	4,700 986	20,412 3502	8,164 922	
	Maiaini	Unawatot	455	1,750	401	
	Maiaini	Midfaewalta	397	1,531	376	
	Ghindae	Harena (MH)	9,640	25,947	4,647	
	Adi Quala	Agrae	1,464	5,500	741	
	Adi Quala	Maisagla	547	2,203	536	
	Adi Keih	Soira	800	3,708	1,483	
	Adi Keih	Hailai	85	403	157	
	Adi Keih	Zula	987	4,233	1,693	
	Sub Total		20,061	69,189	19,120	34.1%
Gash-Barka	Laelay Gash	Adi Keshi		35,313		
	Shambuko	Korekon		1,039		
	Shambuko	Kotobia		4,615		
	Molqui	Tologamja		1,992		
	Molqui	Jejah		7,570		
	Molqui	Dembe-Doran		4,022		
	Afabet	Mekete		21,955		
	Goluj	Gergef				
	Goluj	Tebeldia		5,877		
	Goluj	Sabunait		5,642		
	Goluj	Goluj		20,467		
	Goluj	Hadiset		5,460		
	Goluj	Adi-Shekgala		3,189		
	Sub-Total			131,804		65.1%
N.R.Sea	Gelalo	Ghindae/Bouya	159	452		0.2%
S.R.Sea	Gindae	Ghindae/Assab	314	1,174		0.6%
Others	Not specified			9,351		
	Grand Total			202,619		100%

Source: Genesis of the Current Humanitarian Situation in Eritrea and the Challenges Ahead Towards Meeting Future Emergency and Recovery Needs, ERREC, March 2001)

13.4 List of villages under Administrative areas in Mai Aini & Tsorona Sub Zones

13.4.1 List of villages In the Administrative areas of Endaba Stifanos and Aiba

No	Name of Village	Households	Population
1	Endaba Stifanos	26	90
2	Godofo	43	160
3	Kermet Guzai	31	126
4	Slolo	31	110
5	Ferasit	40	122
6	Unkura	13	40
7	Begena	68	115
8	Timro-Mekie	9	30
9	Gefafin	22	85
10	Aiba	150	540
11	Enda-Haji	32	128
12	Berik-Hutsa	81	330
Total		546	1876

13.4.2 List of villages In the Administrative areas of Gemae

Name of Village	No Households	Population
1. Gemae	88	310
2. Debasit	72	238
3. Solomia	32	126
4. Mihrad Chele	74	265
5. Enda Sherif	34	125
6. Dibi *127	58	211
7. Korboli *	40	141
8. Egri-Mekel*	58	194
9. Hamato (Tigray)	6	31
Total	462	1641

13.4.3 List of villages of Origin for IDPs in Mai-Wuray

No.	Villages	Households	Population
1	Kinin	147	810
2	Kinito	119	469
	Sub Total	366	1279
3	Hadish Adi	115	445
4	Hashaso	158	568
5	Tselim-Kelay	119	113
6	Gergera	90	294
7	Adi-Mesgeno	73	328
8	Adi-Shaho	83	275
9	Debe-Haish	24	59
	Sub Total	569	2374
10	Sebao	130	528
11	Una-Shehak	136	441
12	Kolo-burdo	42	245
13	Adi-Kutu	57	143
	Subtotal	356	1357
	Grand total	1291	5010

13.5 - List of Health Facilities destroyed by Border War in Debub Region

			Number	Degree of	Present
No.	**Location**	**Type**	**of Beneficiaries**	**Destruction**	**Status**
1	Tsorena	Health center	31771	Total	destroyed
2	Maimine	Health center	41761	Partial	Repaired
3	Senafe	Health center	80000	Total	Destroyed
4	Dabre	Health station	4856	Partial	Repaired
5	Serha	Health station	8031	Total	Destroyed
6	Ubel	Health station	6500	Partial	Repaired
7	Forto	Health station	15775	Partial	Not repaired
8	Enda Gergis	Health station	27295	Partial	Repaired
9	Golo	Health station	NA	Partial	Repaired
10	Akran	Health station	NA	partial	Repaired
Source: MoHealth branch office Zoba Debub					

13.6 - Health Services in Emergency Camps

Name	Type of Facility	Common Diseases	Staff	Remarks
Shellab	Clinic	Malaria, diarrhea, TB, skin diseases	2	Commonly used with surrounding villages
Adi-Keshi	Health station	Malaria, diarrhea, URI, skin diseases	4	It is overstretched
Korekon	Health station	Malaria, diarrhea, TB	3	
Koitebia	One Health station	Malaria, diarrhea, TB	3	Serves IDPs and Host Community
Debe-Doran	Clinic	Malaria, diarrhea, skin diseases, ARI, TB and respiratory	2	Serves IDPs and Host Community. It is overstretched.
Mai-Alba	None		None	They go on foot to Adiquala 42 kms
Una-Watot	None	Malaria, diarrhea, TB	None	They go to Endaba-Stefanos
Endaba-Stefanos	Mini-clinic	Malaria, diarrhea, low blood pressure and respiratory problems	2	It is overstretched. It serves the host population, IDPs and 8 surrounding villages.
Gema'e	None	Malaria, diarrhea, TB	None	They go to Tsorona
Mai-Wuray	None	Malaria, diarrhea, TB	None	They go to Genzebo
Tsorena: Unanazo	Health center	Malaria, diarrhea, skin disease	4 nurses, 11	Serves the population of the sub-region including those in camps
& Kudo -Weiba		diseases, TB, relapsing fever, and other respiratory infections.	health assistants, 1 lab. technician, 3 cleaners	
Metera	None	Dysentery, coughing, and fever	None	Senafe Hospital
Afoma	None		None	Senafe Hospital
Tawlie/Hahaile	None	Diarrhea, malnutrition, respiratory infections, TB.	None	Senafe Hospital
Denden	Mini-clinic	Malaria, diarrhea, malnutrition and respiratory	1 nurse who comes from Ghindae hospital	Previously there were 1 nurse and 2 health assistants
Debai-Sima	None	Pneumonia	None	the IDPs go to Assab 57 km

13.7 - War Damaged Educational Establishments

Location	Number of Schools Damaged				Estimated Costs of Damages in 000' Nakfa			
	Heavy	Medium	Light	Total	Heavy	Medium	Light	Total
GashBarka								
Barentu		2	3	5		86	39	125
Gogne	3		2	5	2,022		20	2,042
Guluj	4	2	1	7	4,505	143	10	4,658
Haykota		1	2	3		80	7	87
La'elay Gash	11			11	21,525			21,525
Mensura		1		1		55		55
Mogolo			4	4			28	28
Molqui	1	2	1	4	371	91	19	481
Shambuko	10			10	8,934			8,934
Tesenei	7		3	10	1,856		29	1,885
Total	36	8	16	60	39,213	455	152	39,820
Debub								
Adi-Keih	1		3	4	125		5	130
Adi Quala	4	2	1	7	2,492	124	8	2,624
Areza		4	3	7		273	14	287
Dubarwa			2	2			12	12
Imni-Haili			3	3			2	2
Mai-Aini	2	3	3	8	3,884	105	16	4,005
Mai Mine		2	1	3		128	4	132
Segeneiti		1		1		25		25
Senafe	28			28	49,818			49,818
Tsorona	8	1	1	10	13,439	75	8	13,522
Total	43	13	17	73	69,758	730	69	70,557
Grand Total	79	21	33	133	108,971	1,185	221	110,377
Equipment & Supplies & Books					11,506			11,506
Other serious damages					13810			13810
Contingency								13569
Grand Total								149,262

Source: MOE, Rapid Assessment of War-damaged Educational Establishments in Gash-Barka and Debub Regions, August 2000, pp 8-9.

13.8 - Extent of School Damages during the Border War

	Extent of Damage	Zone	Sub-zone	No.	No. Students	Costs
				Schools		in 000 Nakfa
1	Heavy	Gash-Barka	Laelay-Gash, Shambuko, Goluj, Gogne, Molqui, and Tessenei	36 (20 were in areas of control of invading forces)		
		Debub	Senafe, Tsorona, Adi Quala, Mai Aini, and Adi Keih	43 (36 were in areas of control of invading forces)		
			Subtotal	79	45,000	108,971
2	Medium	Gash-Barka	Goluj, Haikota, Molqui, Barentu, and Mensura	8		
		Debub	Tsorena, Adi Quala, Mai Aini, Areza, Mai Mine, and Segeneiti	13		
			Subtotal	21	16,000	1,185
3	Light	Gash-Barka	Goluj, Hykota, Molqui, Barentu, Mogolo, Tessenei, Gogne	16		
		Debub	Tsorona, Adi-Quala, Mai Aini, Areza, Mai Mine, Adi Keih, Imni-Haili, and Dibarwa	17		
			Subtotal	33	19,000	221
			Grand total	**133**	**80,000**	**110,377**

13.9 - Make Shift Educational Facilities in Emergency Camps

Name	School Structure	Type of School	No. Students	No. Teachers	Remarks
1. Shellab	Corrugated sheet cover of 26 class rooms	Elementary	1500	33	Early marriage of girls and school discontinuity is prevalent
2. Adi-Keshi	Three schools with 52 class rooms	Two elementary (1-5) & one junior (6-7)	3500	61	Early marriage of girls (at 13-14) often results in discontinuity of schooling and boys too old to go to schools discontinue to seek jobs.
3. Korekon	Two tonkobet and corrugated sheet	Elementary (1-5) and Junior (6-7)			
4. Koitebia	One of tonkobet and corrugated sheet	6-Jan	2100	18	
5. Debe-Doran	Tent of 11 classrooms	Elementary(1-5)	750	13	No water. Each student is required to bring 2 small jerrycans of water per week.
6. Mai-Alba	Building	Elementary(1-3)	305	4	
7. Una-Watot	Building with 6 classrooms	Elementary (1-5)	460	6	Almost 50% are unable to continue their junior education in either Tsorena or Maiaini
8. Endaba-Stefanos	No		230	5	The students attend in Aiba in a nearby village
9. Gema'e	No		198		Has 198 students who attend in Tsorena, 14 kms away.
10. Mai-Wray					Has access to one elementary and one junior school
11.Tsorena (Unanazo & Kudo-Weiba)					
12. Metera	Building	Elementary schools			Shortage of teachers
13. Afoma	no				Uses schools in Senafe
14. Tawlie/Hahaile	no				Uses schools in Senafe
15. Denden	Tent school	elementary (1-3)	139 (39 girls)		
16. Debai-Sima	None existent				

BRIEF BACKGROUND OF THE AUTHOR
TECHESTE AHDEROM

Academic Record includes:

- BSc in Building Engineering (STRUCTURAL) – Ethio-Swedish Institute of Building Technology (ESIBT), Addis Ababa
- Post Graduate Diploma in Housing – Baucentrum, Rotterdam, Holland
- MCP – Master's Degree in City Planning- Yale University, New Haven, CT
- CTE - Traffic Engineering – Yale University, New Haven, CT
- M Arch- Master's Degree in Architecture – Iowa State university, Ames, Iowa

Profession/Work Experience includes:

- Head, Central Design Office – Ethio-Swedish Institute of Building Technology (ESIBT), Addis Ababa
- Dept Head/Asst. Professor, Dept of Architecture and Town Planning, Addis Ababa University, Addis Ababa
- Coordinator, Infrastructure Facilities - National Development Thru Cooperation Campaign, Ethiopia
- President/Associate Professor, Asmara University, Asmara
- Chief Urban Planner/Manager - Addis Ababa Master Plan Project (AMPPO)
- General Manager/Prof. - National Urban Planning Institute (NUPI)
- Principal Representative - BIC United Nations Office, New York
- Senior Technical Advisor on Recovery - UNDP Eritrea/Uganda

The Author has over 30 Research/publications to his credit (Few Published and the rest in Manuscript Form)

www.ingramcontent.com/pod-product-compliance
Lightning Source LLC
LaVergne TN
LVHW070212110826
845147LV00003B/559

* 9 7 8 1 7 3 4 0 0 7 7 0 1 *